# Exam Ref 70-774 Perform Cloud Data Science with Azure Machine Learning

Ginger Grant
Julio Granados
Guillermo Fernández
Pau Sempere
Javier Torrenteras
Paco González
Tamanaco Francísquez

*seven mediocre writers !*

**Exam Ref 70-774 Perform Cloud Data Science with Azure Machine Learning**

**Published with the authorization of Microsoft Corporation by:**
**Pearson Education, Inc.**

ISBN-13: 978-1-5093-0701-2
ISBN-10: 1-5093-0701-X

Library of Congress Control Number: 2017963300
1   18

**Trademarks**

Microsoft and the trademarks listed at *https://www.microsoft.com* on the "Trademarks" webpage are trademarks of the Microsoft group of companies. All other marks are property of their respective owners.

**Warning and Disclaimer**

Every effort has been made to make this book as complete and as accurate as possible, but no warranty or fitness is implied. The information provided is on an "as is" basis. The authors, the publisher, and Microsoft Corporation shall have neither liability nor responsibility to any person or entity with respect to any loss or damages arising from the information contained in this book or programs accompanying it.

**Special Sales**

For information about buying this title in bulk quantities, or for special sales opportunities (which may include electronic versions; custom cover designs; and content particular to your business, training goals, marketing focus, or branding interests), please contact our corporate sales department at corpsales@pearsoned.com or (800) 382-3419.

For government sales inquiries, please contact governmentsales@pearsoned.com.

For questions about sales outside the U.S., please contact intlcs@pearson.com.

| | |
|---|---|
| **Editor-in-Chief** | Greg Wiegand |
| **Senior Editor** | Trina MacDonald |
| **Development Editor** | Troy Mott |
| **Managing Editor** | Sandra Schroeder |
| **Senior Project Editor** | Tracey Croom |
| **Editorial Production** | Backstop Media |
| **Copy Editor** | Christina Rudloff |
| **Indexer** | Julie Grady |
| **Proofreader** | Christina Rudloff |
| **Technical Editors** | Naveed Hussain & Robin Lester |
| **Cover Designer** | Twist Creative, Seattle |

# Contents at a glance

# Contents

## Chapter 3  Operationalize and manage Azure Machine Learning Services    107

# Introduction

The 70-774 exam focuses on the features and functionalities available to properly perform data science activities using Azure Machine Learning. It covers the tasks needed to properly prepare data to be analyzed in Azure Machine Learning and how to understand and find the key variables that are describing data behavior. This book also covers how to to develop Machine Learning Models, identifying the best suited algorithm, and describing the train and validation steps that need to be taken to obtain the best in class models. The book also covers how to deploy, manage, and consume Azure Machine Learning Models, and how to leverage other services.

This book is focused on data scientists or analysts who are interested in learning about the use of Azure cloud services to build and deploy Azure Machine Learning Models. We also cover how to build intelligence systems that can complement other services like Cognitive Services APIS, templates from the Cortana intelligence Gallery, HDInsight, or R Server services.

This book covers every major topic area found on the exam, but it does not cover every exam question. Only the Microsoft exam team has access to the exam questions, and Microsoft regularly adds new questions to the exam, making it impossible to cover specific questions. You should consider this book a supplement to your relevant real-world experience and other study materials. If you encounter a topic in this book that you do not feel completely comfortable with, use the "Need more review?" links you'll find in the text to find more information and take the time to research and study the topic. Great information is available on MSDN, TechNet, and in blogs and forums.

## Organization of this book

This book is organized by the "Skills measured" list published for the exam. The "Skills measured" list is available for each exam on the Microsoft Learning website: *https://aka.ms/examlist*. Each chapter in this book corresponds to a major topic area in the list, and the technical tasks in each topic area determine a chapter's organization. If an exam covers six major topic areas, for example, the book will contain six chapters.

# Microsoft certifications

Microsoft certifications distinguish you by proving your command of a broad set of skills and experience with current Microsoft products and technologies. The exams and corresponding certifications are developed to validate your mastery of critical competencies as you design and develop, or implement and support, solutions with Microsoft products and technologies both on-premises and in the cloud. Certification brings a variety of benefits to the individual and to employers and organizations.

> ***MORE INFO*** **ALL MICROSOFT CERTIFICATIONS**
>
> For information about Microsoft certifications, including a full list of available certifications, go to *https://www.microsoft.com/learning*.

# Acknowledgments

When you receive a request for writing a technical book, you always have the challenge of assuring that your readers will fully understand your explanations and samples. But when the book is written by a team, the challenge becomes easier since from the beginning you can share and understand each other's work. Without the involvement of Pearson and SolidQ teams, it would had been much more difficult to accomplish this task. We would also like to thank our families and friends who have been supporting us during the long days of work required to make this happen.

# Microsoft Virtual Academy

Build your knowledge of Microsoft technologies with free expert-led online training from Microsoft Virtual Academy (MVA). MVA offers a comprehensive library of videos, live events, and more to help you learn the latest technologies and prepare for certification exams. You'll find what you need here:

*https://www.microsoftvirtualacademy.com*

# Quick access to online references

Throughout this book are addresses to webpages that the author has recommended you visit for more information. Some of these addresses (also known as URLs) can be painstaking to type into a web browser, so we've compiled all of them into a single list that readers of the print edition can refer to while they read.

Download the list at *https://aka.ms/examref774/downloads*.

# Errata, updates, & book support

We've made every effort to ensure the accuracy of this book and its companion content. You can access updates to this book—in the form of a list of submitted errata and their related corrections—at:

*https://aka.ms/examref774/errata*

If you discover an error that is not already listed, please submit it to us at the same page.

If you need additional support, email Microsoft Press Book Support at *mspinput@microsoft. com.*

Please note that product support for Microsoft software and hardware is not offered through the previous addresses. For help with Microsoft software or hardware, go to *https:// support.microsoft.com.*

# Stay in touch

Let's keep the conversation going! We're on Twitter: *http://twitter.com/MicrosoftPress.*

# Preparing for the exam

Microsoft certification exams are a great way to build your resume and let the world know about your level of expertise. Certification exams validate your on-the-job experience and product knowledge. Although there is no substitute for on-the-job experience, preparation through study and hands-on practice can help you prepare for the exam. We recommend that you augment your exam preparation plan by using a combination of available study materials and courses. For example, you might use the Exam ref and another study guide for your "at home" preparation, and take a Microsoft Official Curriculum course for the classroom experience. Choose the combination that you think works best for you.

Note that this Exam Ref is based on publicly available information about the exam and the author's experience. To safeguard the integrity of the exam, authors do not have access to the live exam.

# CHAPTER 1

# Prepare data for analysis in Azure Machine Learning and export from Azure Machine Learning

The first step in creating a machine learning experiment is to evaluate the data to determine how you can use it in your algorithms. Initially you need to determine how you wish to load the data. Is your data stored in Hadoop or a database? Is your data in the cloud or stored in an on-premise server? Are you just starting out and would like some sample datasets to use to learn how to understand machine learning concepts?

> **IMPORTANT**
> **Have you read page xv?**
> It contains valuable information regarding the skills you need to pass the exam.

## Skills covered in this chapter:

- Skill 1.1: Import and export data to and from Azure Machine Learning
- Skill 1.2: Explore and summarize data
- Skill 1.3: Cleanse data for Azure Machine Learning
- Skill 1.4: Perform feature engineering

Azure Machine Learning (ML) provides features to handle all of these scenarios. It can read in data from anything from an ARFF formatted file to a zip file. You can read data directly in from an Azure data source with the Import module, or use one of the many sample data files included within the application to help you hear concepts without having to go find data. To save results, intermediate data, and working data from your experiments you may use the Export Data module. The Import Data module can be configured to store data outside Azure Machine Learning Studio into other storage locations like Azure Blob Storage, Azure SQL Database, and Hive Queries.

ARFF — Attribute relation file format (used with weka typically)

Once the data has been loaded, Azure Machine Learning has a number of different modules to help explore the data. In addition to viewing the data using the visualize option for each dataset, Azure Machine Learning also provides a module to Compute Elementary Statics, which provides the ability to see at a glance the mean, median, and mode of any column in a dataset, along with several other useful statistical items. When you need to compare two columns, something data scientist call multivariate analysis, Azure Machine Learning provides the ability to visually compare values by selecting them. There are a number of different visual methodologies provided for looking at a single column, which allows you to create univariate distributions of data by looking at box plots, scatter grams, and a number of other visualizations. If the built-in tools included in Azure Machine Learning do not contain the desired analysis within Azure Machine Learning Studio this section details how to use existing R or Python code to create any desired summary or visualization by importing the code directly or by using zip archives.

After examining the data, it is likely that some of the data may need to be modified because it is missing or contains information not needed for analysis. Some of the columns, such as a database id field, may not be needed in a predictive algorithm, and may need to be removed. You may need to modify data if it has several different sources to create key values in order for the data to be joined together. Azure Machine Learning contains functions to easily perform those actions, which are discussed in this chapter.

Some algorithms require modifications to the data in order to perform properly. Columns may need to be classified as different datatypes or as categorical. If the data contains a result used in testing, but is not included in data to be used in anything other than training data, it must be marked as a label. All of these concepts are thoroughly described in this chapter to provide a good understanding of their use.

# Skill 1.1: Import and export data to and from Azure Machine Learning

The primary function of Azure Machine Learning is to analyze data, both manually and automatically. The data analyzed can come from a variety of sources including Azure blob storage, a Hadoop cluster, a website or a SQL database either on-premise or in an Azure SQL Database. To use data in an Azure Machine Learning experiment, part of the initial process is to import it into the Azure Machine Learning Environment to begin the development process. In the process of creating a result from an experiment it may also be important to exporting data for further analysis and distribution.

To import data into an Azure Machine Learning experiment, from within a Microsoft Azure Machine Learning Studio experiment, click on the menu item Data Input And Output, then drag the Import Data control on to the Workspace (see Figure 1-1).

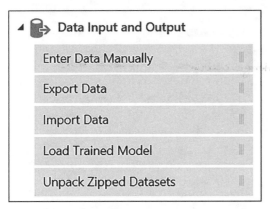

**FIGURE 1-1** Data Input And Output Menu

## Import and Export data from and to Azure blob storage

Azure blob storage is a service that stores unstructured data in the cloud as objects, which are commonly known as blobs. Blob storage can store any type of text or binary data, including text data, media files, and pictures. Data stored in Azure blob storage can contain any data, and can be updated and accessed from anywhere.

> **NEED MORE INFORMATION AZURE STORAGE INTRODUCTION**
>
> There are several books and online resources that describe this topic in detail. A good place to start is "Azure Storage Introduction" at: *https://docs.microsoft.com/en-us/azure/storage/common/storage-introduction*.

## Importing data from Azure blob storage

The easiest way to import data into machine learning is to use the Launch Import Data Wizard. To import data, select the Launch Import Data Wizard button. The wizard contains a number of different screens with contextually-based prompts on what to enter in various fields (see Figure 1-2).

**FIGURE 1-2** Import Data window

The data wizard provides a series of screens with prompts to validate the information, and will validate it as well. The wizard can be used to import any data type as shown in Figure 1-3.

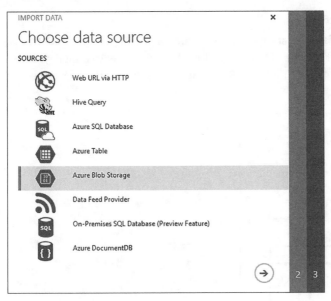

**FIGURE 1-3** Import Data Wizard

If you choose not to use the Import Data Wizard, the properties window default option is Azure Blob Storage. Completing the blanks listed will provide the ability to access data stored in Azure Blob Storage, starting with the first drop down box.

- **Authentication type** This can be Storage Account, Public, or SAS. Most of the time the Storage Account will be selected. To use Public or SAS, you must first generate a time-limited URL in Azure. There is no validation in the properties window, and an incorrect URL can be entered but there will be no error until the code is run.

- **Account name** This contains the name of the storage blob.

- **Account key** This needs to be copied from the properties page of the blob on Azure.

- **Path or directory** This is set based upon the location of the data within the Azure storage blob. In this example, the file being referenced is within the folder output001 and is called dateout, which is why the whole path is output001/dateout. Notice that the actual filename is not being used, but the extension is.

The blob file format accepts ARFF, which is a file format containing header and data information, CSV, TSV, CSV with encoding, and Excel. CSV with encoding is used to include values in the ASCII character set which are higher than 127 and used for characters such as é. If the text does not include data, which requires characters other than the basic latin character set, and uses CSV. If you select Excel you will be prompted to select an Excel data format of either Excel sheet or table, along with the name of the Excel sheet or embedded table name.

## Export to Azure blob storage

Unlike the Import module, there is no wizard for the Export module. Configuring the control for the storage module requires the name of the Azure Blob Storage, Azure Account Key, path, and storage format (see Figure 1-4). CSV, TSF, and ARFF formats are supported, which is the same as for Import.

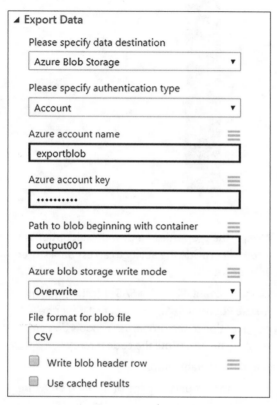

**FIGURE 1-4** Export Data to Azure Blob Storage

In the example above, the blob storage write mode is set to Overwrite, which means the data will be re-written every time the dataset is run. If you want to write data only when the data changes, select the Use Cashed Results option. If the blob storage write mode is set to Error, which is the default, you will get an error if the file already exists.

## Import data from an Azure SQL database

The process for extracting data from an Azure SQL database is similar to the process for importing data from a CSV. Both use the Import Data module and provide the ability to either use the wizard to fill in the form, or enter the information (see Figure 1-5).

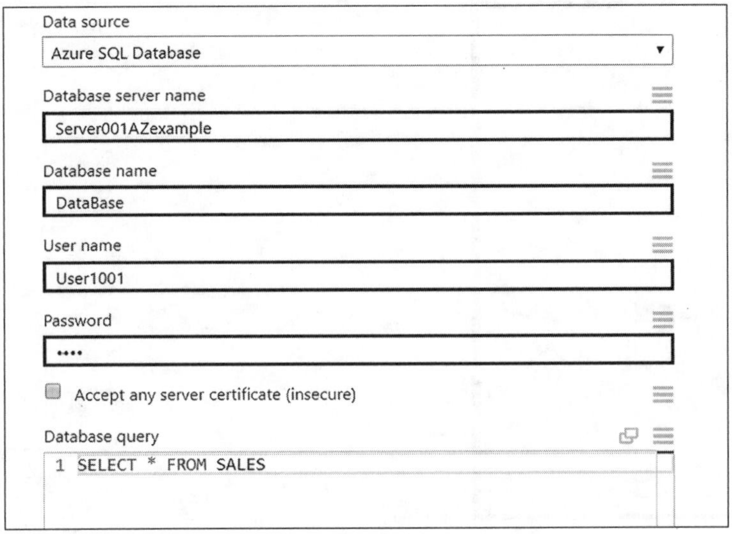

**FIGURE 1-5** Azure SQL Database properties

To complete the form, you will need to know the subscription ID of the Azure account being used, and the name of the database server. The wizard contains dropdown boxes, which connect to your Azure account to run. The properties form expects you to know and correctly spell the names of the items required.

## Export data to Azure SQL database

In the Export module, select Azure SQL database as the destination. The module fields will change for the necessary required fields. Complete the database server name from Azure, as well as the database name, user account name, account password and data table. To specify what data will be inserted into the specified Azure SQL database table, the first step is to identify the columns in their respective order. The column order should correspond to the column names listed in the Comma-Separated List Of Columns To Be Saved field. After that is complete, the next option which needs a value is the number of records added per batch. This value will be used to insert a number of records before Azure creates a write function. If it is a smaller file, you can set the value to the number of records in that file.

## Import data from a local file

To import data from a local file as a new dataset, click on the plus sign and select Import from the bottom of the experiment. Select the Import data set menu and click New, and then select a local file to import (see Figure 1-6).

**FIGURE 1-6** Data Import menu

If the dataset has already been imported into Azure Machine Learning, the new version will overwrite the existing file. There are a number of different kinds of file formats that can be used in an Azure Machine Learning

> *NEED MORE INFORMATION?* **AN R OBJECT OR WORKSPACE .RDATA FILES?**
>
> R workspace objects can be saved into a named image file object with a file suffix of .Rdata so that the objects used in one session can be readily used to start new sessions. For more information see: *http://rfaqs.com/r-workspace-object-image-file.*

## Import data via Hive Queries

Hive queries are part of the Apache Hadoop ecosystem, and they are used to query data stored in HDFS clusters. The language used in Hive queries is called HQL, and is derived from SQL.

> *NEED MORE REVIEW?* **USING HIVE WITH HDINSIGHT**
>
> There are several books and online resources that describe Hive in detail. A good place to start is "What is Apache Hive and HiveQL on Azure HDInsight?" *https://docs.microsoft.com/en-us/azure/hdinsight/hdinsight-use-hive.* Another resource is this introductory course: *https://channel9.msdn.com/Series/Get-Started-MS-Big-Data/03.*

Azure Machine Learning allows data to be accessed from a variety of different locations, including Hadoop, and provides the ability for data to be accessed via a Hive Query (see Figure 1-7). There is a built-in interface to access data stored in Hadoop by using Hive, an Azure HDInsight cluster. To access the data via Hive, you need to know the HCatalog server, user account, password storage account name, and key from your previously configured HDInsight cluster on Azure. Once the connection is established, the Hive query to access the data can be created.

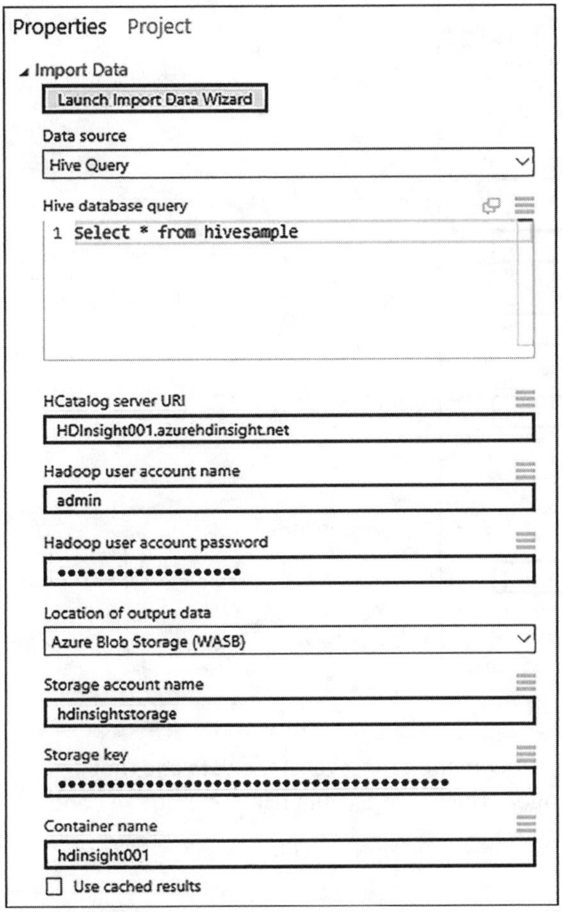

**FIGURE 1-7** Import Data to a Hive dataset

Note that it is possible to enter incorrect data into this section of the form and no validation to occur. The only way to validate that the information in this form is correct is to use the wizard.

## Export Data via Hive Queries

Storing data to an HDFS cluster from Azure Machine Learning is done via the Export module and selecting a Hive Query. Add the Export module to an Azure Machine Learning experiment, and configure the data source as a Hive Query (see Figure 1-8). The Hive Table name will be the location where the data is stored.

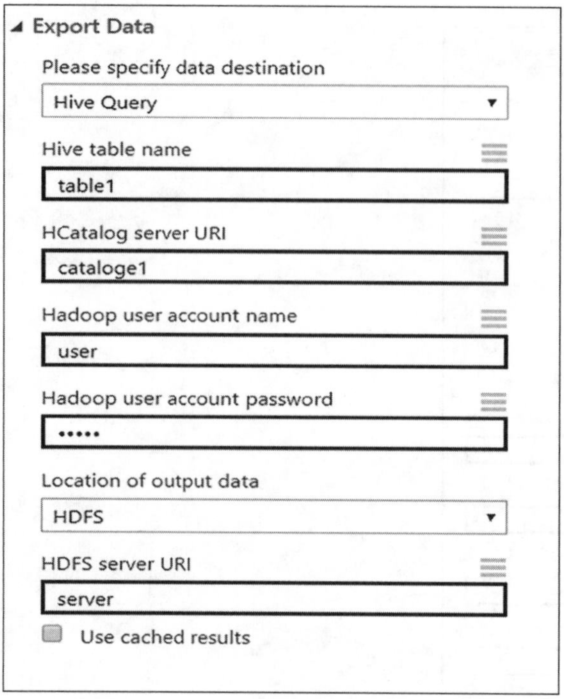

**FIGURE 1-8** Export Data for Hive Queries

To write data to the table every time the experiment is run, even if the data does not change, uncheck the Use Cached Results option. The Azure account name, storage key, and default container should be copied from Azure.

## Import data from a website

Data used in an Azure Machine Learning experiment can also be extracted from a web-based data source (see Figure 1-9). Accessing data from a website does not provide any ability to filter the information. Any and all filtering of the data will need to be performed within an Azure Machine Learning Experiment.

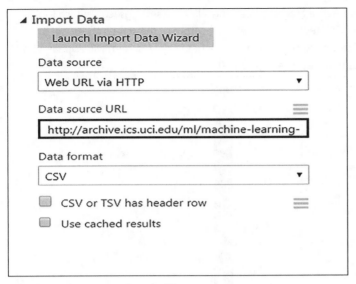

**FIGURE 1-9** Import Data via web URL

## Importing data from an On-Premise database

The <u>Microsoft Data Management Gateway is required</u> to access data from an On-Premise database into Azure Machine Learning. There are some very specific requirements when it comes to installing the Microsoft Data Management Gateway.

> **NOTE THE DATA MANAGEMENT GATEWAY**
>
> It is not possible to import data from On-Premise Database using a free Workspace.

- Only One Data Management Gateway can be installed on a single computer.
- A Power BI Gateway and a Data Management Gateway cannot be installed on the same computer.
- The gateway does not need to be installed on the database server, but the performance improves the closer the gateway is to the database server.  Microsoft does not recommend installing on the database server, so the gateway does not compete for resources with the server.
- The Data Management Gateway cannot be shared across workspaces.
- Only the workspace owner can create a gateway.
- The local computer needs to have the ability to access data in front of any firewall that may be in place.  The default port in use is 8050.

To add a data gateway from Azure Machine Learning, click the settings icon, which looks like a gear, and click on the Data Gateway menu. At the bottom of the screen there will be an icon shaped like a plus. Click on the plus icon to add a gateway. A screen will appear with prompts for you to add a data gateway (see Figure 1-10).

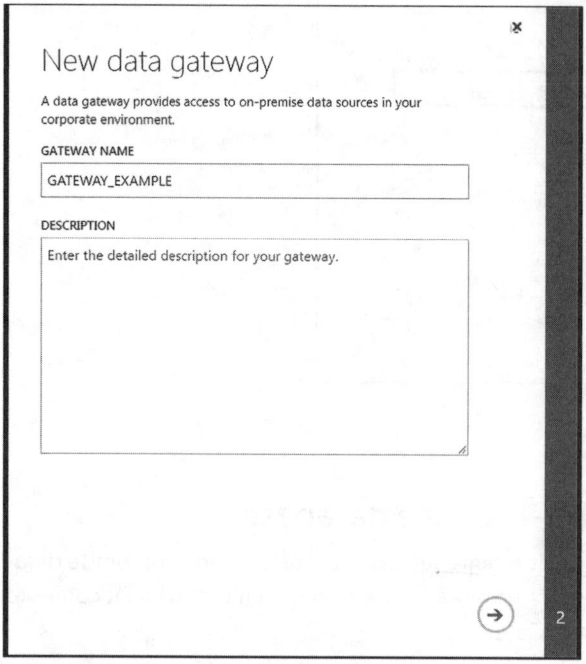

**New data gateway**

A data gateway provides access to on-premise data sources in your corporate environment.

GATEWAY NAME

GATEWAY_EXAMPLE

DESCRIPTION

Enter the detailed description for your gateway.

**FIGURE 1-10** New Data Gateway

> **NOTE DATAGATEWAY INSTALLATION**
>
> It's important that you have permissions as owner of the workspace to be available to install a new data gateway.

For the Data Gateway to work, a Data Gateway application will need to be installed on a PC. Just click and download Data Management Gateway and install. This application provides access to the database for Azure Machine Learning to use. The first screen of the Data Gateway PC application allows the language to be selected (see Figure 1-11).

**FIGURE 1-11** Microsoft Data Management Gateway Setup

The installation wizard is simple. Just click Next to install the application, then run the Data Management Gateway and insert the registration key from Azure Machine Learning (see Figure 1-12).

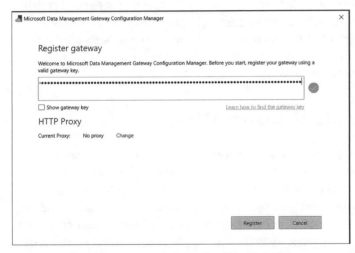

**FIGURE 1-12** Data Management Gateway Configuration Manager

Once the online gateway contains the key, the data gateway can be configured and a connection made to the local database. The connection can be tested by clicking Test in the Data Management Gateway, and completing the Test Connection Form (see Figure 1-13).

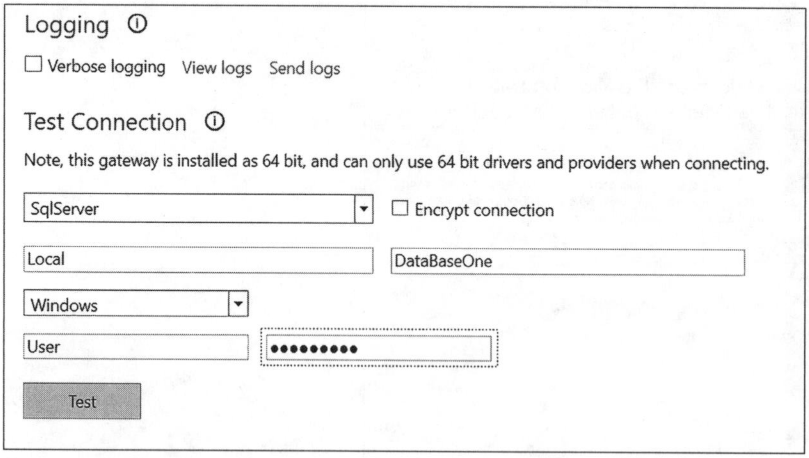

**FIGURE 1-13** Test Connection

Upon clicking the Test button, a window will be returned indicating whether or not a successful connection has been made between the local database and Azure Machine Learning. Success is required to be able to import data from On-Premises SQL Database to Azure Machine Learning.

When creating a data source using data from a database, it is important to remember that decimal and money data types are not supported in Azure Machine Learning. If you create a query using these data types, your SQL statement must cast these values to floats or integer data types for Azure Machine Learning. You will receive and error running the Import from SQL Server if the data types are not modified.

# Skill 1.2: Explore and summarize data

Exploring the data provides insight into how the data can be used as part of an experiment. Examining the statistical values and the distribution of data values is important to determine how the data can be used in experiments. Datasets that contain missing data or data containing many inaccuracies may not be suitable for use in an experiment. It is important to understand everything possible regarding the data including the data types, distribution, continuity, and the accuracy because it may be necessary to change them in order to comply with the data formats required of various algorithms, and the results of an experiment depend upon quality of the data.

**This skill explains how to:**

- Create univariate summaries
- Create multivariate summaries
- Visualize univariate distributions
- Use existing Microsoft R or Python notebooks for custom summaries and c ustom visualizations
- Use zip archives to import external packages for R or Python

The distribution data within a dataset shows all of the possible intervals or values of the data and their frequency. The distributions can be categorical or continuous in nature. Categorical, or nominal data, is qualitative and represents characteristics of the data such as gender, race, and eye color. Data can be divided into groups, but you can't clearly see the order in those groups. A categorical ordinal has a categorical variable with an order, such as the economic status (low, medium, or high).

The analysis of categorical data generally involves counting the number of observations that fall into each group. Continuous data is quantitative and represents measurements that can be classified as groups. For example, instead of showing age as any value, it can be made into categories by assigning the various ages into bins or groups by combining the data into intervals: 0-12 child, 13-18 teenager, and 19 and above adult. Instead of a continuous group, the column Age can be made into a category with three values representing these three groups.

## Create Univariate summaries

To review data in one column, it is helpful to create a univariate summary. This kind of analysis is used to describe the content of the data through the analysis of the results of summarizing, grouping and locating patterns with in a single column of data. Using the sample datasets in Azure Machine Learning is a good way to explore the data and perform univariate summaries in Azure Machine Learning because there are some default measures to explore the data, depending on the type of data. To visualize the data, create a new blank experiment. Using the menu on the left side of the Azure Machine Learning workspace, click on the Saved Datasets option, and then select the Iris Two Class Data dataset. Click on the dot at the bottom of the menu and select Visualize as shown in Figure 1-14.

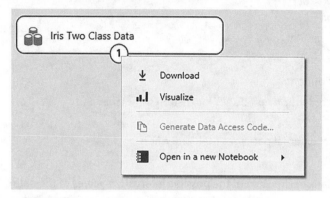

**FIGURE 1-14** Dataset Menu for a dataset

Click on the sepal-width column and view the Statistics on the right side of the screen (see Figure 1-15).

| Statistics | |
|---|---|
| Mean | 33.2409 |
| Median | 29 |
| Min | 21 |
| Max | 81 |
| Standard Deviation | 11.7602 |
| Unique Values | 52 |
| Missing Values | 0 |
| Feature Type | Numeric Feature |

**FIGURE 1-15** Univariate Statistics sample

If the data selected for analysis is numeric, Azure Machine Learning displays statistics showing summary and statistical information on the data included. The values are displayed as statistical functions, and include the mean, also known as the average, the mode which is the most common value, and the median that is the value in the middle. The standard deviation is also provided, which shows the distance a value is away from the mean for all of the values of the column, which in this example is age. The frequency of missing values is displayed, which provides an indication of how this column can be used in a machine learning experiment. If the dataset has high number of missing values, you will need to determine what to do with the column as you may want to include it in the experiment. There are a times when you will entirely replace the missing values or discard the column.

The Visualize option, available when you click on the dot underneath each module, provides a way to visually explore the contents of each column with histograms and box plots, as well as provides the ability to compare visualizations for each value (see Figure 1-16).

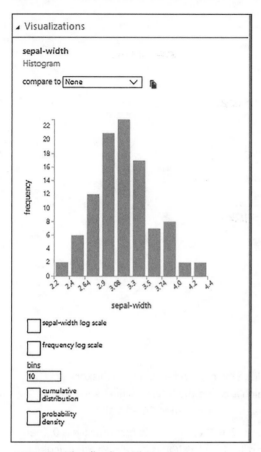

**FIGURE 1-16** Visualizations Histogram

To switch the display from a Histogram to a Box Plot, click on the icon on the top left of the screen. Like Histograms, Box Plots are only available for numeric columns because Box Plots provide information regarding the value of the median and the values above and below the median. In a Box Plot, data is separated into four equal parts known as quartiles. The number at the top of the first quartile is used to represent the value at the bottom of the box. The minimum and maximum values may appear as data points above and below the values in the box plot. The median is the straight line in the middle of the box, and the top of the box is the value in the upper quartile (see Figure 1-17).

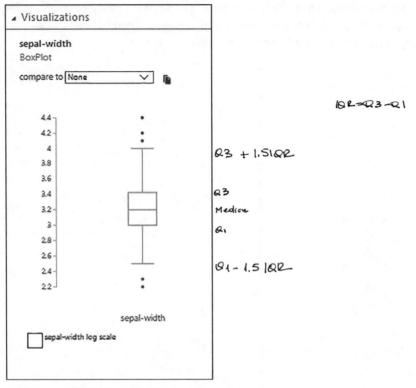

FIGURE 1-17  Visualization Box Plot

The lines at the top and bottom of the box plot, which are referred to as whiskers, are calculated based upon the values in the box, which is called the Interquartile Range (IQR). The actual minimum value is used when the actual value is greater than Q1 – 1.5 *IQR.

For example, in this dataset there are six values: -2, 0, 1, 2, 2.5, 3. The first quartile is 0, the second quartile or median is 1, and the third quartile is 2. The IQR is 2 because it is calculated as Q3-Q1 or 2-0. The minimum value is 0 - 1.5 * 2 = -3, since the actual minimum value is -2, which is used as the whisker since it is greater than the calculated value. The upper whisker is calculated as Q3+1.5*IQR or 2+1.5*2=5. Since the actual maximum value is 3, which is less than the calculated maximum value, the actual maximum number is used. For situations where the actual minimum or maximum values are greater than the calculated amounts, the actual values are represented as dots on the chart and are considered outliers.

> **NEED MORE REVIEW?  ABOUT HISTOGRAMS AND BOX PLOT**
>
> This online resource describes this topic in more detail at: *https://blogs.office.com/en-us/2015/08/18/visualize-statistics-with-histogram-pareto-and-box-and-whisker-charts/*.

# Create Multivariate Summaries

The major purpose for this kind of analysis is to describe the behavior and the relationships of two or more variables, and to summarize, group, and find patterns in the data. There are a number of different modules employed in an experiment to perform analysis on more than one variable. This step is important to find patterns within the data. Principal Component Analysis (PCA), Group Categorical Values, and Group Data into Bins, are components that can be found under Data Transformation in the Scale and Reduce.

We can examine the contents of several columns by creating a multivariate summary on the sample Iris Two Class Dataset. If you look at Figure 1-16, you may notice the Compare To drop down box. This drop down box contains the other columns in the dataset. Selecting the Petal-Width column, creates a multivariate summary displaying the values of both columns in a scatter chart (see Figure 1-18). The labeled X and Y axes show the values of each column displayed respectively. The two columns display uniquely separate values in this data set.

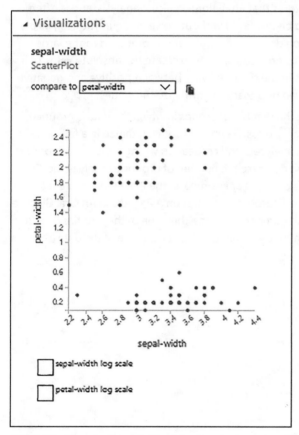

**FIGURE 1-18** Visualizations multivariate summary

# Visualize univariate distributions

Azure Machine Learning also provides the ability to provide deeper data visualization analysis with multiple options available to further visualize the data. Using the Pima Indians Diabetes Binary Classification dataset, right-click and select Visualize. Select the Age column, and the following options appear as checkboxes on the bottom right side of the window. View the screen on the bottom right underneath the histogram to see the following options, which appear as checkboxes.

- Age (years) log scale
- Frequency Log Scale
- Bins
- Cumulative Distribution
- Probability Density

The Log Scale provides different features that are helpful in visual analysis, and is often used to provide a large range of data to be displayed without noise being introduced as the smaller values at the bottom of the graph drop off the scale when compared to the larger values. Another reason to analyze data using a Log Scale is to create the absolute value of a given set of numbers. If there are values in the data that vary between positive and negative values, to obtain clearer analysis it is often necessary to normalize the values.

The Bins option allows you to change the number of groups in which the data is grouped. By default the data is often added to large groups. Having the data contained in a few larger groups loses the detail of the data being analyzed, and can lead to wrong conclusions about the dataset. It is advisable to increase and decrease the number of groups to analyze the distribution of data from different points of view. For example, in the Pima Indians Diabetes Binary Classification, if the column Plasma Glucose Concentration A 2 Hours In An Oral Glucose Tolerance Test is selected with the default number of 10 bins, then one of the bins has over 200 values. Modifying the value of bins from 10 to 20, changes the perspective of the data (see Figure 1-19).

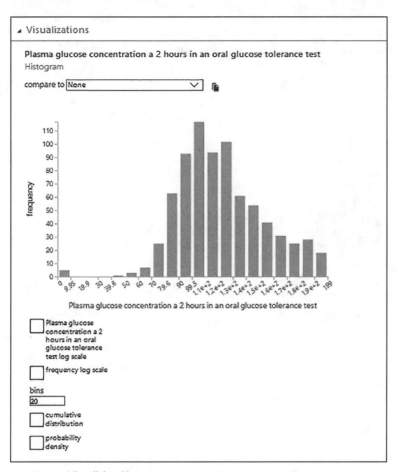

**FIGURE 1-19** Visualizing Bins

Setting the number of Bins to 20, the frequency values decrease to 110, and the values increase more naturally than if there are 10 bins in a histogram.

The cumulative distribution shows the probability that if a random number is taken from the dataset it belongs to, the value range is less than or equal to the value of the range. For example, in the Pima Indians Diabetes Binary Classification, when the column Plasma Glucose Concentration a 2 Hours In An Oral Glucose Tolerance Test set the bins to 10, and the Cumulative Distribution option is checked, the graph illustrates that the probability to achieve values <=60 is remote (see Figure 1-20).

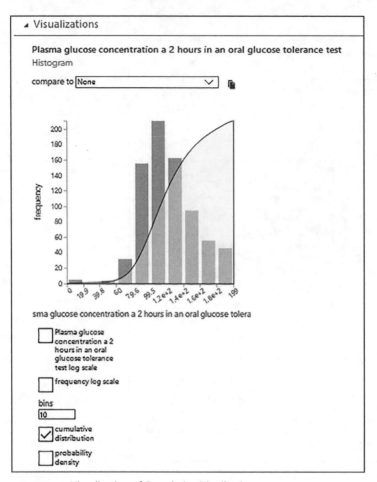

**FIGURE 1-20** Visualization of Cumulative Distribution

A further review of the data shows that most of the values in the data set are higher than 60. Probability density provides a random number taken from the data set belonging to the value point, which is equal to the value of the range and is not a cumulative value. It is easy to see where most of the values are with the Pima Indians Diabetes Binary Classification when the column Diastolic Blood Pressure (mm Hg) is viewed with the Probability Distribution option checked (see Figure 1-21).

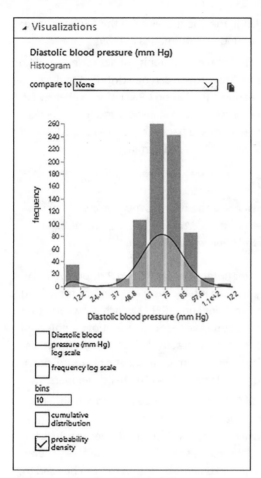

**FIGURE 1-21** Visualization Probability Density

Looking at this visualization, it is clear that the highest probability is between 61 and 73, because there are more values in the data set for those values.

## Use existing Microsoft R or Python notebooks for custom summaries and custom visualizations

Before introducing advanced visualization techniques, let's define some basic concepts. First, what are R and Python? The R language is an open source project derived from a language called S for "statistics," which was created at Bell Laboratories in the 1970s, and was released as an open source language in 1996. The Python language is interpreted, interactive, and is free software. It is an object-oriented programming language, the successor of the ABC language, and created by Guido van Rossum at Centrum Wiskunde & Informatica in 1989.

One of the main reasons for using Python or R is that the community of data scientists who use these languages has grown a lot in recent years. This growth can be attributed to the inclusion of many specialized packages for Machine Learning. R relies on CRAN (Comprehensive R Archive Networks) servers. Python has the SciPy ecosystem, with statistical and data processing packages such as Pandas or Numpy. Both languages have packages for creating advanced visualizations that complement those available in Azure Machine Learning.

> ***NEED MORE INFORMATION*** **R AND PYTHON**
>
> **Introductions to each language can be found in more detail at:** *https://mran.microsoft.com/documents/what-is-r//docs.microsoft.com/es-es/azure/storage/common/storage-introduction.* **And also at:** *https://docs.python.org/3/faq/general.html#what-is-python.*

Azure Machine Learning also implements Jupyter notebooks for writing Python and R.  A Jupyter notebook uses an implementation of IPython, an interactive web interface for writing code. Jupyter notebooks are a multilingual Read Eval Print Loop (REPL), which allows you to create and share documents while documenting the code in one location. A Jupyter notebook makes it easy to mix code and text in the same document interactively, because the interface provides for the ability to run code run directly from the document and get a response, providing a good method for documenting and working collaboratively with other developers.

Although Notebooks are an implementation of Python, they can be used to run either R or Python version 2 or 3.  Python notebooks are pre-loaded with Anaconda, and other libraries can be added using pip or conda. R Notebooks use Microsoft R Open (MRO) version 3.30. Microsoft may choose to include other versions at a later data as they become available. R libraries can be installed using the format install.packages("pkg name"). Notebooks can be used to build an ML model using R or Python code, and deploying it to Azure Machine Learning, or to call an existing experiment as part of Azure Machine Learning.

> ***NEED MORE INFORMATION?*** **JUPYTER NOTEBOOK INTRODUCTION**
>
> **Jupyter Notebooks is an open source web application that provides a location to create and share documents containing both code and the code documentation. This link describes them in detail:** *https://jupyter.org/index.html.*

There are two options for adding Notebooks within the Azure Machine Learning Studio. The first method is to add a Notebook by selecting the Notebook icon on the left side of the screen in Azure Machine Learning Learning Studio, and clicking on the +New Icon in the bottom left corner (see Figure 1-22).

FIGURE 1-22 Adding Jupyter Notebooks

The other method is to incorporate a Notebook from inside an Azure Machine Learning experiment by clicking on any of the dots on the bottom of the components, and selecting Open in a new Notebook. You then select the kind of Notebook that you wish to use, either Python 3, Python 2, or R (see Figure 1-23).

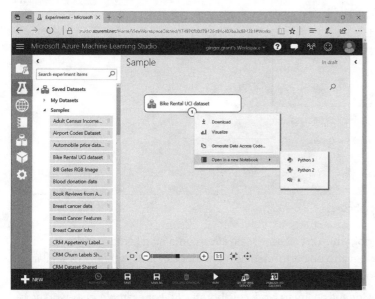

FIGURE 1-23 Add Jupyter Notebook within an Azure Machine Learning Experiment

If the Azure components do not provide the information needed for summarization, you can always include R notebooks with the required information. Notebooks allow you to use existing code created with R or Python in an Azure Machine Learning experiment to customize the fit in ways not provided for in existing modules. For example, if you wish to review the kernel density of different variables, you may want to use an R library to perform this data analysis and draw a graph to display the results (see Figure 1-24).

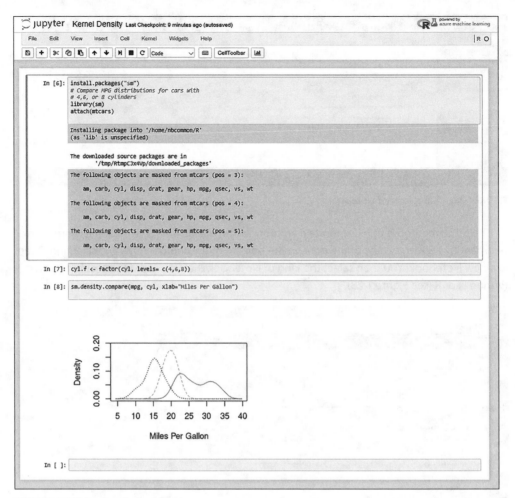

**FIGURE 1-24** Using Jupyter notebooks

Here is a sample notebook which creates a visualization containing kernel density for an R dataset. The same work can also be performed using notebooks with Python, in a similar fashion to the example shown in R.

Jupyter notebooks provide the ability to work collaboratively. For example, a co-worker sent me this notebook as a starting point to perform some analysis to the Pima Indians Diabetes dataset (see Figure 1-25).

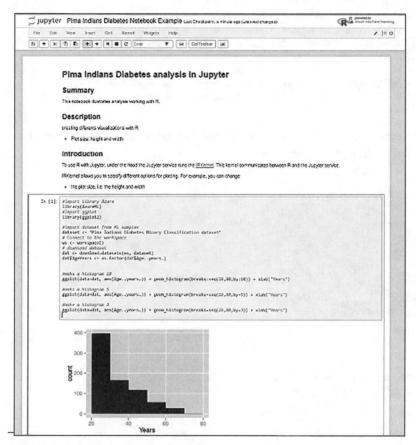

**FIGURE 1-25** Example Jupyter notebook

The first step in the analysis is to create three histograms to establish which data groups provide the best ability to analyze the data in the greatest detail.

**R code Example for Creating Histogram**

```
#import library Azure
library(AzureML)
#Import ggplot
library(ggplot2)
#import dataset from ML samples
dataset <- "Pima Indians Diabetes Binary Classification dataset"
# Connect to the workspace
ws <- workspace()
# download dataset
dat <- download.datasets(ws, dataset)
dat$AgeYears <- as.factor(dat$Age..years.)

#make a histogram 10
ggplot(data=dat, aes(Age..years.)) + geom_histogram(breaks=seq(20,80,by=10))
 + xlab("Years") + labs(title="Histogram for Age group by 10 values ",
x="Age", y="Frequency")
```

```
#make a histogram 5
ggplot(data=dat, aes(Age..years.)) + geom_histogram(breaks=seq(20,80,by=5))
+ xlab("Years") + labs(title="Histogram for Age group by 5 values",
x="Age", y="Frequency")
#make a histogram 3
ggplot(data=dat, aes(Age..years.)) + geom_histogram(breaks=seq(20,80,by=3))
+ xlab("Years") + labs(title="Histogram for Age group by 3 values",
x="Age", y="Frequency")
```

After the code has been created, the Jupyter notebook also contains the visualizations that are created as part of the R code (see Figure 1-26).

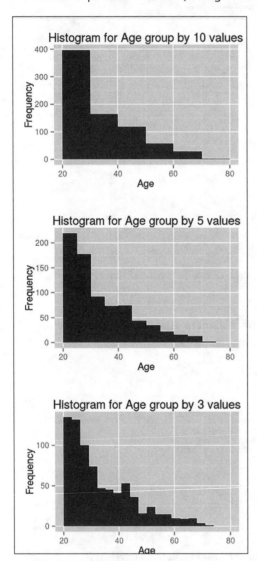

**FIGURE 1-26** Jupyter Notebook contents

Looking at the results, it is easy to develop a conclusion based on the three visualizations. When the data is displayed in groups of three, you can see peaks in the graph that in the other groups can't be seen as having larger groups soften the data. Upon review, we know that groups of three are the best option for analyzing this data. We add another histogram with the value of the mean and the cumulative probability curve (see Figure 1-27).

```
#The visualization provides more information for the  3rd group
#it's important  add median line and accumulative distribution
p<-ggplot(dat, aes(Age..years.)) + labs(title="Histogram for Age", x="Age",
y="Frequency") +stat_ecdf(color="red") +
geom_bar(breaks=seq(20,80,by=3),col="blue",fill="blue",alpha = .2 ,aes(y =
 (..count..)*10/sum(..count..)))
p+ geom_vline(aes(xintercept=mean(Age..years.)),color="red", linetype="dashed",
 size=1)
```

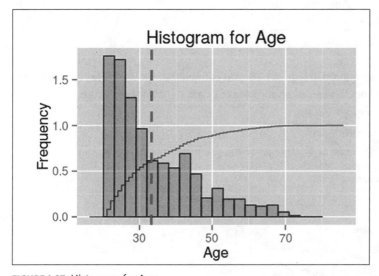

**FIGURE 1-27**  Histogram for Age

Upon reviewing this analysis, you decide to create a multivariable analysis. Initially we will create a scatter plot to display the Age versus the number of times pregnant (see Figure 1-28).

```
# Generate a plot of Age versus Number of time pregnant
ggplot(data = dat)
        + geom_point(mapping =
        aes(x = Age..years., y = Number.of.times.pregnant)
        ,breaks=seq(1,15,by=1), alpha = 1/50) +
         xlab("Age years") +ylab("Number of times pregnant")
```

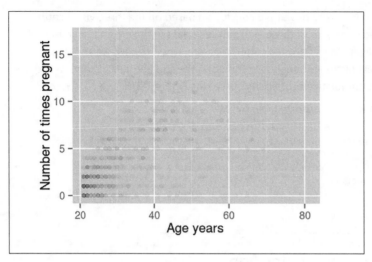

FIGURE 1-28 Scatterplot generated as part of Jupyter notebook

When reviewing the information in Figure 1-28, you can see that most of cases are between 0 to 5 number of children and 30 years of age. To see the data behavior better, the next step adds a regression line (see Figure 1-29).

```
# Fit a regression line to this data
ggplot(data = dat, mapping = aes(x =  Age..years., y = Number.of.times.pregnant)) +
geom_point(alpha = 1/50) +geom_smooth(color = "red") + xlab("Age years") +
ylab("Number of times pregnant")
```

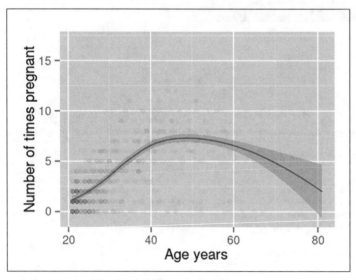

FIGURE 1-29 Regression line added to the scatterplot

The regression line shows that the average number of children with the current population is growing up to 50 years, and it also shows that for the final values, the degree of uncertainty increases. You could have an error of +/- 1 child, because you must have less data than people with ages greater than or equal to 50 years.

Lastly, create some additional visualizations to compare the data by body mass category. The first step is to create a categorical variable from BodyMassIndexWeight, which is a continuous variable number.

```
#Create categorical variable from BodyMassIndex

#Underweight: BMI is less than 18.Normal weight: BMI is 18.5 to 24.9
#Overweight: BMI is 25 to 29.9
#Obese: BMI is 30 or more

dat$BodyMasscat<-cut(dat$Body.mass.index..weight.in.kg..height.in.m..2., c(-
Inf,18.5,24.9,30,Inf),
labels=c("Underweight","Normal","Overweight","Obese"))

# Facet by BodyMassCategory
ggplot(data = dat, mapping = aes(x = Age..years., y = Number.of.times.pregnant)) +
      geom_point(alpha = 1/50) +
      geom_smooth(color = "red") +
      facet_wrap( ~ BodyMasscat, nrow = 2) +
xlab("Age years") +
ylab("Number of times pregnant")
```

The results of the R code are also displayed in the Juypter notebook (see Figure 1-30).

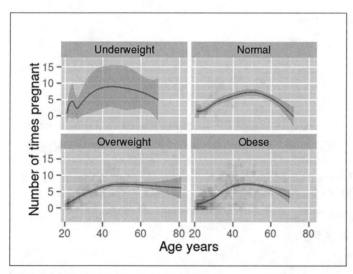

**FIGURE 1-30** Example of Scatter plot comparing more than two variables

With the facet function, you can create comparisons of two or more variables, in this case allowing you to see the relationship of the Number of Children versus Age for each of the categories that have been defined. From the graph, you can see that there are very few cases where the data shows underweight. Having a few items in this category may be the reason why the regression line shows such a large range of variations, because it is harder for the algorithm to fit such a line where there are few observations. Upon further review of the data, most of the data lies in the obese and overweight categories.

## Using zip archives to deploy custom R modules

Within Azure Machine Learning, code written in R can be deployed by uploading a custom R module to an Azure Machine Learning workspace that can be called from within an Azure Machine Learning experiment.

> **NOTE WHAT LANGUAGES ARE SUPPORTED IN CUSTOM MODUELS?**
>
> Currently, R is the only language supported in custom modules, but support for additional languages is scheduled for future releases.

The R code needs to be uploaded as part of a zip archive containing the R source file and an XML definition file. Additional files can be included to provide further functionality, but a zip file must contain those two components. Here is an example of a source file created in R that appends to datasets.

```
CustomAddRows <- function(dataset1, dataset2, swap=FALSE)
{
    if (swap)
    {
        return (rbind(dataset2, dataset1));
    }
    else
    {
        return (rbind(dataset1, dataset2));
    }
}
```

The XML file needs to contain the base language, the script file, the name of the R function, the attributes of the inputs and outputs of the function, and any parameters that may be required. The values in the XML file need to match exactly the elements in the corresponding R file. The output is not defined in the R script, but the order must match that of the inputs in the R function. A sample of the XML file code is included here. These two files need to be combined to create one zip file, which can be uploaded to Azure Machine Learning.

```
<!-- Defined a module using an R Script -->

<Module name="Custom Add Rows">
    <Owner>Microsoft Corporation</Owner>
    <Description>Appends one dataset to another. Dataset 2 is concatenated to
Dataset 1 when Swap is FALSE, and vice versa when Swap is TRUE.</Description>

<!-- Specify the base language, script file and R function to use for this module. -->
    <Language name="R"
      sourceFile="CustomAddRows.R"
      entryPoint="CustomAddRows" />
```

```
<!-- Define module input and output ports -->
<!-- Note: The values of the id attributes in the Input and Arg elements must match
the parameter names in the R Function CustomAddRows defined in CustomAddRows.R. -->
    <Ports>
        <Input id="dataset1" name="Dataset 1" type="DataTable">
            <Description>First input dataset</Description>
        </Input>
        <Input id="dataset2" name="Dataset 2" type="DataTable">
            <Description>Second input dataset</Description>
        </Input>
        <Output id="dataset" name="Dataset" type="DataTable">
            <Description>The combined dataset</Description>
        </Output>
    </Ports>

<!-- Define module parameters -->
    <Arguments>
        <Arg id="swap" name="Swap" type="bool" >
            <Description>Swap input datasets.</Description>
        </Arg>
    </Arguments>
</Module>
```

To add the module to Azure Machine Learning, click on the +New icon at the bottom left of the screen, and select the module from the left side of the list (see Figure 1-31).

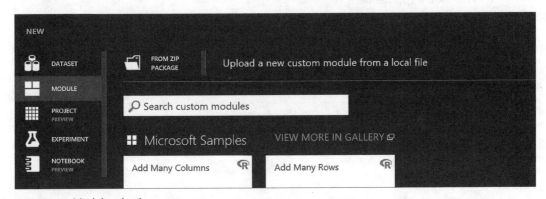

**FIGURE 1-31** Module selection

Click on the From Zip Package option and a pop up window will appear prompting for the location of the zip file to upload to Azure Machine Learning. Once the file has been loaded successfully, a message will appear at the bottom of the screen, letting you know that the module has been added. The new component will appear in the Custom menu in the Experiment section of the Azure Machine Learning Studio.

# Skill 1.3: Cleanse data for Azure Machine Learning

The expression *Garbage In Garbage Out* can definitely be applied to machine learning. One of the keys to a successful experiment is the importance of transforming the data to a format that can be used as a good set of inputs for an algorithm. Data not needed for the experiment may need to be excluded. Incorrect or outlier data may need to be removed. Missing data needs to be handled in some way. Are you going to exclude it? Categorize it as missing? Substitute a missing value for a default value? Azure Machine Learning provides modules designed to address fixing the data to improve the results. The cleansing is done on the data with the experiment, so it will not change the input data.

Data used in a machine learning experiment needs to be in a specific format. Missing data needs to be modified in a method that allows for the data to be processed correctly. Perhaps you wish to filter the data to process different values separately or exclude values of a certain kind. Depending on the type of missing data and the percentage of the missing values, you may decide to eliminate the column or fill in the missing values with either a default value or a calculation, such as the mean of the existing values. The choice of which method employed will of course depend upon the experiment.

> **This skill explains how to:**
>
> - Identify and Address Missing Data
> - Apply filters to limit a dataset to the desired rows
> - Identify and Address Outliers
> - Remove columns and rows of Datasets

Azure Machine Learning contains a number of built in components designed to help the data cleansing process, including filtering, handling missing data, removing outliers, and completing columns and rows.

> **NEED MORE REVIEW?** **ADDITIONAL CLEANSING DATA INFORMATION**
>
> To learn more about cleansing data for Azure Machine Learning, the topic is described in detail at: *https://docs.microsoft.com/en-us/azure/machine-learning/machine-learning-data-science-prepare-data*.

## Identify and address missing data

There are different approaches you can employ to resolve the problem of missing data. For instance, you can perform missing value substitution only if 3% or fewer of the rows contain missing values. In that case it might make sense to complete the field with the median value of the existing values if it is a number or the most common feature in a category. The method selected will be determined by knowing your data and using a value that makes the most sense.

From the Manipulation section, select the Clean Missing Data module to your workflow, and review the properties (see Figure 1-31). Select the columns to be cleaned, all of which will have the same rule applied. The options for when the cleansing will be applied are data driven. The Minimum Missing Value Ratio that evaluates the ratio of the value should be modified. If the ratio of missing values is less than the value specified, cleansing will not occur. The Maximum Missing Value Ratio will not cleanse data if the ratio is higher than the number specified (see Figure 1-32).

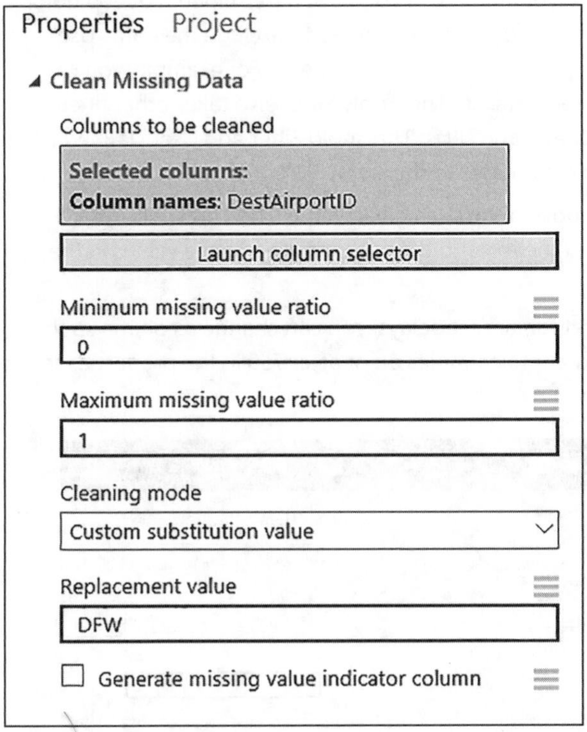

---

**Properties** Project

⊿ **Clean Missing Data**

Columns to be cleaned

**Selected columns:**
**Column names:** DestAirportID

Launch column selector

Minimum missing value ratio

0

Maximum missing value ratio

1

Cleaning mode

Custom substitution value ▽

Replacement value

DFW

☐ Generate missing value indicator column

---

**FIGURE 1-32** Clean Missing Data module

There are several different cleaning methods available. To replace the missing value with a value of your choice, select the default Custom substitution value from the dropdown box and enter a replacement value. If you want to indicate which value has been changed, check the Generate Missing Value Indicator Column option. This will add a new column to your dataset indicating which values were generated by this module. Among the different options available in the Cleaning mode dropdown box include the ability to delete missing columns or rows of data thatch are missing.

If there is a lot of data missing, it might make sense to remove the column entirely, because it is not possible to interpolate what the missing information may be. In that case, use the Select from Dataset module to include only the columns you wish to include into the experiment.

**NEED MORE REVIEW** **ON PROCESSING MISSING VALUES?**

For a more detailed review on how to handle missing values with the Clean Missing Data module: *https://msdn.microsoft.com/en-us/library/azure/dn906028.aspx*.

Apply filters to limit a dataset to the desired rows. Using the exploration techniques discussed earlier helps determine how good your data is. If you have determined that you don't wish to include some of it, there are various modules you can use to exclude the data. Use the Apply Filter module to exclude columns that meet a given criteria. For example, you can exclude all numeric columns from the used dataset. The Apply Filter also takes other filters as input. The FIR, IIR, Median Filter, Moving Average Filter, Threshold Filter and User Defined Filter are all designed to be inputs along with the dataset to the Apply Filter.

Use two modules to exclude values above or below a given value. The Threshold Filter allows you to set the threshold value, and the threshold value is applied to the values in the Apply filter.

For example, using the sample dataset for airport delays, you can change a column so that the CRSDepTime Departure column only contains values on or after 759 in the properties section (see Figure 1-33).

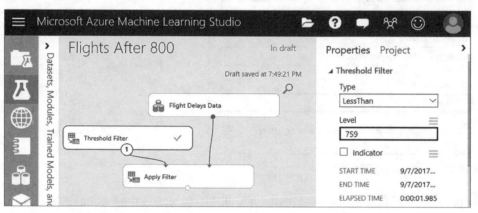

**FIGURE 1-33** Threshold Filter

Notice that the Threshold Filter is set to remove everything Less Than 759. After running Apply Filter, all of the values below 759 are excluded from the data. If you need to apply two different filters in your experiment, you need to apply the filters to different workflows as there is only one filter applied, the Apply filter. The one filter can be used to filter multiple columns. There are four other filter types you might need to apply in your experiment, FIR, IIR, User Defined, which lets you set more IIR or FIR properties.

Using this module does not change your source dataset. Instead, it creates a new dataset in your workspace that you can use in the subsequent workflow. You can also save the new, cleaned dataset for reuse.

This module also outputs a definition of the transformation used to clean the missing values. You can re-use this transformation on other datasets that have the same schema, by using the Apply Transformation module.

Another filtering technique is to remove the duplicate rows that you may have found while analyzing your data. For example, while reading the product table, two records are found with the same productid. One record can identify that the data is not unique, and the other record can identify how one of the duplicate rows should be removed. To resolve this issue, add the Remove Duplicate Rows module to the experiment. Select the duplicate column name for evaluation to remove the records with multiple copies. This module is designed to look at the keyed columns removing the rows that have matching values.

---

**NEED MORE REVIEW? ON FILTERING**

To learn about how adding a filter can transform the data read: *https://msdn.microsoft.com/en-us/library/azure/dn905876.aspx* and *https://msdn.microsoft.com/en-us/library/azure/dn905843.aspx*.

---

Perhaps you wish to decrease the number for records contained within a dataset. The Partition and Sample module provides the ability to divide the number of records in several ways. There are a number of different reasons for wanting to split a dataset into groups. In subsequent chapters, we will cover why splitting it is useful for training data in an experiment, but you may also wish to apply this technique when evaluating the data. With the Azure Machine Learning component Partition and Sample, the data is randomly split into subsamples. The data is trained multiple times and each subgroup is at one point the test group. The accuracy is based upon the average of each run of the data. The individual subsamples created are known as folds.

To ensure that the dataset is not biased or skewed, you may want to apply a cross validation process. This technique consists of randomly splitting the data in N partitions or folds. When training a model using this option, it will be trained multiple times and the number of times is equal to the number of partitions specified in the Specify Number of Folds to Split Evenly Into field. The accuracy is based upon the average of each run of the data. If you aren't using this technique, it is common to split the data into groups with a random sample of the data for evaluation or training. It is also possible to partition the data based upon values within it then make changes to only one of the groups.

To split data into groups of rows, select Assign To Folds if you want to create groups for cross-validation (see Figure 1-35). If the Use Replacement In The Partitioning option is checked, the groups will contain multiples of the same records. If the option is unchecked, each group will contain unique records in each group. If a randomized split is not checked, the records will be added to each group in an orderly format in the same manner that cards are dealt by a dealer. If the option is checked, the records will be added to each group in a random fashion. Creating a random seed will cause the partition to be created differently every time the partition is created, which will decrease the chance of over fitting. If the default value of 0 is selected, the records added to each partition will be added in the same manner every time the module is run. Partitions can be created evenly, or the records contained can be divided up in uneven groups by providing a comma delimited list such as: .1, .2, .4, .25, .05, which adds up to 1. If you need the data to be split based upon the value in a single column, change the stratified split option to true and select a categorical column of either a string or an integer to serve as the strata column (see Figure 1-34).

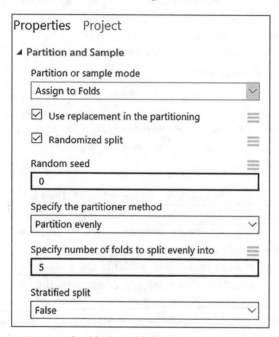

**FIGURE 1-34** Partitioning with the Partition and Sample Window

## Identify and Address Outliers

Some algorithms have issues when data contains a few results that are greatly different from the majority of the values. Data outside a range of values may indicate that the data is incorrect. Worse, data outliers can skew the algorithm training by modifying the mean values and provide longer training times, and thus less accurate models.

To remove outlier values, go to the Scale and Reduce menu and select the Clip Values module. This module contains parameters that can be set to replace or remove data above or below a certain threshold. To remove data above a threshold, select the Threshold option ClipPeaks. To apply the modification to lower boundaries, from the dropdown box select

Subpeaks. Both upper and lower boundaries will apply the modification if the option ClipPeak-sandSubPeaks is selected (see Figure 1-35).

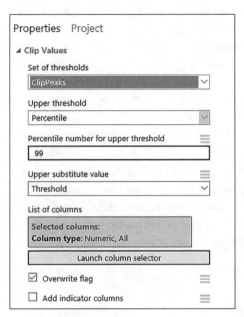

**FIGURE 1-35** Set Thresholds

The same rules can be applied to all of the data in a dataset, when all numeric columns are selected, ensuring that all of the data in a dataset will follow a normal distribution. Individual columns can be selected if the impact is limited to a column or two.

> **NEED MORE REVIEW ON OUTLIERS?**
>
> Detecting outliers and determining how to handle them is discussed in more detail here: *https://msdn.microsoft.com/en-us/library/azure/dn905918.aspx.*

## Remove columns and rows of datasets

The data used in an experiment may need to be cleaned to either remove rows of data that contain erroneous data or columns not needed in the experiment. There are several modules that can be used to accomplish this task: Clean Missing Data, Remove Duplicate rows, and Select Columns in Dataset. With Clean Missing Data, you have the option to remove rows or columns containing missing data. Removing Duplicate Rows will parse through the entire dataset eliminating any duplicates. With the Select columns in Dataset module, you have the ability to decrease the data being analyzed by selecting a smaller set of columns.

# Skill 1.4 Perform feature engineering

Feature Engineering tasks on a set of data are performed to improve the outcome of an experiment by creating features that help improve the learning process, leading to better results. Feature selection can improve the performance of a model by determining which columns can provide improved accuracy, while using less data, as they identify the important columns and remove unneeded and redundant information from the model. This technique is not universally applied to all models, because there are cases that the person performing the application will understand the data well enough to provide this analysis. After the model has been trained, there are further steps that can be implemented to improve variable selection including using the Permutation Feature Importance module, discussed in subsequent chapters.

Azure Machine Learning (ML) provides a selection of different tools to help the process of selecting the data needed in an experiment. There are ways to automate some portion of the tasks, but the columns and processes used will be determined by the kind of data being analyzed, along with the result. The data being analyzed may come from multiple sources, which means that the features needed for the experiment must be gathered into one dataset.

> **This skill explains how to:**
> - Merge multiple datasets by rows or columns into a single dataset by columns
> - Merge multiple datasets by rows or columns into a single dataset by rows
> - Add columns that are combinations of other columns
> - Manually select and construct features for model estimation
> - Automatically select and construct features for model estimation
> - Reduce dimensions of data through principal component analysis (PCA)
> - Manage variable metadata
> - Select standardized variables based on planned analysis

## Merge multiple datasets by rows or columns into a single dataset by columns

When analyzing data for an experiment, the data may come from multiple source locations. Azure Machine Learning offers the ability to create one dataset in a manner similar to how two tables are joined in SQL Server, by using a Join module, which can be found underneath the Manipulation menu. For a join to occur, only one column from each table can be used to create the join because that is the only supported join type. The join takes two inputs and creates one output based upon matching the selected value from each dataset.

The matching criteria has four different options, which appear in the dropdown box (see Figure 1-36). If the Joint Type Inner Join is selected, the columns from both datasets must equal one another.

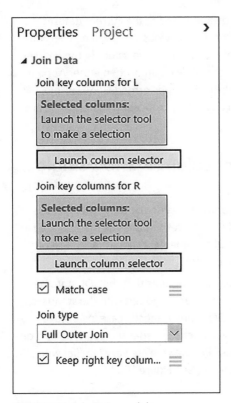

**FIGURE 1-36** Join Data module

A Left Outer Join returns all of the records from the dataset on the left input and those records on the right dataset where they values match. If there are no matching values on the right dataset, those values will be missing. If Full Outer Join is selected, all of the columns from the left dataset and the right dataset are returned. When the values do not match one another, either the left dataset values will be returned with no matching values from the right, or all of the values for the right dataset will be returned with no matching values from the left dataset. The last join option is the Left Semi-Join, which will return all of the values from the left dataset when the join columns match.

The single output dataset from a join will have columns that must have unique names. If there are two columns with the same name, one of them will have a number appended to the name of the column to create a unique name.

When merging data, the columns need to have matching values and there may be some steps required to create values in two different datasets, which can be used to create a join. One way that the data can be modified is through the Apply Math Operation module found in the Statistical Functions menu. This module can perform many different calculations to a given number, such as Square, Round, Mod, RoundUp, RoundDown, and Truncate, to name a few. You can use the Columnset option within the Apply Math Operation to perform math operations on two columns, for example if you want to add the values of two columns together to derive a value for another column. The results can be appended to the current dataset causing a new column to be added. If Inplace is selected, the previous value will be overwritten with the output of this module. ResultOnly will not return any of the values in the dataset, just the computed value. The name of the column which will be created when either Append or ResultOnly options are created are named to reflect the math performed. For example, Truncate(logTime_$1) would be the name of a column created by truncating the values in a column called logTime.

## Merge multiple datasets by rows or columns into a single dataset by rows

Azure Machine Learning also contains the ability to modify the values by using the datasets as tables. Select the SQL Transformation module, and the dataset can then be manipulated in a version of SQL known as SQLite. SQLite uses a minimalist implementation of ANSI SQL. This version of SQL will allow a maximum of three datasets as input.

Each dataset will be assigned a name: t1, t2 or t3. SQL Lite requires that the SQL statement be completed by a semi-colon. Comments to the SQL code can be added with the standard slash and asterixis /* comment*/ or two dashes --. The SQL code is mostly case insensitive because there are few exceptions to this rule. Using a SQL query provides the ability to add different filters contained within the SQL in a where clause. People who are very familiar with SQL will find this method a faster way of creating different filters (see Figure 1-37).

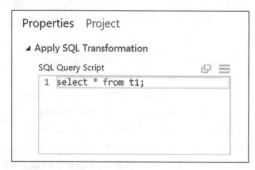

**FIGURE 1-37** SQL transformation window showing a query from the table t1

**NEED MORE REVIEW?**

The SQL Transformation module uses a language called SQLite. For more information regarding the language and how it is used in Azure Machine Learning check out this link: *https://msdn.microsoft.com/en-us/library/azure/dn905914.aspx*.

# Manually select and construct features for model estimation

Some algorithms, used in machine learning, such as support vector machines, require that data be normalized. Data normalizing is a process of standardizing the data values so that the values fall within the same range, generally from 0 to 1. For the data to be compared between columns, it is helpful if the values in the columns are near the same values. Big differences in the ranges will result in skewed results. Other times the data may need to be modified so that the data has a standard distribution from zero. For classification algorithms, normalizing the data prior to processing it can improve the results. While normalization can be important, it is important to determine whether your model requires modifying the data, because there are of course times, for example when using linear models, when normalization can adversely impact the results.

There are two different methods for eliminating the features not needed in an experiment. One method manually removes them by using the Select columns module and choosing to select a subset of columns, and the other method is using an automated method for selecting only the features you need. Often times your dataset may include a value such as a primary key, a value which is not useful in analysis. It is possible to remove the column and then add it back to the dataset later, which might be useful in a later step where perhaps you might wish to add the primary key back to write the output to a database.

To increase the predictive accuracy of a given model, you may want to create new features using the existing raw data as a source. Adding features may mean pivoting the data to create columns from row values, concatenating features together to make a new column, or record patterns in text data by transforming text values using the Feature Hashing module.

Feature Hashing is often used in datamining to analyze text. When looking to determine sentiment analysis on a block of text, it is important to determine the patterns of the words, their order, and use of key phrases. These are analyzed by hashing the text into indices. For example, if one is analyzing review data, one might compare the numeric rating assigned to the review with the text in the review detail column. The Hashing Bitsize determines how many feature columns will be returned. The bitsize is two and the value of the Hashing Bitsize is the exponent used to create a feature. If the Hashing Bitsize = 3, then the number of columns created will be $16 = 2^3$. N-size refers to the number of sequential words to be included in the hash. In data mining the next word is considered important, which means that the value should at least be set to 2, to cover a word on each side. The possible values for N-grams are 0-10. Columns generated contain the name of the column used plus an underscore, the word Hashing and he number for columns create, starting at 1 (see figure 1-38).

Target column(s)

Selected columns:
Column names: Col2

Launch column selector

Hashing bitsize

8

N-grams

2

| START TIME | 1/21/2015 3:57:59 PM |
| END TIME | 1/21/2015 3:57:59 PM |
| ELAPSED TIME | 0:00:00.000 |

**FIGURE 1-38** Feature Hashing

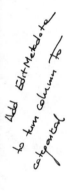

*(handwritten note) Add Edit Metadata to turn column to categorical*

For some algorithms, it may be best to pivot the row values in a categorical column to features, using the Convert Indictor to Values module, which is found in the Manipulation menu. Select one or more categorical columns. The new columns will be named with a name of the column with value in the column appended to it. The values in the column will be set to 0 or 1. This technique will be useful if you are trying to normalize the data to values between 0 and 1. To convert the values, select a categorical feature in the dataset. If you try to convert a column that is not categorical, this error will occur, Error 0056: Column with name <column name> is not in an allowed category. If there are missing values, a new column called Missing will be created. The values contained within the column can be text or numeric; either can be used. There is an option that is turned off by default, to overwrite categorical columns. This will add the new columns and make the original disappear. The original feature still exists and can be added into the dataset later by selecting it.

## Automatically select and construct features for model estimation

Azure Machine Learning can help determine which features in a dataset have the greatest predictive powers. The Filter Based Feature Selection Module applies statistical tests to the variables contained within and scores the best columns based upon which one would contain the most predictive features. The methods used for selecting a metric are selected by you within the module.

To implement this feature within an experiment, select the Filter Based Feature Selection model from the left menu of Azure Machine Learning Studio and connect it to your experiment so that it has data to analyze. The menu options selected will determine what kind of analysis is completed (see Figure 1-39).

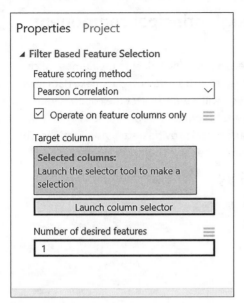

**FIGURE 1-39** Properties of the Filter Based Feature Selection module

The first option is to select the scoring option used. The simplest is the Count-based method, which calculates a score by counting the different values and weighing them accordingly. There are a number of different statistical options to choose from: Pearson Correlation, Mutual Information, Kendall Correlation, Spearman Correlation, Chi Squared, and Fisher Score. Each of these statistical algorithms applies a different method for weighting the variables.

> **NEED MORE REVIEW? ON THE STATISTICAL METHODS**
>
> Each of the standard methods used is described in more detail here: *https://msdn.microsoft.com/library/azure/dn913071.aspx.*

The method selected not only needs to be appropriate from an algorithm perspective, but the data in your experiments needs to contain data formatted in the following manner:

- Pearson Correlation—Numeric features only
- Mutual Information—Text or numeric features
- Spearman Correlation—Numeric features only
- Chi Squared—Text or numeric features
- Fisher Score—Numeric Features only
- Counts—Text or Numeric

The values selected in the targeted column will be for the label. All of the features in the dataset will be analyzed. The number of desired features will return the new feature columns. You should not increase this number to be greater than the number of features contained in the dataset.

# Reduce dimensions of data through principal component analysis (PCA)

Principal Component Analysis (PCA) is an automated method for reducing the number of columns in a dataset by encoding the variances into one value. It's often used to make data easy to explore and visualize. When using this module, you will need to select the columns you wish to reduce, and the number of dimensions that you want them to be reduced (see Figure 1-40). This technique can also decrease the required resources and provide better visualizations. The downside is that PCA can lead to a precision loss due to the use of compressed data.

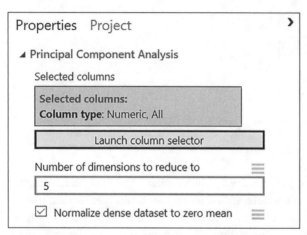

**FIGURE 1-40** Principal Component Analysis module

Prior to using PCA in an experiment, make sure that all the features and labels have been defined. Select the number of columns to include for input and the decreased number for output. If there are few missing values and you want to normalize the data to have a mean of 0, check the option Normalize Dense Dataset to Zero Mean.

> **NEED MORE INFORMATION ON PCA?**
>
> PCA is a very complex topic and you may want to learn more about the methodologies it uses for reducing columns in a dataset. The following link provides some visualizations that help describe PCA: *http://setosa.io/ev/principal-component-analysis/*.

# Add columns that are combinations of other columns

There are times when creating an experiment you may want to group values into categories as evaluating fewer elements can improve the performance of some algorithms . For example, if the dataset contains a column called education-num, you may only want to see three different categories of data: High School or Less, Some College, and College Degree. Group Categorical Values, which is an option in Data Transformation, acts as an in-place lookup table that can combine the values into groups of values. The component always creates an unknown value for items not specified, meaning if you want three groups specify four groups as there will be one group specified for unspecified values (see Figure 1-41).

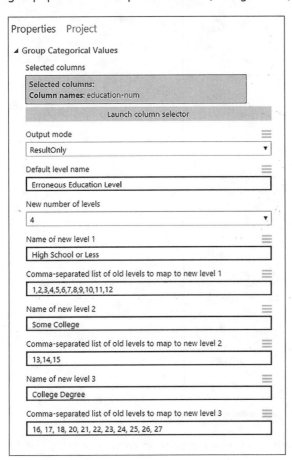

**FIGURE 1-41** Group Categorical Values

As shown in Figure 1-41 the default value will be mapped to a value called Erroneous Education Values. Data will only appear in the default value if the data is outside the ranges specified. Since all of the good data is specified, data is in this category only if it is not valid. After the experiment is run, the data created by this module can be shown in a histogram (see Figure 1-42).

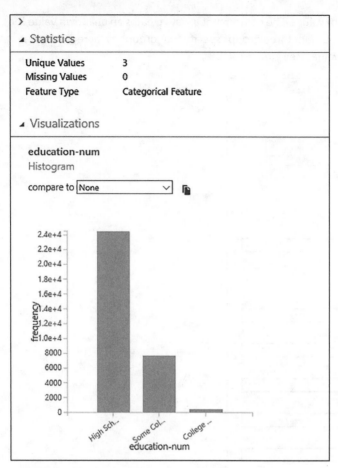

**FIGURE 1-42** Visualization of the output of Category Grouping Module

Notice there are only three categories listed in Figure 1-41 because no data existed that did not appear in the list of comma separated values.

## Manage variable metadata

To ensure that your data is processed as expected in an experiment, it may be necessary to modify some of the metadata using the Edit Metadata module, which can be found in the Data Transformation menu in the Manipulation section. Perhaps your experiment would perform better if more data elements were categorical, or a numeric column is defined as text instead of a number, or you may wish to define a column as a feature that is required for another module (see Figure 1-43).

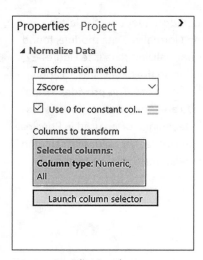

**FIGURE 1-43** Edit Metadata

These tasks are all performed within the Edit MetaData module, which is shown in Figure 1-43. After the columns are selected, the operations specified will be applied to all the selected columns. If you want to change some columns to categorical and others to numeric without being categorical, you will need two Edit Meta Data modules to perform both tasks. Azure Machine Learning supports a number of different data types, including: String, Integer, Double, Boolean, DateTime, and TimeSpan—,each of these values are listed in the Data Type dropdown box. Changing a value to categorical may improve the predictability, and the dropdown box allows you to turn it on or off.

The Fields options are used to change the characteristics of your variables, and this dropdown box allows you to set or clear three different values: Features, Labels, and Weights. While it is not possible to set a column score to a column in Azure Machine Learning currently, it is possible to do so in a custom R or Python Module, and the Fields dropdown will let you clear it. By default, all columns are defined as features, but if you want to perform mathematical operations on a column, you will need to clear the feature flag. If your test data contains the value, which in later datasets you are trying to predict, the column containing the values needs to be set as a label as part of the data preparation needed to run a predictive algorithm. Weights are often used in machine learning to reduce the importance of other columns by applying a weight to a given column to determine that some are more influential, which is often applied in classification tasks when trying to come with distinct groups.

## Select standardized variables based on planned analysis

Different analysis techniques require different methods of standardization. If you are interested in performing anomaly detection you may want to look for outliers. When doing a predictive experiment, it may be more useful to standardize the data. The normalization module provides the ability to transform numeric data to a specific column or to the entire dataset. The data being normalized must be numeric.

The Normalization module can be found within Scale and Reduce menu on the left in Azure Machine Learning Studio. The Azure Machine Learning Normalize Data module, found under Scale and Reduce, contains five different methods for normalizing data (see Figure1-37). ZScore, a process of standardizing data, changes the distribution so the data values to appear in a standard distribution with a mean of 0 and a standard deviation of 1. This provides a data distribution that appears like a bell curve when graphed. If you are looking to review a series of values to determine which one causes the most variance, a technique often used in Principal Component Analysis (PCA), you may want to use a ZScore to normalize the values in a column as this improves the ability of the algorithm to determine the relationship between different components (see Figure 1-43).

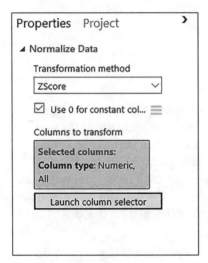

FIGURE 1-43 Normalize Data Properties Menu

MinMax standardization is used to normalize data between 0 and 1. For example, the dataset contains temperature data from Phoenix, Arizona from 2006 to 2016. The maximum temperature in Fahrenheit can be 124 and the minimum temperature can be 27. The first value in our column is 97. To standardize the value of 97 using MinMax, take the observation value 91 and subtract the minimum value 27. Divide that by the Maximum value minus the minimum value and apply the range. The value in the column when MinMax is applied is ((97-27)/ (124-27)) = .721649485. This transformation is helpful when you are trying to find a general solution and wish to compare numbers in the same ranges in different columns using in K-means clustering algorithms.

# Thought experiment

This thought experiment allows you to demonstrate the skills and knowledge gained by reviewing the topics covered in the chapter. The answers are included in the next section.

You have been asked to look at sales data from Contoso Bike Company to create an experiment in Azure Machine Learning to determine what products they should market to customers who have already purchased a bike. The last six months of the sales data is located in an Azure SQL Database and after six months the data is moved to an HDInsight Cluster. There was a problem in some of the data loaded to the HDInsight Cluster and some of the fields have missing data. You want to be able to analyze the last two years of data.

The first step in the process is of course preparing your data for analysis to create the experiment. Use the information provided, to answer the following questions.

1. You will need to ask the Azure Administrator for some information to be able to connect to the HDInsight Cluster. Which of the following items do you need to have to be able to import data from HDInsight using Hive?

   **A.** Azure Resource Group

   **B.** User Account Password

   **C.** Container Name

   **D.** Database Name

   **E.** File Name

   **F.** Server URI

   **G.** Storage Key

   **H.** Storage Methodology

   **I.** User Account Name

2. Contoso bike company has eliminated their sportswear department seven months ago and do not want to include any product sales of sportswear in the experiment. After reviewing the data, you determine that eliminating all of the rows with a product type of sportswear is required. What Azure module will you use to do eliminate these rows from the experiment?

3. In the experiment, you have determined that instead of looking at all of the prices individually, that you want to replace the Price column from the actual price data to instead contain store as equally sized price groups instead and stored as a category. Which Azure module would you use do this?

4. Luckily, the data is stored in the same format in both HDInsight and in the Azure SQL DB. What Azure Machine modules can you use to merge the data together?

5. When creating a machine learning experiment, the dataset you are using contains an identity field in Column 1. You have determined that the identity field is not needed in the experiment. What can you do to omit Column 1?

# Thought experiment answers

This section contains the answers to the thought experiment in this chapter.

1. To connect to an HDInsight Cluster you will need:
   - Server URI
   - The Hadoop User Account Name
   - User Account Password
   - Container Name
   - Storage key

2. Use the Group Data into Bins module. Using the Quantiles option the data can be grouped into a number of equally sized bins. To replace the value in the price column, ensure the output mode Append is selected. To make the column categorical, select the option Tag Columns as category.

3. The Azure module

4. Use the Azure module Join Function. The option Full Outer Join would be selected from the dropdown box to return all of the values from both datasets.

5. Use the Select Columns module and exclude the identity column.

# Chapter summary

Preparing data to be used in Azure Machine Learning is a process that requires many different steps to be performed.

- The first step in an experiment is accessing the data, which can be accomplished by importing small data files Machine Learning Environment, but Azure Machine Language also provides the ability to use the data from the source by using the Import Data module to directly access data from an Azure SQL Database, Azure Blob Storage, or Hive with HDInsight. As Azure Machine Learning is not limited to using only cloud based data storage, using the Azure Data Gateway allows data stored in an on premises to be referenced within an Azure Machine Learning experiment. Data can also be exported from an Azure Machine Learning experiment to provide interim information about the data by using the Export module. Providing the connection information for Azure Blob Store, Azure SQL Database, or an HDInsight Cluster provides the ability to store results from within the Azure Machine Learning environment.

- Once data has been loaded, using the Visualization menu on the data provides the ability to view statistical information on any single column providing univariate analysis of a single field by viewing a histogram or box blot of a column. For a multivariate summary, a second column can be selected for analysis providing the ability to visualize the data. For a more complex analysis, Azure Machine Learning provides the ability to use Jupyter notebooks providing the ability to create custom analysis in either R or Python.

If you have R or Python analysis components already created, Azure Machine Learning provides the ability to use them within an experiment by using zip Archives within an experiment.

■ Prior to using data in an experiment, the data needs to be cleansed to ensure an optimum result. Using the Clean Missing Data module, data can be cleansed by selecting the option in the Cleaning mode to Remove Entire Row or Remove Entire Column. The missing data can also be substituted by setting the Cleaning Mode to replace the missing value with a fixed value entered in the Replacement Value field or selecting one of the other options such as Replace with Mean or Replace with Mode values to replace the missing value. If the analysis performed has determined there are a number of outliers, the Threshold Filter component can be used to removed data above or below a specified value or by selecting range criteria. Missing data can be processed in a number of different ways with the Missing Data module. Rows or columns that contain missing data can be removed, or you have the ability to specify replacement values, which can include a fixed value or using a calculated value such as mean or median.

■ To format data in a method, which can best be consumed by an algorithm, requires that ensuring the data in a dataset contains the necessary features. Data may come from multiple sources and may need to be combined into one dataset using the Merge Component or by using a SQL Transformation Component. Columns may need to be reduced by automatic methods such as the Principal Component Analysis (PCA) Module. The format of the data may need to be modified to perform better for certain algorithms. Columns may need to be classified as different datatypes or as categorical. If the data contains a result that is used in testing but will not be included in data to be used in anything other than training data needs to be marked as a label. All of these concepts are thoroughly described to provide a good understanding of their use.

# CHAPTER 2

# Develop machine learning models

Once the data has been loaded and cleaned up, it is time to learn how to create the model that best fits that data. There are many algorithms to build your model in the machine learning ecosystem. Most of them are implemented in different tools, platforms and languages, since their theoretical fundamentals are public and well documented. However, knowing which one will better fit your datasets is not as straightforward as it might seem. Sometimes, algorithms "surprise" you, performing much better on a certain dataset than you expected, while on others underperform. It is important to test and compare algorithms, and identify and understand why such differences occur in order to choose the best combination of steps for your particular problem. This chapter focuses on the choice of the most appropriate machine learning algorithm, the training of several models considering multiple parameter configuration options, and the evaluation and choice of the best model.

## Skills covered in this chapter:

- Skill 2.1: Select an appropriate algorithm or method
- Skill 2.2: Initialize and train appropriate models
- Skill 2.3: Validate models

## Skill 2.1: Select an appropriate algorithm or method

This skill covers the basic types of machine learning problems and the modules that Azure Machine Learning has to deal with them. Depending on the machine learning problem that you are tackling, different algorithms, evaluation methods, and even expected results may vary. Such problems will be presented both as abstract situations and with particular examples (that might be similar to the ones you would face in your business scenarios) from Azure Machine Learning sample datasets for a better understanding.

Azure Machine Learning comes with a broad range of pre-built algorithms. Figure 2-1 shows a list of the different types of Azure Machine Learning algorithms and how they are categorized.

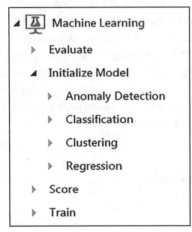

**FIGURE 2-1** The collection of Azure Machine Learning models by type are located under Machine Learning > Initialize Model

There are cases where it is clear what type of algorithms to use. For example, you cannot use a binary classifier when you want to predict a real number. However, there are many different types of algorithms that would fit the task of predicting real numbers. Which algorithm is best for that task? That kind of choice is what will be addressed in this skill, and it is important to note that the rules exposed here should be taken as a rule of thumb. It is difficult to know how an algorithm will behave until it is tested in the dataset under consideration. When faced with a new problem, you can apply the rules proposed throughout the chapter, but the most accurate way to find the best model on that specific domain is to use validation techniques (see Skill 2.2).

## Select an appropriate algorithm for supervised versus unsupervised scenarios

Which algorithms to use when building our machine learning models depends primarily on the data you have and what your purpose is. Use *supervised learning* methods for data with a target value that you want to predict. If you do not explicitly have the value you want to predict, use *unsupervised algorithms*. There are other types of machine learning problems, but the two just mentioned are by far the most widely used in the industry, and the only ones for which Azure Machine Learning provides modules.

Inside the supervised learning algorithms, depending upon the type of target you want to predict, you find *regression* (continuous values) and *classification* (discrete values) problems. Inside classification problems you have two different types: *binary* (predict which two categories or classes a sample belongs) or *multiclass* (predict two classes or more than two classes). Stock prediction is an example of a regression algorithm, and customer churn is an example of binary classification, and a digit recognition system is an example of multiclass classification.

*Anomaly detection* is a special case of classification algorithms. The anomaly detection algorithms are actually binary classifiers between two classes: anomalous sample and not anomalous sample. Anomalous cases have almost no representation in the training set (typically less than 1% of the samples). With a very small number of positive samples it's better to train an anomaly detector rather than a binary classifier. The number of anomalies is enormous and cannot be covered with the observations in your dataset, so you cannot train a model that is able to learn what an anomaly is. Instead, a model is trained to learn the common characteristics of class members, and it is able to know when a sample does not fit the class. It is common to train these models with only normal samples, and why they are called one-class classifiers. The detection of outliers in sensor data is one such example.

In Azure Machine learning within the unsupervised learning algorithms, you can find only one module that is used for *clustering* problems. Sometimes you do not need to predict a value (either continuous or categorical), but you need to understand the underlying structure of the data. Clustering algorithms group samples according to the characteristics they have in common. This type of exploration is very useful to get a better insight into the data. Customer segmentation is a good example of clustering.

This taxonomy is based on the Azure Machine Learning modules shown in Figure 2-1, however, there may be many variations or different types of learning that are not shown in the graph.

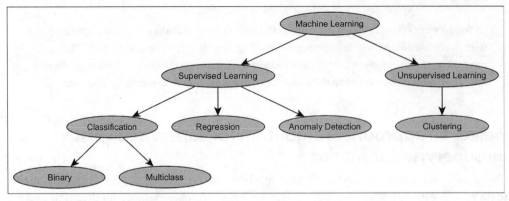

**FIGURE 2-2** Taxonomy of the Azure Machine Learning models

## Time series

There is a special case of problems called *times series* in which the data is ordered chronologically. The main objective of this type of problem is to predict the values following the last sample you have (forecasting). It's also common to find anomalous values in the data sequence. For the latter case, Azure Machine Learning has the Time Series Anomaly Detection module.

## Recommender systems

*Recommender systems* are another special case that provide suggestions to users (recommendations) on a certain type of items. The results are intended to best suit the user's needs or tastes. More about this will be covered in Chapter 3, "Operationalize and Manage Azure Machine Learning Services."

## Criteria to select models

Here is the criteria to take under consideration when selecting a model:

- **Nature of the problem**  This model covers what you want to find or predict. Before selecting an algorithm, the first and easy step is to identify what kind of problem of the exposed in Figure 2-2 you are facing. This limits the range of algorithms you can use.

- **Model complexity**  Choose between algorithms of the same group requires examining model complexity. The simplest models use lines to fit the data. Linear models can work well in simple datasets, but in cases where the data structure does not fit a line, they may have poor performance. There are models that are better able to adjust to the data thanks to decision boundaries or adjustment curves that are more complex than a straight line. In general, the more complex the models are, the more accuracy you can get, but, a model with high capacity can cause an overfitting: the model has learned the training set perfectly well, but is not able to generalize out of it. Techniques such as regularization help to avoid this problem.

- **Training speed**  Resources are finite, so the training speed of a model can lead you to choose between models. Perhaps the training time for a single model is not a problem, but doing hyperparameter optimization with k-fold cross validation (more information about this in Skill 2.2) hundreds or thousands of times can be unfeasible.

- **Memory usage**  Each algorithm uses a different amount of memory. In some cases, there may not be enough memory, so the training stops and you can't obtain a model. Perhaps in Azure Machine Learning memory usage is less important than if you are running something on your own machine.

- **Number and structure of the input features**  There are algorithms that work better with more features than others. For example, SVMs deal better with a high number of features compared to logistic regression. The structure of the input features is also important, because convolutional neural networks can take advantage of the proximity of pixels to each other.

- **Number of hyperparameters**  The more hyperparameters the model has, the more exploration you must do to be sure you have found the best values. More details on hyperparameters are covered in Skill 2.2.

The following sections cover almost all of the Azure Machine Learning algorithms. The modules aren't thoroughly covered, but you can rely on the documentation and example experiments.

# Select an appropriate algorithm for predicting continuous label data

If the target is a continuous value, you are facing a regression problem. Figure 2-3 shows the list of all the regression models that you can train with Azure Machine Learning.

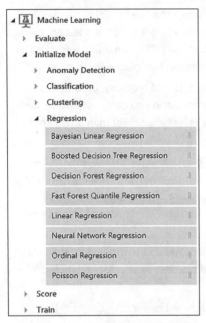

**FIGURE 2-3** List of regression algorithms

All of these methods fit the task of predicting continuous values. They will be commented on, and the most significant characteristics that can lead you to choose one against the other will be listed.

One of the oldest and most basic machine learning algorithms is linear regression. This model fits a straight line (hyperplane when dealing with higher number of dimensions) to the data. It is fast and simple to capture complex patterns. Figure 2-4 shows a simple example of an experiment using the Linear Regression module. Actually, the structure of the experiment does not differ much from one model to another. Every experiment has the initialization of the model, a training module, and scoring and evaluation of the model on a data set not seen during training. In the following skills, you will look in more detail at the split data and score and evaluation process.

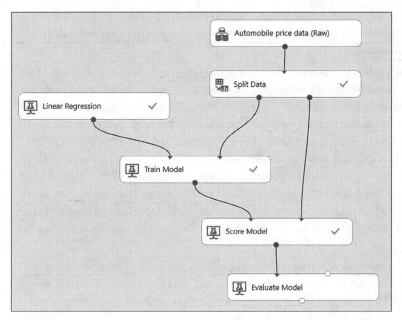

**FIGURE 2-4** Linear regression example

If you select the Linear Regression module, you will see a list of the available parameters of that model (solution method, L2 regularization, and random seed) on the right panel, as seen in Figure 2-5.

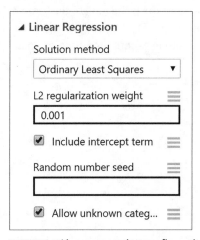

**FIGURE 2-5** Linear regression configuration parameters

Each model, in addition to the internal parameters, has some modifiable parameters that affect the training. These types of parameters are called hyperparameters, and we will cover them in more detail in Skill 2.2.

The Bayesian Linear Regression model allows you to create a regression model using Bayesian statistics. Like linear regression, Bayesian linear regression is a simple linear method, but it is more accurate in small datasets.

There are different models that are tree-based. Decision trees are another classic machine learning model that are even used in fields such as economics. They are based on successive decisions that can be painted schematically. This makes them interpretable models. Nevertheless, when talking about a forest (set of trees) this interpretation becomes more complicated because the final decision is made based on the values returned by many trees. Trees can be used in both classes. This model is really an ensemble of trees (see section about ensembles in this chapter). In short, this model provides good accuracy and fast training. On the other hand, it uses a lot of memory. There is another module called Decision Forest Regression that, apart from good accuracy and fast training, uses less memory. When memory is not a problem, it is too difficult to say which one is better, but the best way to know is by testing those models in a specific dataset.

Another option is to use Neural Network Regression. They can achieve great accuracy, but they are slow to train. The next section discusses more about neural networks since it is also an algorithm that can be used in binary and multiclass classification. Many of the concepts mentioned there also apply to regression neural networks.

There are certain types of regressors whose scope is very specific. Fast Forest Quantile Regression is designed to predict distributions and Poisson Regression is useful for predicting event counts (assuming that the label has a Poisson distribution).

Another special type of regression is the Ordinal Regression module. It is useful when data is ordered. This module uses a binary classifier to answer the question: Is the rank of the sample x greater than k? By repeating these questions with different values of k, the model obtains the position of each sample. Figure 2-6 shows how to construct a simple experiment using ordinal regression.

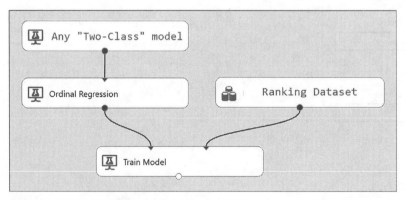

**FIGURE 2-6** Use of the Ordinal Regression module

# Identify an appropriate algorithm for classifying label data

Within supervised learning problems, besides predicting a continuous value, there are models that allow you to predict categorical values. Classification problems aim to assign a class from among several classes to a given example.

Furthermore, within the classification problems you can find mainly two types: *binary classification* (predictions between two classes) and *multiclassification* (two or more classes). Technically you can use any multiclass algorithm on any binary dataset and, using the one-versus-all approach, you can also use the binary algorithms in multiclassification tasks.

In Figure 2-7 you will find a list of all the classification models that Azure Machine Learning has. Models whose name begins with "Two-Class" are binary classification models and the others are multiclass.

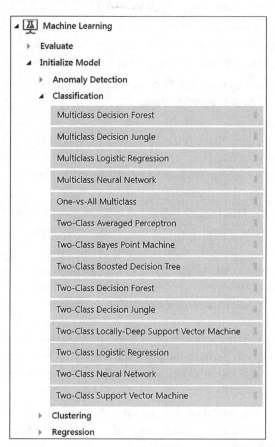

**FIGURE 2-7** List of classification models

## Binary models

Logistic Regression is one of the best known and basic algorithms. The Two-Class Logistic Regression module implements that method. As the regression linear model, offers fast training times but can suffer of sub-optimal prediction performance when the input datasets are complex and do not follow a linear distribution. The same applies for Two-Class Averaged Perceptron and Two-Class Bayes Point Machine. The Two-Class SVM module is also linear, but the training method is slower than the models listed above. The algorithm finds the line that best separates the data, that is, the line that maximizes the margins between the samples of different classes. This characteristic makes this model ideal when dealing with many features.

There is another kind of SVM that uses a different kernel instead of the linear one. That kernel provides more accuracy without increasing training time too much. The module that implements that model is called Two-Class Locally-Deep SVM.  *(diff kernel)*

Just like with the regression models, there are several classification models that use decision trees: Two-Class Decision Forest, Two-Class Decision Jungle, and Two-Class Boosted Decision Tree. Those models do not have linear decision boundaries, so they can reach high accuracy.

The last binary model available in Azure Machine Learning is Two-Class Neural Network, but you will review neural networks in the "Multiclass models" section.

## Multiclass models

For multiclass problems Azure Machine Learning also has two tree-based models: Multiclass Decision Forest and Multiclass Decision Jungle. Forest can consume a lot of memory in comparison to Jungles.

Multiclass Logistic Regression is an extension of the logistic regression module for multiclass problems. It has the qualities of linear models, fast training, and simple decision boundaries.

Azure Machine Learning allows you to easily implement neural networks by using the Multiclass Neural Network module. Neural networks are mathematical models inspired by how the humans believe the brain works. Neural networks are composed by smaller units called neurons that are activated or not depending on the value of their inputs. The combinations of those neurons (typically arranged by layers) endow the neural network with the ability to produce more complex decision boundaries than other simple models like logistic regression. Usually, more complex boundaries give better predictions on complex data. In general, neural networks provide you with a high power of generalization, but especially when you have a lot of data to learn about.

The number of parameters to be configured in a neural network is higher than in other models, as shown in Figure 2-8. As mentioned earlier in this Skill, tuning these parameters takes longer, which may lead to us not using this model with other alternatives.

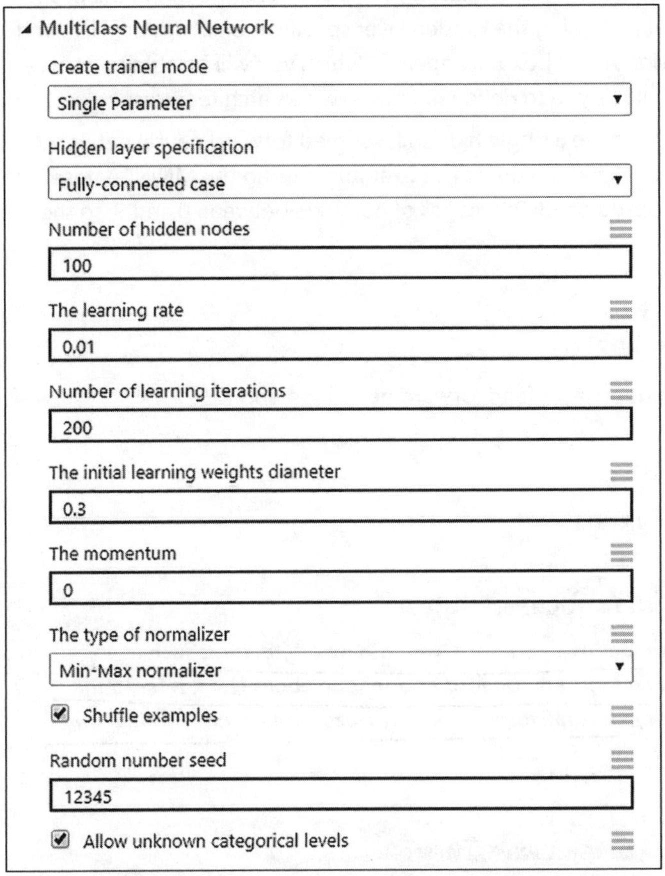

**FIGURE 2-8** Configuration options of the neural network module

Another weak point of neural networks is the training time. The training of a neural network is quite slow compared to other models, especially in Azure Machine Learning, which does not use GPU acceleration. The training of neural networks with GPUs will be discussed in Chapter 4, "Use Other Services for Machine Learning."

One factor that can help to rule out the use of a neural network is when predictions are applied to a business and that business needs to get the reasons that have driven the network to make that decision. Neural networks are very much like a black box that is quite difficult to interpret. Other models like those based on decision trees are more easily interpretable. However, modules such as Permutation Feature Importance can help to obtain the most important features for any model.

By default, the architecture of neural networks is limited to a single hidden layer with sigmoid as the activation function and softmax in the last layer. You can change this in the properties of the model (see Figure 2-8), opening the Hidden layer specification dropdown list, and selecting a Custom definition script. A text box will appear in which you will be able to insert a *Net# script*. This script language allows you to define neural networks architectures.

As an example of Net# code you have a single hidden layer feed forward neural network (the default neural network) with 200 hidden units. This example is using the MNIST dataset as input. The MNIST dataset is composed of 28x28 images of numbers between 0 and 9, so the output is between 10 classes.

```
input Picture [28, 28];
hidden H1 [200] from Picture all;
output Result [10] softmax from H1 all;
```

The next code creates a two hidden layer feed forward neural network.

```
input Picture [28, 28];
hidden H1 [200] from Picture all;
hidden H2 [200] from H1 all;
output Result [10] softmax from H2 all;
```

> *NEED MORE INFORMATION?* **NET# DOCUMENTATION**
>
> In addition to increasing the number of layers, with Net# other architectures such as convolutional networks can be defined. For detailed information about Net#, refer to the Microsoft documentation: *https://docs.microsoft.com/en-us/azure/machine-learning/studio/azure-ml-netsharp-reference-guide*.

> *NEED MORE INFORMATION?* **AZURE ML EXPERIMENTS**
>
> If you want to see examples of neural networks with different architectures defined in Net# you can clone the following experiments. From this first example of a neural network with a hidden layer, you can continue exploring more advanced experiments. They will appear in the Related Items section. All examples work on the MNIST dataset, which is among the default Azure Machine Learning datasets. *https://gallery.cortanaintelligence.com/Experiment/Neural-Network-1-hidden-layer-3*.

Another way to implement a multiclass algorithm is the One-vs-All Multiclass module. With this method, you can use any binary classifier module in a multiclass problem. The way this module deals with it is by training a binary classifier on each class versus all the other classes. It uses all of the samples of a class to create a binary classifier of the "X" class, and uses the remaining samples as the "no X" class. The process is repeated for each of the classes, resulting in a classifier per class. To predict which class a sample belongs to, the class of the classifier that has obtained the highest confidence is returned.

Figure 2-9 shows an outline of how to build a multiclass model using the One-vs-All Multi-class module. The module expects a binary classification model as input, and it has one output that you must plug into any of the available training modules.

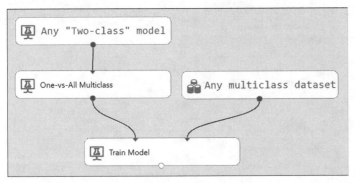

**FIGURE 2-9** Use of the One-vs-All Multiclass module

# Identify and appropriate algorithm for grouping unlabeled data

The way of grouping samples according to the characteristics they share with each other is called *clustering*. After this process, similar samples will end in the same group. Applying a clustering algorithm to our data shows the internal structure of it. A very common example of clustering is applying clustering algorithms to customer data. This is to help better understand the different types of customers a company has. Clusters can also be used for anomaly detection and even for classification.

As is shown in Figure 2-10, Azure Machine Learning provides us with a module called K-Means Clustering. Although Azure Machine Learning does not have other clustering algorithms apart from K-Means, it could be expanded with those available in the different R and Python libraries.

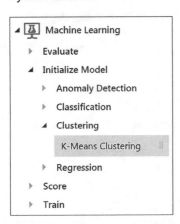

**FIGURE 2-10** There is only one clustering algorithm in Azure Machine Learning: K-Means

You are going to build an example of clustering with the Iris Two Class Data (which is among the default Azure Machine Learning datasets). The experiment should be as shown in Figure 2-11.

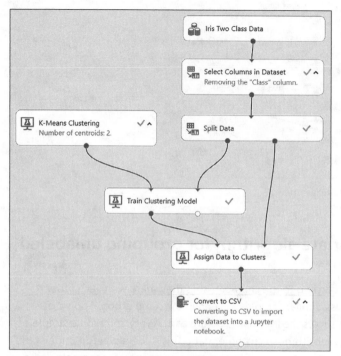

**FIGURE 2-11** Clustering experiment with K-Means

After executing it, open the output dataset of the Convert to CSV module with a Python 3 Jupyter Notebook (see Chapter 1, "Prepare Data for Analysis in Azure Machine Learning and Export from Azure Machine Learning" to remember how to load a dataset into a notebook). Insert a new code cell below the cell that loads the dataset in the frame variable. You will build a visualization of the dataset without showing any class distinction; you will paint all samples of the same color, using the code below. Notice that the code assumes that there is a pandas dataframe in the variable frame with the dataset. The resulting plot is shown in Figure 2-12.

```
%matplotlib inline
import seaborn as sns

sns.set(style="ticks", color_codes=True)
sns.pairplot(frame, vars=["petal-length", "sepal-length", "petal-width", "sepal-width"])
```

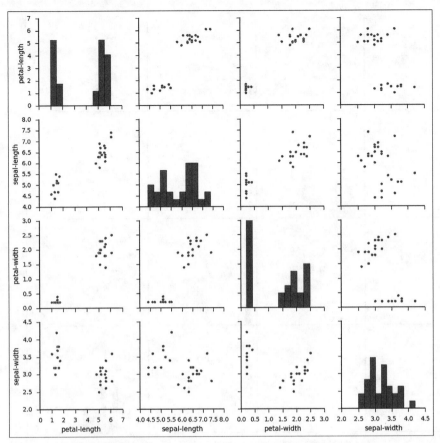

**FIGURE 2-12** Unlabeled matrix scatterplot of Iris features—.only 30% of samples are shown

You can see two clearly differentiated groups. The experiment has applied clustering with the option of searching for two groups, and it would be good if these groups matched the two groups that we have detected visually. Figure 2-13 show the results. To get that plot you have to select as the color of the points the column "Assignments." This column contains the cluster number assigned by the algorithm.

```
sns.pairplot(frame, hue="Assignments", vars=["petal-length", "sepal-length",
"petal-width", "sepal-width"])
```

The colors of each sample are assigned by the clustering algorithm and there is a direct correspondence between those colors and the class to which that sample really belongs.

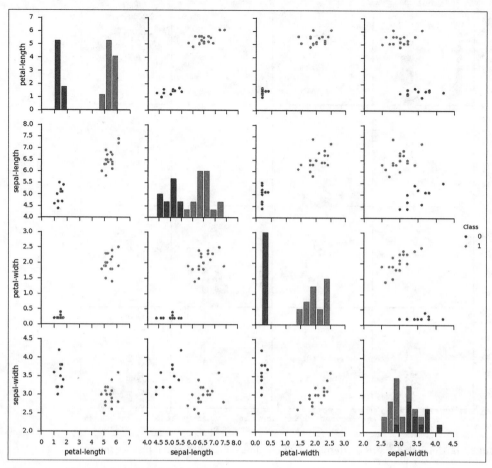

**FIGURE 2-13** Matrix scatterplot of Iris features

This little experiment shows that there is a relationship between classification and clustering algorithms. Normally there are common features among the samples in a class, and that is why classification algorithm can learn to discern between classes. Clustering algorithms perform the same task, but in an inverse way.

Like many other methods, the result after a K-Means training can vary depending on the initial value of the clusters. Therefore, among the configuration options of the model, there are different methods to perform this initialization. In the Azure Machine Learning implementation, you can also use a label to improve this initial cluster selection. Since this is optional, it can still be considered an unsupervised method. However, if all of your data is labeled, consider using a supervised classification algorithm.

# Identify when to select R versus Python notebooks

The decision of when to use a notebook powered by R or Python is up to the data scientist. With both languages you can get pretty much the same results. It depends on the data scientist experience. Usually, if you have a statistics background you will probably feel more comfortable with R because you have used it before. If you come from a computer science background you probably feel more comfortable with Python, even if you have not used it before. That is because Python is very similar to other computer languages you have used. For example, Python has native support for Object-Oriented Programming (OOP) and, in contrast, for using OOP in R you will need a workaround (like using R6 or RevoPemaR packages).

It is also possible that the availability of certain functions or libraries may make you choose between one language or another. For example, if you know about a function that exists in R and is not implemented yet in any Python library, you will probably use R. The opposite may also be true. Although almost all of the functionalities exist in both languages, it is possible to choose one language over another because the same task can be done in 3 lines instead of 10, due to how the API of certain libraries are organized.

Another reason that can bring us to use one language versus another is the popularity of that language in a concrete field. For example, it seems that there is more deep learning code written in Python than in R. That does not mean that R is worst for deep learning, it only means that Python has more active development of deep learning libraries. After all, native libraries (written in languages like C++) are the ones that execute the part of the code with the highest computational cost, and Python and R are only an interface that calls that native code.

# Select an appropriate ensemble

Ensembles are a way to combine several models to improve predictions. Ensembles are quite similar to "Ask the audience" lifelines, in which several persons are asked about something and another person makes a decision based on the results of the others.

Certain models have an inherent ensemble, for example, some may be based on forests (a collection of trees). Apart from a specific algorithm, Azure Machine Learning has no specific module that allows you to create ensembles, but you can easily create and experiment with ensembles. In the following paragraphs you will review the most common types of ensembles that are easily implementable in Azure Machine Learning, as well as those that are not.

The most direct form of ensemble is stacking, where the outputs of several models (base models) trained on the entire dataset are passed through another element that, in some way, weighs the results returned by the other models. Using this method usually results in an improvement over the use of a single classifier. In the next skills you will find examples of stacking. In Figure 2-14 you can see a diagram of how to implement a stacking ensemble. The "Join predictions" node in Figure 2-14 can be implemented, for example, calculating the arithmetic mean of each of the outputs from the previous models.

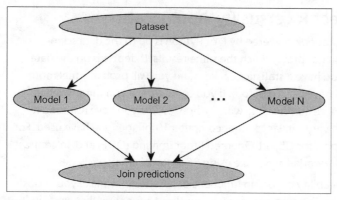

**FIGURE 2-14** Stacking ensemble method

Other types of ensembles are those based on bagging (also referred to as bootstrap aggregation). This technique divides the training set in different subsets that can be overlapped (sampling with replacement). A different model is trained on each of the subset and, like in stacking, the results of each classifier are combined. The Random Forest algorithm is very similar to a bagging of Trees, but with some additions. Figure 2-15 shows an overview schema of this method.

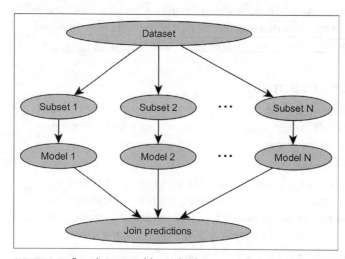

**FIGURE 2-15** Bagging ensemble method

Another common type of ensemble is boosting. This type of ensemble trains a first model on the initial dataset. Then, looking at the errors that this first model has made, it generates another dataset in which it assigns more weight to those samples where the first model has failed. In this way, the second model will pay more attention to the errors of the first model. The process is repeated N times and the outputs of the N models are combined. Azure Machine Learning uses this type of ensemble in algorithms such as Boosted Decision Trees. Figure 2-16 shows a diagram that sums up the boosting ensemble method.

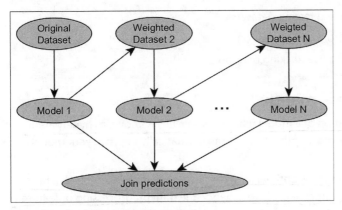

FIGURE 2-16 Boosting ensemble method

Stacking and bagging can be easily implemented in Azure Machine Learning, but other ensemble methods are more difficult. Also, it turns out to be very tedious to implement in Azure Machine Learning an ensemble of, say, more than five models. The experiment is filled with modules and is quite difficult to maintain. Sometimes it is worthwhile to use any ensemble method available in R or Python. Adding more models to an ensemble written in a script can be as trivial as changing a number in the code, instead of copying and pasting modules into the experiment.

> **NEED MORE INFORMATION?**  **R AND PYTHON ENSEMBLES DOCUMENTATION**
>
> To review further details about ensembles, refer to the sklearn documentation (Python): *http://scikit-learn.org/stable/modules/ensemble.html*, and caret documentation (R): *http://topepo.github.io/caret/train-models-by-tag.html#ensemble-model.*

# Skill 2.2: Initialize and train appropriate models

Machine learning algorithms are getting faster and more precise every day. Therefore, they have more parameters to tweak and adjust its behavior and performance depending on the data provided. In order to do that, some procedures are used to avoid known problems and maximize the models' precision and performance. In this section, you will learn to apply them to overcome the aforementioned problems and create the best possible model.

# Tune hyperparameters manually

The search for the ideal combination of a model parameter's values is known as hyperparameters optimization. Adjusting the most optimal values can dramatically improve your model performance.

Each hyperparameter combination is optimal for a certain algorithm and a certain dataset. This means that if your dataset changes, even if you change the data preprocessing or feature engineering prior to the model training, a new hyperparameter search is required. This is a common scenario in any machine learning language or tool, and Azure Machine Learning is no different. Every algorithm has its own set of parameters to be tuned. Each of them controls a certain aspect of the behavior of the algorithm. Thus, for instance, Forests will have the number of trees built as a parameter, yet with Logistic Regression you will be able to adjust the values of the L1 and L2 regularization parameters.

To illustrate how to manually change the default hyperparameters in the Azure Machine Learning Studio, create a new experiment. Drag the Steel Annealing multi-class dataset from the Samples section. Next, drag the Multiclass Decision Forest module from machine learning initialization modules and, finally, a Train Model module from the Machine Learning Train section. Connect them as shown in Figure 2-17.

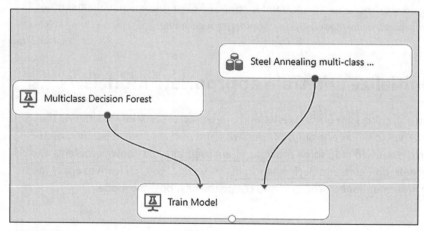

**FIGURE 2-17** Initial configuration of the experiment

Once you have set up the experiment, click on the Multiclass Decision Forest and check the configuration menu on the right side of the screen. See Figure 2-18.

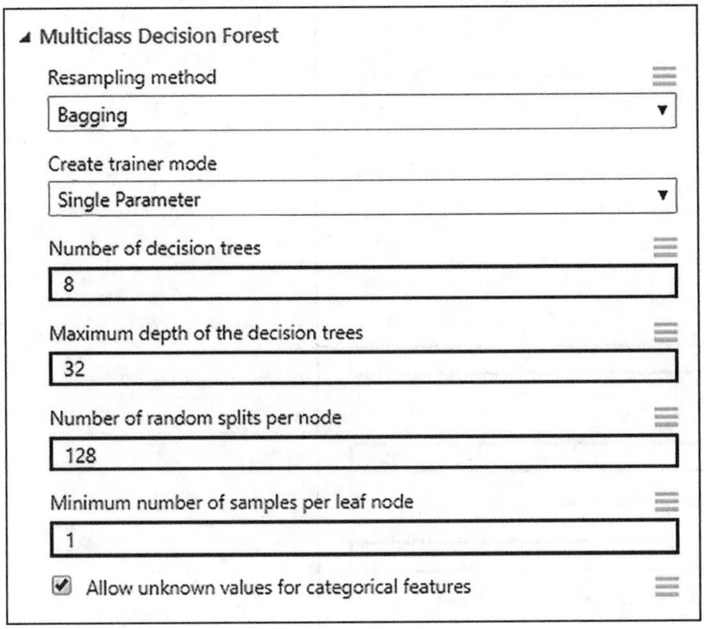

**Multiclass Decision Forest**

Resampling method
Bagging ▼

Create trainer mode
Single Parameter ▼

Number of decision trees
8

Maximum depth of the decision trees
32

Number of random splits per node
128

Minimum number of samples per leaf node
1

☑ Allow unknown values for categorical features

**FIGURE 2-18** Initial hyperparameter configuration

Note that only single values are allowed in the configuration menu shown in Figure 2-18. You can edit any of them to force the algorithm to use that combination the next time you run the experiment. Randomly changing these values would take an enormous amount of time, but if you know the parameters and their effects on the algorithm behavior and the dataset you are working on, this is a way to adjust your model configuration and performance.

## Tune hyperparameters automatically

In complex algorithms and datasets, manual hyperparameter tuning consumes too much time even for an expert. Azure Machine Learning allows you to automatically test different hyperparameter configurations to check which one fits your algorithm and dataset the best.

To create ranges of parameters to explore, change the Create trainer mode from Single parameter to Parameter Range in your model's initialization module. Then, you can specify different values to be tested separated by commas or use the Range Builder to graphically increase the width of the range while configuring the number of points to be selected from within the range. See Figure 2-19.

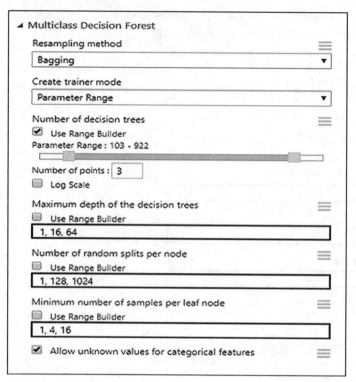

**FIGURE 2-19** Range hyperparameter builder

Azure Machine Learning will create a Cartesian product of combinations from the values you define in this module. This grid can be used subsequently to train as many models as individual combinations or less to test their performance.

In order to create that grid and explore the hyperparameters for your model, navigate to the Train section under Machine Learning in the main Azure Machine Learning Studio and drag and drop a Tune Model Hyperparameters module into the canvas.

Connect the Multiclass Decision Forest initialization module to the leftmost connector and the Steel Annealing multi-class dataset to the center connector.

In the Tune Model Hyperparameters module, launch the column selector in the module's Properties and select Classes to indicate that you are looking for hyperparameters to predict that particular column, as shown in Figure 2-20.

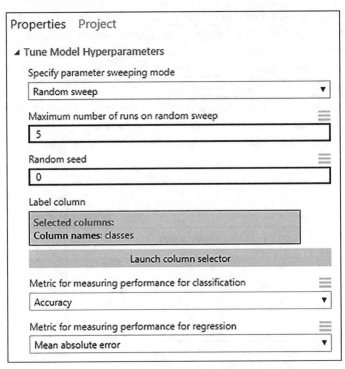

**FIGURE 2-20** Tune model hyperparameters random sweep configuration

There are three modes in Azure Machine Learning to tune the hyperparameters for your model:

- **Random Sweep** If you have selected a certain parameter range in your module initialization, it creates N random combinations of parameters within that range. Otherwise, Azure Machine Learning explores N possible hyperparameters over a system-defined range. By default, it explores five combinations as shown in Figure 2-18. You can change that value to increase the exploration space, increasing the training time with it, but exploring a wider range of random hyperparameters.

- **Entire Grid** Azure Machine Learning uses every single hyperparameter combination from the grid created in Figure 2-19 and creates a model out of each of them. Then, using the Metric For Measuring Performance selected, chooses the best model and makes it available as the rightmost output of the module. This option can be very time-consuming depending on the type of algorithm you are training and the number of combinations of the grid.

- **Random Grid**   Azure Machine Learning takes N random combinations from the grid created in Figure 2-19 and creates a model out of each combination. Again, selecting Metric For Measuring Performance identifies the best model and makes it available. This option has been proved less time-consuming and almost as effective when exploring the hyperparameter space as the "Entire grid" option.

Regardless of which option you choose, Azure Machine Learning always informs you of the results of the exploration in the leftmost output of the module, the Sweep results. For example, if you select Random grid with five random picks, you obtain results similar to these (see Figure 2-21).

| rows | columns | | | | |
|------|---------|---|---|---|---|
| 5 | 5 | | | | |
| | Minimum number of samples per leaf node | Number of random splits per node | Maximum depth of the decision trees | Number of decision trees | Accuracy |
| | 4 | 1024 | 16 | 512 | 0.976786 |
| | 4 | 1024 | 16 | 786 | 0.975 |
| | 4 | 1024 | 16 | 103 | 0.975 |
| | 16 | 1024 | 16 | 786 | 0.957143 |
| | 16 | 1024 | 64 | 376 | 0.957143 |

**FIGURE 2-21**  Random grid results

In Figure 2-21 the results are sorted in a descending order using the performance measure you selected in the Tune Model Hyperparameters module. However, when a more extensive exploration is performed, it is possible that the absolutely best model had taken too much time to train, and other models with less time consuming combinations may be offering a very similar performance, being a better option for production environments.

> **NEED MORE INFORMATION  OPTIMIZE YOUR ALGORITHMS IN AZURE ML**
>
> Several books and blog posts online describe this topic in detail. A good place to start is "Choose parameters to optimize your algorithms in Azure Machine Learning" at: *https:// docs.microsoft.com/en-us/azure/machine-learning/studio/algorithm-parameters-optimize*.

To explore such scenarios and understand where your "hot" hyperparameter areas are, you can use a custom visualization R or Python module. In this case, you might want to use an R Script module connected to the Tune Model Hyperparameters result output. A script like the following might help you to visualize where your hyperparameters are best set to optimize your model's performance:

```
R Code to create a hyperparameter space visualization
library(ggplot2)
dataset1 <- maml.mapInputPort(1) # class: data.frame
```

```
names(dataset1) <- c("minSamples", "randomSplits", "maxDepth", "numberOfTrees",
  "Accuracy")

      ggplot(dataset1, aes(x = randomSplits, y = maxDepth)) +
    geom_raster(aes(fill=Accuracy)) +
    scale_fill_gradientn(colours = c("blue", "yellow"))

maml.mapOutputPort("dataset1");
```

Depending on how wide your hyperparameter space is, the results may vary. In this example, you are first visualizing the Random Splits parameter against the Maximum Depth of each tree and showing the Accuracy measure as a heatmap.

You can visualize all of the graphs generated in an Execute R module, and right-clicking on the rightmost output of the module, and selecting Visualize (see Figure 2-22).

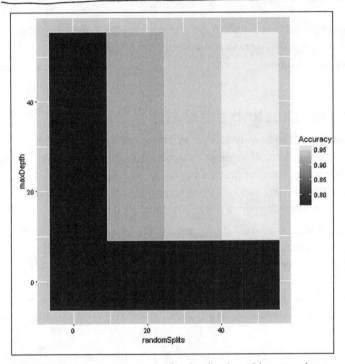

**FIGURE 2-22** Hyperparameter results visualization with custom heatmap

Using graphs to visually summarize the results you can understand that the higher the maximum depth of the trees and the random splits considered to build them, the higher the performance of the algorithm. Moreover, you can notice that the parameter that has a bigger impact is the number of random splits, since the upper left corner of the heatmap is still blue (even having a maximum depth of 48 levels per tree).

Other, more advanced hyperparameter space exploration techniques are also relatively common among the data science community, like Bayesian Optimization, Sequential Model-based Algorithm Configuration (SMAC), Tree-structured Parzen Estimator (TPE) or even Quasi-Monte Carlo methods, to name a few. Although they are not included natively in Azure Machine Learning, you can install the R or Python packages (as shown in Skill 1.2) that implement frameworks that ease their use and execute them inside R or Python modules inside Azure Machine Learning

> **NEED MORE INFORMATION ON ADVANCED HYPERPARAMETER TUNING?**
> **ADVANCED HYPERPARAMETER TUNING**
>
> To have a deeper knowledge of the hyperparameter tuning routines and techniques, take a look to some of the blog posts, documents and papers from the data science community and universities at:
>
> *https://www.iro.umontreal.ca/~bengioy/cifar/NCAP2014-summerschool/slides/Ryan_adams_140814_bayesopt_ncap.pdf* and *http://blog.revolutionanalytics.com/2016/06/bayesian-optimization-of-machine-learning-models.html.*

## Split data into training and testing datasets

When you are training a model, you want it to be very precise. Within your designing process, the way to know it is precise is comparing its results against data that you already know the results about, either if it is a classifier, a regressor, or a recommender of any type. However, if you test your model against data that has been used in the training process, the algorithm has already "seen" those precise cases, and its performance will be synthetically good.

In other words, you will not know if your model will perform good predictions when faced against yet unknown data, like the cases that it will have to predict when put in production. Since you are not yet able to evaluate how good your model is against unknown data, you may be falling into an overfit scenario, where your model is overspecialized on the data it has been trained with, but is not useful for yet-to-be-seen cases. If each rule in your model is built for each case of your training data, it will perform much worse against cases that are not identical to any of the ones used for training.

The most common and the first step that is applied in almost every machine learning experiment, regardless of the programming language or tool it is designed in, is to divide your dataset into two parts: the training set and the test set. Both sets must contain different completely disjointed sets of observations, and are not in risk of falling in an overfit scenario like the one described in the previous paragraph. That is why the split is done as randomly as possible (even the complete randomness is not as easy as it might appear in computer science). As a rule of thumb, 70% of the data is assigned for training, while the other 30% is used for testing. This might be adapted depending on the dataset and its distribution and the amount of observations.

In Azure Machine Learning, you can easily implement this split using the Split Data module before training your models. You can find this module in the Data Transformation section, under the Split and Sample sub-section. Connecting its only input to your already used Steel Annealing multi-class dataset and configuring it to use 70% of the data for training will look like what is shown in Figure 2-23.

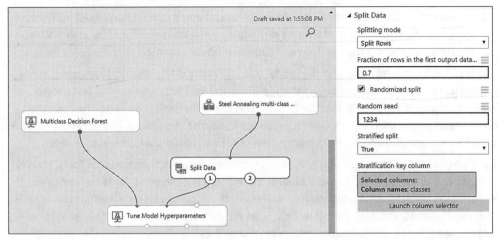

**FIGURE 2-23** Split data module configuration

Note that the stratified split option is set to TRUE. In a classification problem like this, selecting your label class as the stratification key column ensures that your output data subsets have a representative sampling of the selected strata column. This reduces potential biasing in the distribution and guarantees that your algorithm will be training over the same distribution of cases from each class that will appear in the test set, thus avoiding overfitting or underfitting (the absence of valid observations of a certain case).

Other options are available for the Split Data module:

- **Recommender split**   Special case of splitting for recommender algorithms. This will be covered in further sections of this book.
- **Regular expression**   Splits your data following a regular expression specified by you.
- **Relative expression**   Splits your data following a specific expression over values in your columns. You would usually use this option when training on data with a temporal axis (regressions or time series) and you want to test against a certain period (such as the last six months of data).

# Including using routines for cross-validation

Although split data for train and test fits most of the data science experiments, there are cases where a most extensive data analysis and validation is necessary. That is where cross-validation comes into play. Cross-validation is a process widely used in data science to examine the variability of the dataset as well as the reliability of the model trained with that data.

Cross-validation divides randomly the training dataset into a certain number of partitions, commonly called folds. In Azure Machine Learning the default number of folds used is 10, but you can change that using the Partition and Sample module with the Assign To Folds option.

One of the folds is set apart and the model trains with the other N folds. The trained model is tested using the fold that had been set aside. Thus, this fold acts now as your test dataset. Precision measures are calculated after this test and saved for further analysis. The measures used depend on the problem you are facing (classification or regression). Please review Skill 2.3 for further explanation about performance metrics for each machine learning problem.

For simplicity, in Figure 2-24 you will find a cross-validation diagram for three folds. Usually, the number of folds is higher to avoid biasing, but not too high to avoid large variability in results. Ten folds is usually a good point to start, and then you can change the number of folds when you understand better the behavior or your model over your dataset. You can find an example of a simple cross-validation process in Figure 2-24.

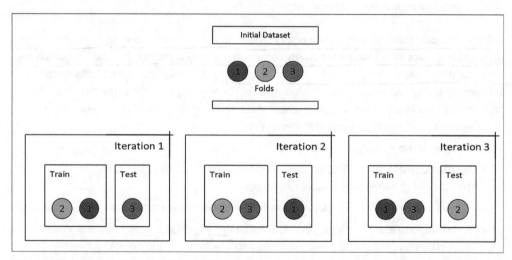

FIGURE 2-24 Cross-validation iterations for three folds

Cross-validation also gives you better information about how well the model will generalize when in production than just splitting in a random fashion. Cross-validation works perfectly with Split data. First, you can split data to ensure that the performance test will perform against totally unknown data, and then you tune your model using cross-validation to obtain even better results.

In Azure Machine Learning, you can find the Cross Validate Model module under the Machine Learning and Evaluate subsection. Drag and drop it on the canvas and connect it to your Multiclass Decision Forest initialization module and your Steel Annealing Multi-Class dataset, as shown in Figure 2-25.

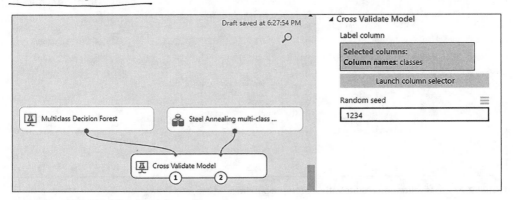

**FIGURE 2-25** Cross Validate Module configuration

When you run the module, you will have two available outputs. The leftmost dataset is the scored results, where you can examine the fold assignations for each row of the dataset and the scorings assigned by the initialized model. See Figure 2-26.

| Fold Assignments | family | product-type | steel | carbon | hardness | temper_rolling |
|---|---|---|---|---|---|---|
| 6 | C | A | 8 | 0 | | |
| 6 | C | R | 0 | 0 | | |
| 7 | C | R | 0 | 0 | | |
| 3 | C | A | 0 | 60 | T | |
| 6 | C | A | 0 | 60 | T | |
| 8 | C | A | 0 | 45 | | |

**FIGURE 2-26** Cross validation results

In Figure 2-27 you can see the scored probabilities for each case in the last columns of the results window for the Cross Validation Model module. In this case you will find different Scored Probabilities since you used a Multiclassification model.

| len | oil | bore | packing | classes | Scored Probabilities for Class "1" | Scored Probabilities for Class "2" | Scored Probabilities for Class "3" | Scored Probabilities for Class "5" | Scored Probabilities for Class "U" | Scored Labels |
|---|---|---|---|---|---|---|---|---|---|---|
| 0 | | 0 | | 3 | 0 | 0 | 1 | 0 | 0 | 3 |
| 0 | | 0 | | 3 | 0 | 0 | 1 | 0 | 0 | 3 |
| 762 | | 0 | | 3 | 0 | 0 | 1 | 0 | 0 | 3 |
| 0 | | 0 | | 3 | 0 | 0 | 1 | 0 | 0 | 3 |
| 269 | | 0 | | 3 | 0 | 0 | 1 | 0 | 0 | 3 |
| 0 | | 0 | | 3 | 0 | 0 | 1 | 0 | 0 | 3 |
| 4880 | Y | 0 | | 3 | 0 | 0 | 1 | 0 | 0 | 3 |
| 0 | | 0 | | 3 | 0 | 0 | 1 | 0 | 0 | 3 |
| 0 | | 0 | | 3 | 0 | 0 | 1 | 0 | 0 | 3 |
| 762 | | 0 | | 3 | 0 | 0 | 1 | 0 | 0 | 3 |
| 0 | | 0 | | 3 | 0 | 0 | 1 | 0 | 0 | 3 |

FIGURE 2-27 Cross validation results with scored probabilities

The rightmost output of the Cross Validation Model module will give you information about the performance metrics collected during the testing process with different folds (see Figure 2-28).

| Fold Number | Number of examples in fold | Model | Average Log Loss for Class "1" | Precision for Class "1" | Recall for Class "1" | Average Log Loss for Class "2" | Precision for Class "2" | Recall for Class "2" | Average Log Loss for Class "3" |
|---|---|---|---|---|---|---|---|---|---|
| 0 | 79 | Microsoft.Analytics.Modules.Gemini.Dll.MulticlassGeminiDecisionForestClassifier | 30 | 0 | 0 | 30 | 0 | 0 | 30 |
| 1 | 80 | Microsoft.Analytics.Modules.Gemini.Dll.MulticlassGeminiDecisionForestClassifier | 30 | 0 | 0 | 29.556817 | 0 | 0 | 30 |
| 2 | 80 | Microsoft.Analytics.Modules.Gemini.Dll.MulticlassGeminiDecisionForestClassifier | 0.693147 | 1 | 1 | 0.071335 | 1 | 1 | 0.01144 |
| 3 | 80 | Microsoft.Analytics.Modules.Gemini.Dll.MulticlassGeminiDecisionForestClassifier | 30 | 0 | 0 | 26.988031 | 0.166667 | 0.017544 | 30 |

FIGURE 2-28 Cross validation performance results

At the final rows in the Cross Validation Model module performance results window, you will find the mean and the standard deviation for each performance metric. Therefore, you can analyze how the performance varies between folds, and that gives you a picture of what is the variance in your data and how well the model generalizes through the folds, which is ultimately one of the aforementioned goals for the cross validation process.

In order to evaluate the model's bias variance (and, as a consequence, the data biasing itself), you must analyze such results and conclude that, the higher the mean of the performance metrics (Precision, Recall) and the lower the standard deviation (less variation), the better. This is useful to establish the model's sensitivity to variation and the data potential biasing. See Figure 2-29 to see the complete set of results with the mean and deviation metrics at the end of it.

| Fold Number | Number of examples in fold | Model | Average Log Loss for Class "1" | Precision for Class "1" | Recall for Class "1" | Average Log Loss for Class "2" | Precision for Class "2" | Recall for Class "2" |
|---|---|---|---|---|---|---|---|---|
| 0 | 79 | Microsoft.Analytics.Module s.Gemini.Dll.MulticlassGem iniDecisionForestClassifier | 30 | 0 | 0 | 30 | 0 | 0 |
| 1 | 80 | Microsoft.Analytics.Module s.Gemini.Dll.MulticlassGem iniDecisionForestClassifier | 30 | 0 | 0 | 29.556817 | 0 | 0 |
| 2 | 80 | Microsoft.Analytics.Module s.Gemini.Dll.MulticlassGem iniDecisionForestClassifier | 0.693147 | 1 | 1 | 0.071335 | 1 | 1 |
| 3 | 80 | Microsoft.Analytics.Module s.Gemini.Dll.MulticlassGem iniDecisionForestClassifier | 30 | 0 | 0 | 26.988031 | 0.166667 | 0.017544 |
| 4 | 80 | Microsoft.Analytics.Module s.Gemini.Dll.MulticlassGem iniDecisionForestClassifier | 0 | 1 | 1 | 0.035101 | 1 | 1 |
| 5 | 79 | Microsoft.Analytics.Module s.Gemini.Dll.MulticlassGem iniDecisionForestClassifier | 15.143841 | 1 | 0.5 | 0.026153 | 1 | 1 |
| 6 | 80 | Microsoft.Analytics.Module s.Gemini.Dll.MulticlassGem iniDecisionForestClassifier | 0 | 1 | 1 | 0.051929 | 1 | 1 |
| 7 | 80 | Microsoft.Analytics.Module s.Gemini.Dll.MulticlassGem iniDecisionForestClassifier | 0.287682 | 1 | 1 | 0.060173 | 1 | 1 |
| 8 | 80 | Microsoft.Analytics.Module s.Gemini.Dll.MulticlassGem iniDecisionForestClassifier | 30 | 0 | 0 | 29.507833 | 0.090909 | 0.016667 |
| 9 | 80 | Microsoft.Analytics.Module s.Gemini.Dll.MulticlassGem iniDecisionForestClassifier | 0.287682 | 1 | 1 | 0 | 0.714286 | 1 |

FIGURE 2-29 Complete Cross Validate Model performance metrics to evaluate variability and generalization

In fact, the Tune Model Hyperparameters module you studied in Skill 2.2 internally uses cross-validation routines to be able to test every hyperparameter combination needed against every fold in the dataset, ensuring the model's generalization against the wider amount of data possible.

In conclusion, including cross-validation routines (both with the module designed for it and/ or using Tune Model Hyperparameters) allows you to evaluate your models against more data, since you use every fold across your whole dataset. In addition, cross-validation routines evaluate both the model and the dataset itself, so you can identify easily biasing in your data, the model's sensitivity to changes in the dataset, and the dataset's variability itself.

# Build an ensemble using the stacking method

The stacking method to create ensembles is one of the methods known as "meta-algorithms," a category that includes bagging, boosting, and diverse voting and averaging techniques, to name a few. You have already seen some of them in Skill 2.1.

In order to create a stacking method in Azure Machine Learning, you will need to keep the same main structure that you used in the rest of your experiments. Thus, data ingestion and preparation are a requirement as they were before.

However, once you have done this, you will have to create your train and test datasets. To achieve this, you will split data with a Split Data module, already discussed in this skill. Then, another split will be needed to create our test dataset. Split percentages are variable in this approach, depending on the case (although the 70-30 baseline is always useful), but also keep in mind the stratification split to keep the label ratios. After this, and as shown in Figure 2-13 in Skill 2.1, you will need to train and score N different algorithms (also known as base algorithms) that will be composing the final ensemble.

Since both the train and testing set will need to have the same features, the scores from each model built on your regular features already present in the source dataset, you will need to run two scoring modules per algorithm. The process for each algorithm in the ensemble should be something like this:

- Initialize the model.
- Tune model hyperparameters with the leftmost output of the second Split Data module.
- Score resulting model with the first and the second Split Data results. The first subset will create the test set to check performance and the second will build the scores used to build the ensemble.
- You will repeat this for each model you want to add to the ensemble.

You will need to split data twice, because if you are going to use the scoring results from the base models for training the final model, you will need both the training and test set the same scoring as features. Thus, the first portion of the data will be used to train the base models, the second will be used to score and create the final training dataset, and the third portion will be used to create the test dataset with the base model's scores.

As you might have realized, all of these results should be combined afterward to create the dataset used for creating the ensemble model and the ensemble test dataset.

The first step for each algorithm used in the ensemble should look like what is shown in Figure 2-30.

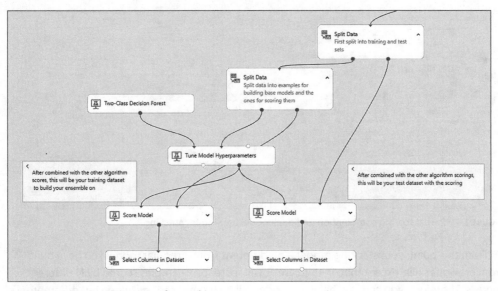

**FIGURE 2-30** Base model training for stacking

From this point on, you will only use the scorings in both test and train datasets to train and test your models. You will have N of this sections in your experiment, depending on how many algorithms you want to use. Using the Add Columns modules, discussed in Chapter 1, you will combine both results for training and testing. Remember to change their names with Edit Metadata modules prior to combine them so you keep track of which score feature comes from which base algorithm. This is especially important when it comes to optimization, since these score features, as any features, can reveal themselves not useful (maybe using the feature selection modules present in Azure Machine Learning) and you may want to change them if you detect they are not adding predictive accuracy to the model.

Once you have combined the results, a final model will be built using these score features. Using a Logistic Regression is common in these scenarios due to its training speed and because the feature space is now dramatically smaller. You will only have N features, where N is the number of base models you used, instead of the dozens or hundreds of features that you may have had in the original dataset. This higher number of features may have made the problem less suitable for a linear approach. However, you can use whichever algorithm to build your ensemble final model.

The Azure Machine Learning Tune Model Hyperparameter module does recognize the data that is consuming and does not let you use score results by themselves, so you will have to "trick it" in some way. See Figure 2-31 to see how applying a simple mathematical operation that does not change the scorings, like summing a zero value, converts them into features from the Azure Machine Learning engine perspective. Changing its metadata with the Edit Metadata module does not work for this purpose at the time of writing this book.

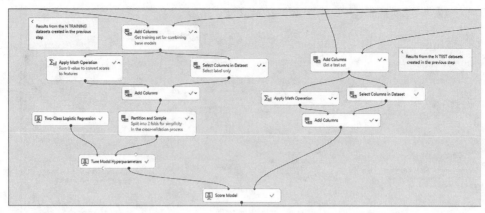

**FIGURE 2-31** Partial scoring combination and final model training for stacking

From this point, your stacking model is no different from a regular model you have built from previous skills, except that, in this case, it will score from samples scored by N different models. Therefore, you can say that your model will be "composed" or "made by" different heterogeneous models.

> **NEED MORE INFORMATION ON STACKING? BUILDING ENSEMBLES USING STACKING**
>
> You can find complete examples of models built using stacking by the community in the Cortana Intelligence Gallery: *https://gallery.cortanaintelligence.com/Experiment/Building-Ensemble-of-Classifiers-using-Stacking-2*, and *https://gallery.cortanaintelligence.com/Experiment/Stacked-Regression-Model*.

This stacking approach, and other ensembling methods, is useful in different scenarios, both in real production models and data science competitions (Kaggle, KDD Cup). Other ensembling techniques are also useful and available in Azure Machine Learning using R or Python modules. The combination of these techniques with the previous routines you learned about in this Skill (Hyperparameter tuning, data splitting, and cross validation) will help you to build more precise and robust models to put in production. You will learn how to evaluate the resultant models in Skill 2.3.

## Skill 2.3: Validate models

It's important to remember that the purpose of machine learning is not to minimize the error on training data, but to minimize the error obtained by running the model on data that it has not seen before. So, as discussed in Skill 2.2, measuring the performance on the training set is not the best way to ensure good performance in a production environment.

In Skill 2.1 you have already seen some complete experiments with training, scoring and evaluation (like the linear regression in Figure 2-4), but the last modules have not been thoroughly explained yet. In Skill 2.2 you have seen how to tune hyperparameters, in which the choice of model was based on a metric. However, not much has been said about the different metrics available. In order to learn where to aim in your optimization process, this skill covers the scoring phase, the different evaluation metrics that you can apply to each type of model, and how to make a model selection in Azure Machine Learning.

**This skill covers how to:**

- Score and evaluate models
- Select appropriate evaluation metrics for clustering
- Select appropriate evaluation metrics for classification
- Select appropriate evaluation metrics for regression
- Use evaluation metrics to choose between Machine Learning models
- Compare ensemble metrics against base models

## Score and evaluate models

The *testing* phase of a model can be decomposed on two steps:

- **Scoring**   Assuming that you already have a trained model, scoring consists of running that model on new samples. Running your model means different things depending on what model you are dealing with: assigning a cluster to a new example, marking a new sample as anomaly, predicting a continuous value, and others. For almost all of the models, this task can be done using the module Score Model. Clustering and recommender models use a special implementation of scoring, using the modules Assign Data to Clusters and Score Matchbox Recommender respectively.

- **Evaluation**   In supervised algorithms, once you have the objective values predicted by your model, you only have to compare them with the real values. This is what is called the evaluation phase. Later on, you will see different metrics that help you to measure how well the models perform. In clustering problems, where you do not have labels, the evaluation is somewhat different, but it uses the same module as the one used in classification, regression, and anomaly detection: the Evaluate Model module. Only recommender algorithms need a special module to be evaluated: the Evaluate Recommender module.

In Azure Machine Learning, the scoring phase is very straightforward. It consists of dragging one of the scoring modules to the canvas (the scoring modules are located in the left panel under Machine Learning > Score) and plugging into it the trained module and the data to score. The output consists of the same input data, plus columns containing the model predictions. The columns added to the dataset are different depending on the model. In addition, you must use this module when you want to create a web service with your pre-trained model to score new samples. More about deploying solutions will be discussed in Skill 3.1. See Figure 2-32 for a more visual clarification about the different scoring modules.

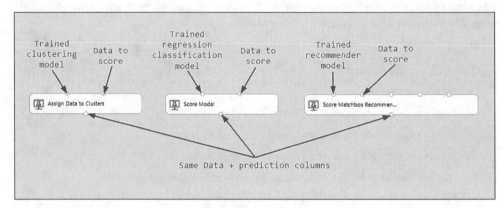

FIGURE 2-32 Inputs and outputs of the different scoring modules

The evaluation phase is not so simple. The way to implement it in Azure Machine Learning is quite straightforward (see Figure 2-33), but the choice of the metric to use is not so trivial. Just as the choice of a model type (regression, clustering, etc.) depends on the problem you are facing, the choice of an evaluation metric depends on the type of model you are using. For example, a metric used to evaluate a binary classification algorithm cannot be used in regression algorithms, but there is more than one evaluation metric for binary classification problems.

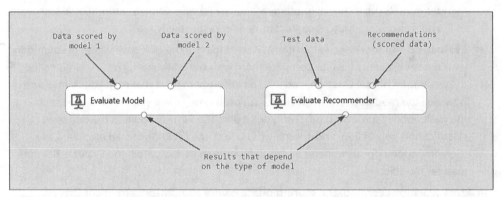

FIGURE 2-33 Inputs and outputs of the different evaluate modules—Evaluate Model can receive 1 or 2 scored datasets and if it receives 2, a comparison is made between the two

In addition to the modules shown in Figure 2-32 for evaluating models, the modules involved in hyperparameter optimization also use metrics, such as the Tune Model Hyperparameters and Sweep Clustering modules. As seen in Skill 2.2, these modules train several models with different combinations of hyperparameters, and return the best model. How do they know what model is best? They carry out an internal evaluation such as the one done by Evaluate Model and Evaluate Recommender, but instead of doing it on the test set they do it on the validation set. The returned model is the one that maximizes or minimizes a chosen metric. Figure 2-34 shows where you can configure the metric to use in the hyperparameter tuning modules.

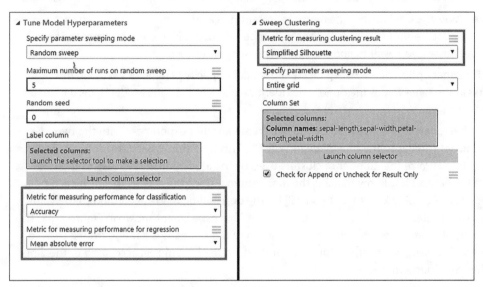

**FIGURE 2-34** On the left are the Tune Model Hyperparameters options where you can select one metric for classification and one for regression. On the right you will find the Sweep Clustering options where you can select the metrics to evaluate the clusters.

The following sections will show the most common metrics that will allow you to compare models and choose the best one. The clustering metrics will be seen first, then the classification (binary and multiclass) metrics, and finally the metrics used in regression problems.

## Select appropriate evaluation metrics for clustering

Since there is not a unique correct answer for clustering problems (unsupervised learning), the results are more difficult to evaluate than results from a supervised learning model. In order to evaluate the clusters, you must use the information returned by the evaluation of the model: number of examples per cluster, separation between clusters, and how close the samples of the center are of the cluster (commonly called centroid) to which they belong. Using this information, different metrics can be computed.

The Sweep Clustering module has an option called Metric For Measuring Clustering Result that allows you to change the metric that will be used for selecting the best model (see Figure 2-34). You can choose one of the following four metrics:

- **Simplified Silhouette**   This metric is a measure of how similar an object is to its own cluster compared to other clusters. Values range from -1 to 1. Higher values are better.

- **Davies-Bouldin**   This metric is defined as a ratio between the dispersion and the separation between each cluster. As you want slightly scattered and separated clusters, the lower values are better.

- **Dunn**   As the other metrics, the aim of this metric is to identify sets of clusters compact and well separated. Generally, a higher value for this metric indicates better clustering.

- **Average deviation**   The metric represents the average distance between each sample and its centroid. It decreases as the number of clusters increase, so it is not the best choice if you want to find the optimal number of clusters.

The other option of the Sweep Clustering module, Specify parameter sweeping mode, works in the same way as the option with identical name of the Tune Model Hyperparameters module.

To better explore these metrics you will create another experiment with the two-class Iris dataset (similar to the one made in Skill 2.1). This time the Sweep Clustering is used in order to optimize the number of clusters used by the algorithm. In the case of the two-class Iris dataset it is know that 2 is the most optimal since the classes to which each point belongs are already known, but you will let the decision be made according to the value of the Simplified Silhouette metric. Look at the final experiment shown in Figure 2-35. The number of clusters selected in the initialization of the k-Means is a range from 2 to 5, so Sweep Clustering will perform four runs and return the best model according to the Simplified Silhouette metric.

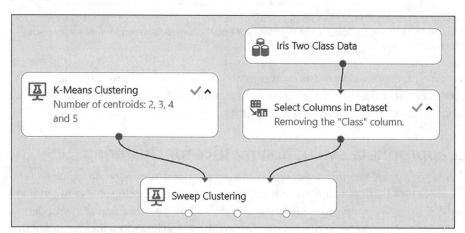

**FIGURE 2-35** A clustering experiment. In the experiment, the number of clusters is evaluated using Sweep Clustering with the Simplified Silhouette metric

If you visualize the third output of the Sweep Clustering module (see Figure 2-36), you will see a table with each of the executions ordered by the selected metric. In this case it is ordered in descending order, but when metrics in which the best value is the lowest value (such as Davis-Boulding), the order is inverted.

rows    columns
4       3

| Cluster Metric | Number of Centroids | Index of Run |
|---|---|---|
| view as | | |
| 0.855614 | 2 | 0 |
| 0.709597 | 3 | 1 |
| 0.603364 | 4 | 2 |
| 0.560317 | 5 | 3 |

Descending order

FIGURE 2-36  Sweep Clustering runs with the Simplified Silhouette metric

The model with two clusters is chosen as the best model by using the Simplified Silhouette metric. If you rerun the experiment with the Average Deviation metric you will get something similar to the Figure 2-37.

rows    columns
4       3

| Cluster Metric | Number of Centroids | Index of Run |
|---|---|---|
| view as | | |
| 0.451865 | 5 | 3 |
| 0.486897 | 4 | 2 |
| 0.546952 | 3 | 1 |
| 0.68278 | 2 | 0 |

FIGURE 2-37  Sweep Clustering runs with the Average Deviation metric

Using the Average Deviation metric, the best model is the one that uses five clusters. This is because this metric approaches zero as the number of clusters increases (being zero when you have as many clusters as samples). So, you cannot use the Average Deviation for finding the best number of clusters (or at least not without a more detailed analysis), but you can use it for choosing another hyperparameter of K-Means.

In datasets with few features like Iris you can visually explore the data and find clusters, but in datasets with a higher number of dimensions and lots of examples, since humans have difficulties with visual representations beyond just a few dimensions, the situation is different, and requires you to be guided by metrics. But besides this mathematical way of evaluating clusters, you should also evaluate them in the context of your data. The best way to achieve this is to ask yourself: Do the groups that the algorithm has found make sense? Can you interpret them in a way that brings some insight into your domain? If both answers are "yes," you can conclude your exploration. If not, you might want to repeat the exploration perhaps with a different number of clusters or other variations in some of the hyperparameters.

## Select appropriate evaluation metrics for classification

When talking about evaluation metrics for classification, a distinction must be made between binary and multiclass models.

When a *binary classifier* gives a prediction, it can be a correct or an incorrect prediction. Every prediction can fall in one of these categories:

- **True Positives (TP)**    The label of the sample is positive and the model predicts that it is positive. This is a success.
- **True Negatives (TN)**    The label of the sample is negative and the model predicts that it is negative. This is a success.
- **False Positives (FP)**    The label of the sample is negative and the model predicts that it is positive. This is an error.
- **False Negatives (FN)**    The label of the sample is positive and the model predicts that it is negative. This is an error.
- Figure 2-38 shows a table summarizing the four cases.

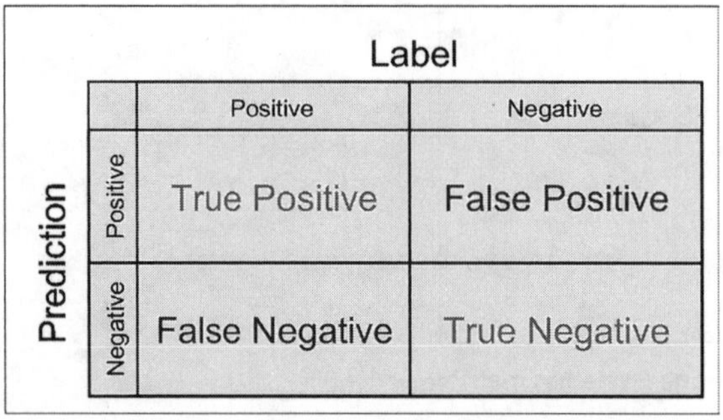

**FIGURE 2-38** Evaluating binary classifiers. In green the correct predictions and in red the incorrect ones

The following metrics are reported when evaluating binary classification models:

■ **Accuracy**   Measures the proportion of correctly classified cases. It gives misleading results on unbalanced datasets (unbalanced datasets contain a large percentage of samples of a unique class). For example, if 90% of our samples are from class 1, our algorithm could have a 90% accuracy just by predicting that all examples are from class 1. Figure 2-39 shows the formula used to compute the accuracy. The value goes from 0 to 1 where 1 is the ideal value. It is very common to express accuracy in percentage.

$$Accuracy = \frac{TP + TN}{TP + TN + FP + FN} = \frac{Correct}{Total\ population}$$

**FIGURE 2-39** Accuracy formula, where TP, TN, FP, FN stand for true positives, true negatives, false positives and false negatives respectively

■ **Precision**   It answers the question: from the cases that have been classified as positives (TP and FP), which ones were classified correctly (TP)? The value goes from 0 to 1 where 1 is the ideal value. This measure is often used when the cost of a false positive is high. See Figure 2-40.

$$Precision = \frac{TP}{TP + FP}$$

**FIGURE 2-40** Precision formula

■ **Recall**   It answers the question: from the cases that should have been predicted as positives (TP and FN) which ones were classified correctly (TP)? The value goes from 0 to 1 where 1 is the ideal value. This measure is typically used when the cost of a false negative is high. See figure 2-41.

$$Recall = \frac{TP}{TP + FN}$$

**FIGURE 2-41** Recall formula

■ **F1-Score**   (Also F-Score) is the harmonic mean of precision and recall. The value goes from 0 to 1 where 1 is the ideal value. Very commonly used when the dataset is unbalanced (skewed). See Figure 2-42.

$$F_1 = 2\ \frac{Precision \cdot Recall}{Precision + Recall}$$

**FIGURE 2-42** F1-Score formula

■ **AUC**   Measures the **A**rea **U**nder the ROC **C**urve. The ROC curve shows how the performance (true positive rate and false positive rate) of a binary classifier changes when the discrimination threshold is varied. The AUC value varies between 0 and 1. See Figure 2-43.

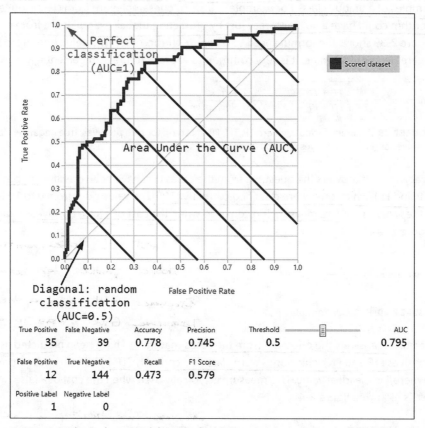

**FIGURE 2-43** The Evaluate Model output for binary models. At the top is the ROC curve and below several previously seen metrics: accuracy, precision, recall, and F1-score

*Anomaly detection* algorithms are evaluated in the same way as a binary classifier. This is because anomaly detectors classify samples into two classes: anomalous and not anomalous. For this type of problem, it is very important not to use accuracy to evaluate the models, due to the small number of anomalous events. Metrics such as F1-Score, which maintain the balance between precision and recall, may be a good option.

The metrics used in multiclass models are slightly different. The table shown in Figure 2-38 is actually a confusion matrix. This case can be extended to more than two classes. Figure 2-44 shows the confusion matrix obtained with an Evaluate Model module from a classifier on the Iris dataset with three classes. The diagonal shows the successes and the other elements of the matrix indicate errors. For example, in the figure you can see that the Iris-Versicolour class is confused with the Iris-Virginica by the classifier 15.4% of the time.

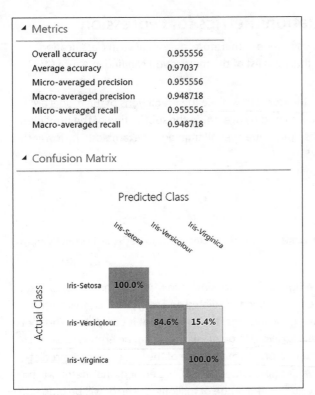

## Metrics

| | |
|---|---|
| Overall accuracy | 0.955556 |
| Average accuracy | 0.97037 |
| Micro-averaged precision | 0.955556 |
| Macro-averaged precision | 0.948718 |
| Micro-averaged recall | 0.955556 |
| Macro-averaged recall | 0.948718 |

## Confusion Matrix

Predicted Class

|  | Iris-Setosa | Iris-Versicolour | Iris-Virginica |
|---|---|---|---|
| Iris-Setosa | 100.0% | | |
| Iris-Versicolour | | 84.6% | 15.4% |
| Iris-Virginica | | | 100.0% |

Actual Class

**FIGURE 2-44** Metrics and confusion in the matrix of multiclassification models

Apart from the confusion matrix, at the top of the results window you can see other measures. Overall accuracy is the total number of correct predictions over the number of samples (accuracy as has been defined before). The averaged metrics are the same as in the binaries (accuracy, precision and recall), but taken per class and averaged. Micro averages consider the total count of samples and macro averages do not take imbalance into account.

In both binary and multiclass classifiers, knowing which of these measures to use depends on the context. For example, if you are considering a fraud detection scenario, false positives are very serious (you are accusing someone of a crime), meanwhile if you are recognizing dangerous objects in an airport camera, false negatives are more dangerous because you are letting people enter in a plane with a knife or a gun. In the fraud detection case, precision is the most appropriate metric; in the airport case recall would give better results. A third example of equally unwanted cases may be a marketing campaign to identify who will potentially buy a product, where both cases are as bad (losing a sale and overestimating stock). In this case, if the dataset is well balanced, you can use accuracy as a measure, but if it is not, it is better to use F-Score.

*[handwritten note: What does this mean you poor excuse of a writer?]*

# Select appropriate evaluation metrics for regression

Regression problems predict continuous numbers; therefore, metrics used in classification problems are no longer useful. Below there is a list of the metrics you can find in Azure Machine Learning.

- **Mean absolute error (MAE)** Measures how close the predictions of the model are to the target value. This metric is calculated by averaging the subtraction of the predicted value and the actual value in absolute value over all training set examples. The lower the value the better. See Figure 2-45.

$$MAE = \frac{\sum_{i=1}^{N} |y_i - \widehat{y_i}|}{N}$$

FIGURE 2-45 MAE definition, where is the number of samples, is the target value of sample and is the predicted value of sample

- **Root mean squared error (RMSE)** This is very similar to MAE, but instead of taking the absolute value of the difference between predicted and target values, this metric squares the difference. After taking the average, the square root is computed. This metric should be used when you want to avoid large errors (because the error is squared). This and the previous metrics depend on the magnitude of the values you are predicting. If you are predicting small values (like values near 0), the error of this metric will be small, but if you are predicting values in the range of millions, the error will be bigger. See Figure 2-46.

$$RMSE = \sqrt{\frac{\sum_{i=1}^{N} (y_i - \widehat{y_i})^2}{N}}$$

FIGURE 2-46 RMSE definition

- **Relative absolute error (RAE)** Thisis a normalized absolute error between expected and target values. It is very similar to MAE but with normalization. Because it is a relative metric, it goes from 0 to 1. It is better the nearer it comes to zero. See Figure 2-47.

$$RAE = \frac{\sum_{i=1}^{N} |y_i - \widehat{y_i}|}{\sum_{i=1}^{N} |y_i - \bar{y}|}$$

FIGURE 2-47 RAE definition, where is the mean of the target values

- **Relative squared error (RSE)** The normalized version of the RMSE. Because it is a relative measure, it goes from 0 to 1. It is better the nearer it comes to zero. See Figure 2-48.

$$RSE = \sqrt{\frac{\sum_{i=1}^{N}(y_i - \hat{y}_i)^2}{\sum_{i=1}^{N}(y_i - \bar{y})^2}}$$

**FIGURE 2-48** RSE definition

- **Coefficient of determination (R2)**  This represents the predictive power of the model as a value between 0 and 1. 0, and means that the model is random (explains nothing); 1 means there is a perfect fit. However, caution should be used in interpreting R2 values, because R2 can be low even if the model is good, and R2 can be high even if the model is not good. See figure 4-49.

$$SS_{res} = \sum_{i=1}^{N}(y_i - \hat{y}_i)^2$$

$$SS_{tot} = \sum_{i=1}^{N}(y_i - \bar{y})^2$$

$$R2 = 1 - \frac{SS_{res}}{SS_{tot}}$$

**FIGURE 2-49** R2 definition, where  is called the residual sum of squares and  is called total sum of squares

In Figure 2-50 you can find a screenshot of the Evaluate Model output if you are using a regression model.

| ◢ Metrics | |
|---|---|
| Mean Absolute Error | 1637.286516 |
| Root Mean Squared Error | 2268.361615 |
| Relative Absolute Error | 0.297707 |
| Relative Squared Error | 0.111291 |
| Coefficient of Determination | 0.888709 |

**FIGURE 2-50** Regression metrics

**NEED MORE INFORMATION?** **EVALUATE REGRESSION MODELS**

Read more about this metrics and how to interpret the values in the next post: *https://medium.com/wandering-in-advanced-analytics/how-to-better-evaluate-the-goodness-of-fit-of-regressions-990dbf1c0091.*

## Use evaluation metrics to choose between Machine Learning models

So far you have seen that if you want to select a model based on a given metric, you only need to select that metric in the Tune Model Hyperparameters, and use the returned model. Then, to estimate its performance in unseen data, you must run the Score Model and Evaluate Model on the test set. In this section you will look at another use of the Evaluate Model module. If you connect two datasets to the module you will get a comparison between the models that have scored those datasets. This way you can compare the resulting two models from their respective Tune Model Hyperparameters. To avoid overfitting, it is better not to adjust parameters based on the test result and simply use this measurement as a final comparison between the best models obtained.

Figure 2-51 shows an experiment that compares two tuned models (logistic regression vs decision jungle).

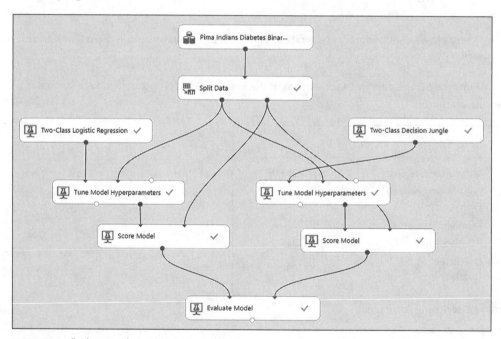

**FIGURE 2-51** Evaluate and compare two models

If you visualize the output of the Evaluate Model module you will see a comparison between the two models, similar to the one in Figure 2-52. The blue curve refers to the first input of the module (dataset scored by logistic regression) and the red curve refers to the second input (decision jungle).

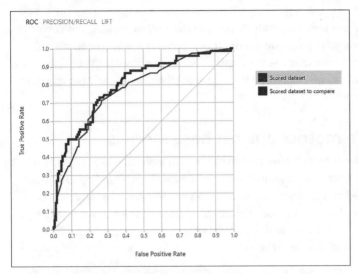

**FIGURE 2-52** Comparative of the ROC curve between two models

In addition to the ROC curve, you have other charts such as lift charts or precision/recall charts. Figure 2-53 shows a screenshot of a precision/recall curve. This graphical representation is very similar to a ROC curve, but this time the model is better the closer the curve is to the top right corner.

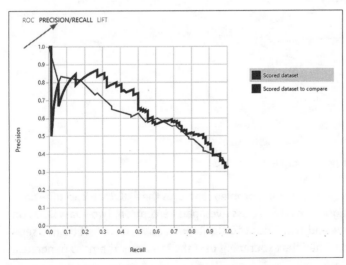

**FIGURE 2-53** Precision/recall plot. At the top of the chart you can switch between plot types.

After exploring the results, it can be concluded that, in this particular case, logistic regression outperforms decision jungle. This is because the blue ROC curve is closer to the upper left corner than the red one (Figure 2-53). In addition to the curve, as mentioned above, the window shows other measures (accuracy, recall, precision and AUC) that are also higher for logistic regression.

Apart from the Azure Machine Learning metrics, you can use a script module and compute your own metrics. For example, you can create a script that computes the Gini coefficient () in binary classifiers if you want to use that specific metric. Therefore, consider the option of evaluating your algorithms with scripts if you see that using another metric can help you get a better model.

## Compare ensemble metrics against base models

If you want to check if an ensemble has higher performance than individual models you can clone the experiment (*https://gallery.cortanaintelligence.com/Experiment/Building-Ensemble-of-Classifiers-using-Stacking-2*) and compare the results. This experiment takes 30 minutes to run. As previously mentioned when talking about ensembles, creating them in Azure Machine Learning is a tedious task that gives rise to highly populated experiments. See Figure 2-54 to better understand the structure of that experiment.

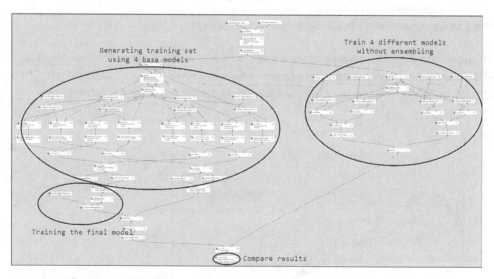

**FIGURE 2-54** Experiment that implements a stacking ensemble

The experiment solves a binary classification problem and uses the AUC metric to tune and select the models. It uses four algorithms (Two-Class Averaged Perceptron, Two-Class Decision Forest, Two-Class Decision Jungle and Two-Class Logistic Regression) that are first trained separately on the entire training test. Then the experiment uses the same algorithms to generate a training set to train the final model. After running the experiment, visualize the last output. You will get a table with five columns, like the one in Figure 2-55. The AUC of the four algorithms are compared with the ensemble and it is verified that the AUC of the ensemble outperforms all the others separately.

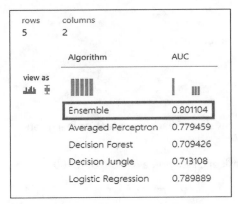

**FIGURE 2-55** Ensemble vs 4 base models. The ensemble outperforms all the others.

Ensembles have been used with great success in data science competitions such as those released on Kaggle. In order to raise a few places in the final classification, some of these ensembles have hundreds or thousands of models. In the business world, pushing to the limit the number of models used in ensembles is not so common. This is due to the fact that most of the time it is not worth investing so many resources (development time and computing power) when the improvement in predictions is only a few decimal places.

# Thought experiment

This thought experiment allows you to demonstrate the skills and knowledge gained by re-viewing the topics covered in the chapter. The answers are included in the next section.

1. Sort the following steps to create a simple but well-done experiment:

   A. Evaluate model.

   B. Split data in training and test.

   C. Use Tune Model Hyperparameters module to find the best combination of hyper-parameters of a given model.

   D. Import dataset to the experiment.

   E. Score model.

2. Is the average deviation the best metric you can use to get the optimum number of clusters to use in the k-Means algorithm?

3. Which of the following metrics do not apply to binary classifiers?

    A. AUC.

    B. Accuracy.

    C. MAE.

    D. Recall.

4. Which of the following modules do not have parameters?

    A. One-vs-All Multiclass.

    B. Two-Class Neural Network.

    C. Decision Forest Regression.

5. Which module would you use to obtain the relevance of each input feature in a given model?

6. Which of the following models best fits the task of classifying a dataset of 10000 samples and 10000 features?

    A. Logistic regression.

    B. Linear SVM.

7. If you connect a neural network with a Tune Model Hyperparameters module configured with Random Sweep and Maximum number of runs on random sweep = 1, how many neural networks are trained during the execution of the experiment? Why? If you connect a validation dataset to the third input of the Tune Model Hyperparameters module, how many neural networks are trained now?

## Thought experiment answers

This section contains the answers to the thought experiments in this chapter.

1. The correct order is D, B, C, E, A. Among the proposed steps there is not a model initialization, but it can be done in any position before the tuning of hyperparameters (Step C).

2. No, because the more clusters you have the less average deviation you get.

3. MAE is used to evaluate regression models.

4. One-vs-All Multiclass module does not have parameters, it only uses a binary model (with its respective parameters) as input.

5. Permutation Feature Importance.

6. Linear SVMs usually works better than linear regression that has so many features.

7.  Without validation dataset 11 (10 of k-fold cross validation + 1 trained with all the data with the best combination of hyperparameters). With the validation set only 1 neural network is trained, so the best model is not trained using the validation set if you provide it.

## Chapter summary

How to get the best model is not an easy task. Below, in summary, there is a list with the most important points learned in this chapter that help you to obtain a good model.

- It has been discussed the different types of machine learning problems that exist and can be solved with Azure Machine Learning. Azure Machine Learning algorithms have been classified into four categories: classifiers, regressors, anomaly detectors, and clustering. In addition to these four types, time series and recommenders have been mentioned as special types.

- You have seen the algorithms that Azure Machine Learning puts at your disposal for each of these problems. In addition, you have seen the different characteristics of these models that can help you when choosing one of them.

- You have seen several alternatives to combine models (ensembles) and you have implemented staking in Azure Machine Learning.

- You have learned about why data partitioning in training and test set is important. You have also reviewed the benefits of cross validation.

- You have learned to do manual and automatic tuning of hyperparameters in all the models.

- It has been explained how to score samples.

- You have learned about the different evaluation metrics that exist in Azure Machine Learning.

# CHAPTER 3

# Operationalize and manage Azure Machine Learning Services

Now that you have already built an optimal machine learning model following best practices to solve your business scenario, the next step is to consume the model and use its predictions to create a business solution. Publishing models, managing them and consuming their predictions in enterprise environments, has been historically difficult. Azure Machine Learning intends to ease this process leveraging well-known cloud mechanisms, such as the Azure Portal, or secure web services, to facilitate the pipelining of machine learning solutions in your organization.

## Skills in this chapter:

- Skill 3.1: Deploy models using Azure Machine Learning
- Skill 3.2: Manage Azure Machine Learning projects and workspaces
- Skill 3.3: Consume Azure Machine Learning models
- Skill 3.4: Consume exemplar Cognitive Services APIs

## Skill 3.1: Deploy models using Azure Machine Learning

Deploying models trained with Azure Machine Learning brings flexibility to the way they are consumed by users and applications because they are exposed as web services. These web services can be called from a REST API to obtain batch or real-time predictions, and therefore they are accessible from web applications, programming languages (.NET, Java, etc.), or even applications such as Excel or Power BI Desktop.

**This skill covers how to:**

- Publish a model developed inside Azure Machine Learning
- Publish an externally developed scoring function using an Azure Machine Learning package
- Use web service parameters
- Create and publish a recommendation model
- Create and publish a language understanding model

## Publish a model developed inside Azure Machine Learning

When you convert a training experiment (like the ones you have been seeing so far in this book) into a Predictive Web Service, Azure Machine Learning automatically conducts two main changes:

- The set of modules used for training are converted into a single module containing the saved model.
- Adds incoming and outgoing ports that the final web service uses as data inputs and outputs.

Once the model has passed the training phase in your training experiment (thus, you are satisfied with its performance), you can create a web service using your model for consumption. In order to create this web service, click Configure Web Service, and then select Predictive Web Service. This automatically converts your training experiment into a predictive experiment. It is useful to create a predictive model from your training experiment because we can continue working on the trained model if we have to apply any changes without affecting the users who are consuming the web service already in place.

Generally, the life cycle of an Azure Machine Learning experiment follows the pattern shown in Figure 3-1.

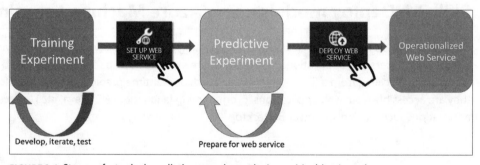

**FIGURE 3-1** Stages of a typical predictive experiment in Azure Machine Learning

In order to go through the web service publication process, in Azure Machine Learning Studio create a new experiment from the left-bottom menu New, Experiment, and finally, select Sample 7: Train, Test, Evaluate For Multiclass Classification: Letter Recognition Dataset (see Figure 3-2).

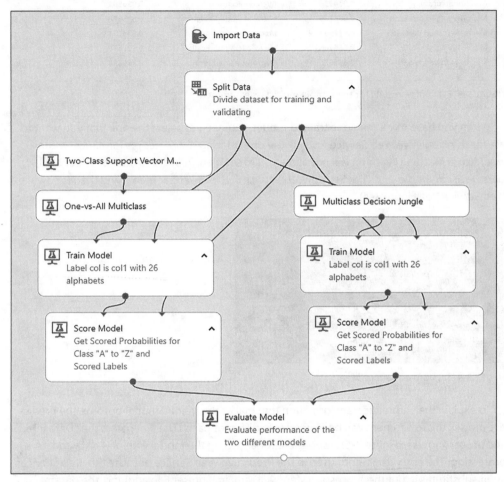

**FIGURE 3-2** New Experiment from Sample 7: Train, Test, Evaluate For Multiclass Classification: Letter Recognition Dataset in the Cortana Intelligence Gallery

To deploy the model, first you run the experiment. This executes each module, including the current models. In Figure 3-2, you have several models trained (a one-vs-all SVM and a Multiclass Decision Jungle). Once you have run your experiment you are able to evaluate and compare the performance of both algorithms. See Figure 3-3 to check the major performance metrics. It shows that the Multiclass Decision Jungle (the rightmost model) offers better performance in this circumstance (see Figure 3-3)

Sample 7: Train, Test, Evaluate for Multiclass Classification: Letter... ❯ Evaluate Model ❯ Evaluation results

| ▲ Metrics | | ▲ Metrics | |
|---|---|---|---|
| Overall accuracy | 0.666366 | Overall accuracy | 0.825678 |
| Average accuracy | 0.974336 | Average accuracy | 0.986591 |
| Micro-averaged precision | 0.666366 | Micro-averaged precision | 0.825678 |
| Macro-averaged precision | 0.674953 | Macro-averaged precision | 0.833171 |
| Micro-averaged recall | 0.666366 | Micro-averaged recall | 0.825678 |
| Macro-averaged recall | 0.664672 | Macro-averaged recall | 0.824898 |

**FIGURE 3-3** Evaluation results for the sample multiclass experiment

When you have more than one trained model, you need to select the one that you want to use for the Predictive Web Service (usually the one offering the better performance). Otherwise, Azure Machine Learning will not allow you to set it up. In order to do that select Multiclass Decision Jungle, and click Set Up Web Service in the lower bar menu, and then Predictive Web Service (see Figure 3-4)

**FIGURE 3-4** Set up Web Service Menu

To explain the automatic transformation that makes the trained model become the predictive model, this experiment can be divided into different parts. The first part is the "Data Input and processing" (see Figure 3-5) responsible for enriching the model with new data and its processing. The entry itself is not used in the Predictive Web Service because the Web Services input substitutes it, but the processing steps will remain if present. In addition, the dataset metadata, such as data types, is used by the predictive model. This is important because you may want to adjust the needed data input in the web service. For example, input data may not be ready at the time of scoring, or some of your data input is subsequently deleted in the data processing pipeline. For a part-by-part description of the experiment from Figure 3-2, see Figure 3-5.

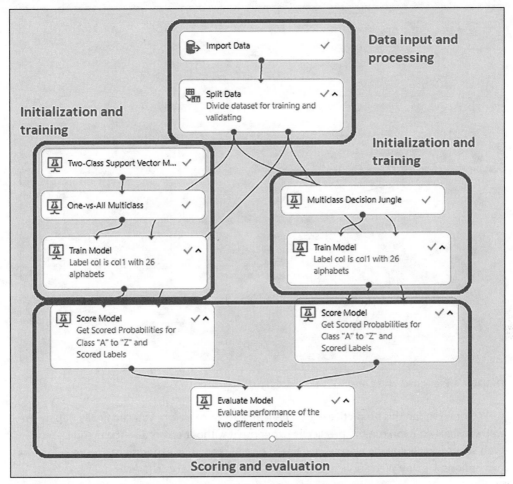

**FIGURE 3-5** Azure Machine Learning experiment parts based on their function

The initialization and training modules are replaced with a single module that contains the trained model, which is also saved in the Trained Models'section of the module palette. The Evaluate Model module is also deleted because it is not needed anymore, the algorithms' performance has been evaluated and the web service only needs to score.

Finally, the automatic deploy includes incoming and outgoing ports that the final web service will use (see Figure 3-6).

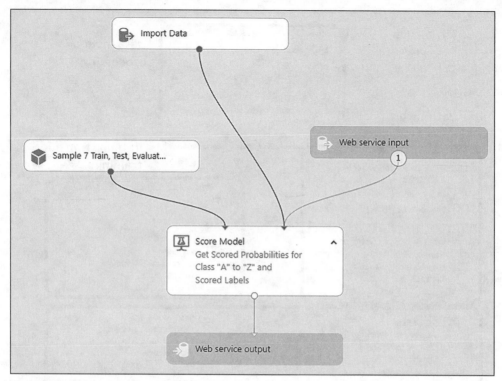

**FIGURE 3–6** Predictive model result

You need to run this predictive experiment at least once before you can finally deploy the web service. After you run the predictive experiment without errors, use the menu Deploy Web Service to deploy the web service based on the predictive experiment. Figure 3-7 shows two options: Deploy Web Service [Classic] and Deploy Web Service [New].

**FIGURE 3-7** Deploy Web Service menu

The main difference between the new web services and the classic web service is that the new web service option enables you to copy between subscriptions; the web service is deployed once, and the resulting web service can be copied to multiple subscriptions in multiple regions. You can also use the ARM APIs to deploy and manage web services using the RESTful APIs. PowerShell cmdlets are also available. With the Classic Web Service option, the web service can only be consumed using Request / Response, Batch, and App.

Another important difference is the pricing tiers where you can deploy your web services. When using the classic mode you can only consume your web services using a fixed rate for production API computing hours and production API transactions. However, if you decide to use the new deployment model you will be able to contract different consumption tiers depending on your usage, potentially saving money (the higher the tier, the more you pay up front, but the cheaper the API transactions and compute hours are).

**NEED MORE INFORMATION?** AZURE MACHINE LEARNING PRICING INFORMATION

Due to the dynamic nature of the cloud-based services, pricing details might change over time. To check the latest pricing options and tiers, please visit: *https://azure.microsoft.com/ pricing/details/machine-learning-studio.*

When deploying a web service using the new model, you need to confirm the service name and its price plan (created in one of the tiers offered in the pricing page; see prior note) to deploy the web service. Click Deploy to deploy the web service under your Azure subscription (see Figure 3-8).

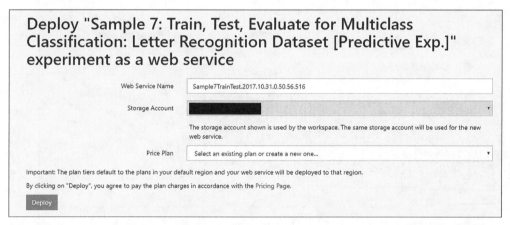

**FIGURE 3-8** New Deploy Web Service menu

**NEED MORE REVIEW?** DEPLOY AN AZURE MACHINE LEARNING WEB SERVICE

There are several books and online resources that describe this topic in detail. A good place to start is "Deploy an Azure Machine Learning web service" at: *https://docs.microsoft.com/ azure/machine-learning/machine-learning-publish-a-machine-learning-web-service.*

Once the web service is deployed, you are able to consume it from a wide range of tools and programming languages. Consumption of this web service to leverage your models' predictions is covered in Skill 3.3.

## Publish an externally developed scoring function using an Azure Machine Learning package

Using external functions in Azure Machine Learning is possible through two different methods. The first method is to use them inside of the Create R Module that you can find under the R Language Modules menu. The second method is to deploy directly from your local development machine.

To explain the first option you can create a new experiment from the New Experiment menu and select the Create R Model from the samples gallery, and then select Open In Studio. The example to be created will be the next one (See Figure 3-9).

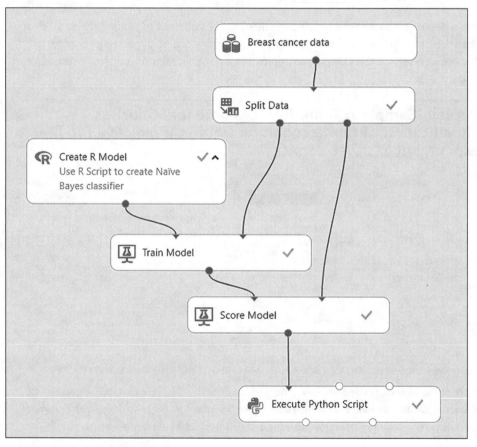

**FIGURE 3-9** Create R Module experiment

When you select the Create R Model module you see two scripts. The first is the Trainer R script and is used to define how the model itself is trained using the available input data (see Figure 3-10).

```
1  #Get library
2  library(e1071)
3  #Select the columns marked as features from the dataset with the predefined get.feature.columns function
4  features <- get.feature.columns(dataset)
5  #Select the columns marked as labels from the dataset with the predefined get.feature.columns function
6  labels <- as.factor(get.label.column(dataset))
7  #Build a dataframe called train.data with features and labels
8  train.data <- data.frame(features, labels)
9  #Get the names of the columns marked as features in the original dataset
10 feature.names <- get.feature.column.names(dataset)
11 #Rename the columns in the new dataframe as all the feature names and the last column (the label) as "Class"
12 names(train.data) <- c(feature.names, "Class")
13 #Build the Naive Bayes model predictint the "Class" label, using the rest of the columns (the features)
14 model <- naiveBayes(Class ~ ., train.data)
```

FIGURE 3-10  Trained R Script module training a Naïve Bayes module

In the comments of the script, you can find the explanation for each step used to transform the dataset. Because it is coming from the leftmost output of the Split Data module and it is configured to split the dataset using a 0.75 ratio, it represents 75 percent of the rows from the original input. In addition, the output from the Trainer R script is an object containing the trained model stored in the "model" object from the R script. Note that you are using pure R code resulting from applying the Naïve Bayes algorithm, not any of the out-of-the-box algorithms present in Azure Machine Learning.

The Scorer R script uses the trained model from the Trainer R Script, and uses whatever dataset that comes to the Score Model module, in this case, the remaining 25 percent of the original dataset coming from the Split Data module. It outputs the scores from the previously trained model using on the test dataset (see Figure 3-11).

```
7  #Charge the library
8  library(e1071)
9  #Use the function predict to score the trained model
10 #with the 0.25 of rows from the Input and get the probabilities
11 #column from the result
12 probabilities <- predict(model, dataset, type="raw")[,2]
13 #with the probabilities if >= 0.5 is from the class 1 else 0
14 classes <- as.factor(as.numeric(probabilities >= 0.5))
15 #the Output is a dataframe with the class and probabilities
16 scores <- data.frame(classes, probabilities)
```

FIGURE 3–11  Score R script

The next steps of the experiment execute the corresponding parts of the script. Thus, the Train Model module executes the Trainer R script and the Score Model module executes the Scorer R script. Finally, the output from the scoring process has to be evaluated. At the time of writing this book, Azure ML does not have the capacity to evaluate results from a personalized external model because it is impossible to set the scoring results as "Scores" like the regular Score Model module does. This is why in these cases R or Python scripts are used to visualize the score metrics. In this example, a Python Module is used, showing the Receiver Operating Characteristic (ROC Curve) that you already saw in Chapter 2 (see Figure 3-12).

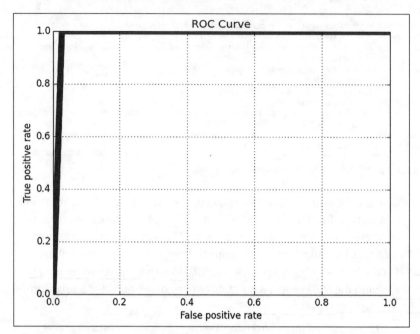

**FIGURE 3-12** ROC Curve using Python script module

You can deploy a web service based on this model following the same process used in the previous subskill, which is to publish a model developed inside Azure Machine Learning.

The second option is to deploy directly from a local environment using R. The advantage of deploying directly from R is that external algorithms from the Azure Machine Learning package can be used without installing them. As you might have noticed, that option was not available when using the Create R Model module. In this case, you are using the XGboost library to create the model and the scorings.

You can develop the following R script in your favorite IDE, like R Tools for Visual Studio, Visual Studio Code, or R Studio. There you can debug, execute, and deploy the model straight to Azure Machine Learning.

```
##Load the libraries
library("AzureML")  # the library to connect to Azure Machine Learning and publish
the model
library("e1071")
```

```
library("xgboost")  # the main algorithm
##Load the Azure workspace. You can find the ID and the pass in your workspace
ws <- workspace(
id = "Your workspace ID",
auth = "Your Auth Pass"
)
##Download the dataset
dataset <- download.datasets(ws, name = "Breast cancer data", quote="\"")
## split the dataset to get train and score data
## 75% of the sample size
smp_size <- floor(0.75 * nrow(dataset))
## set the seed to make your partition reproducible
set.seed(123)
## get index to split the dataset
train_ind <- sample(seq_len(nrow(dataset)), size = smp_size)
##Split train and test data
train_dataset <- dataset[train_ind, ]
test_dataset <- dataset[-train_ind, ]
#Get the features columns
features<-train_dataset[ , ! colnames(train_dataset) %in% c("Class") ]
#get the label column
labelCol <-train_dataset[,c("Class")]
#convert to data matrix
test_gboost<-data.matrix(test_dataset)
train_gboost<-data.matrix(train_dataset)
#train model
bst <- xgboost(data = train_gboost, label = train_dataset$Class, max.depth = 2, eta = 1,
nround = 2, objective = "binary:logistic")
#predict the model
pred <- predict(bst,test_gboost )
#Score model
test_dataset$Scorelabel<-pred
test_dataset$Scoreclasses<- as.factor(as.numeric(pred >= 0.5))
#Create
# Scoring Function
predict_xgboost <- function(new_data){
predictions <- predict(bst, data.matrix(new_data))
output <- data.frame(new_data, ScoredLabels =predictions)
output
}
#Publish the score function
api <- publishWebService(
ws,
fun = predict_xgboost,
name = "xgboost classification",
inputSchema = as.data.frame(as.table(train_gboost)),
data.frame = TRUE)
```

*amateurs !* (handwritten annotation)

To see the new web service go to the Web Services menu in Azure Machine Learning (see Figure 3-13).

FIGURE 3-13 Web service deployed

Note that you need to install a zip utility on your system so you do not encounter an error when trying to publish to Azure Machine Learning. To do that, install R Tools from *https://cran.r-project.org/bin/windows/Rtools/* and then install the directory to the system path. For example, if it is installed in C:\Tools, you should add C:\Tools\bin to your system path, and then restart R.

> **NEED MORE REVIEW?** **XGBOOST**
>
> If you want to know more about the XGBoost package, you can visit the official documentation page at: *http://xgboost.readthedocs.io/en/latest/*.

## Use web service parameters

In some cases, it may be necessary to change the behavior of the experiment in Azure Machine Learning while the web service is still running. To achieve this, you can use the Azure Machine Learning parameters. The data source may be modified to use different origins (maybe more up-to-date copies when retraining), or maybe the destination of the experiment results need to point to a different storage location.

As an example, create a new experiment using the Create R Model Template. Once it is created, from the Data Input and Output menu select Export Data Module and connect it with the output of the Execute Python Script module (see Figure 3-14).

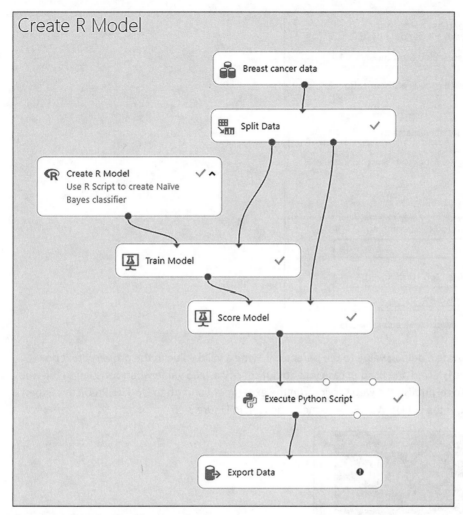

**FIGURE 3-14** Experiment with export data

The next step is to configure the Export Data Module configuration properties as parameters to the model. Click the three-bar icon next to the module properties, and select Set As Web Service Parameter for each property (see the Figure 3-15).

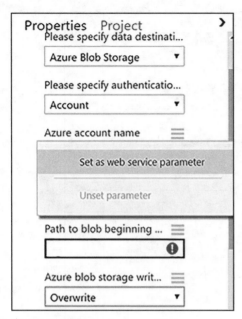

**FIGURE 3-15** Web service parameters

To provide a default value to the parameter, write a valid value in the property text box. That value is saved and used in case you do not specify a valid value when consuming the web service. To re-publish the web service, run the experiment and go to Update Predictive Experiment under the Set Up Web Service menu, as seen in Figure 3-16.

**FIGURE 3-16** Update predictive experiment

Now the results of the experiment can be stored in any account and path provided in the web service call. You can check the parameters in the Web Services menu. Select the web service name, go to configuration, and in the bottom of the page there appears the new parameters (see Figure 3-17).

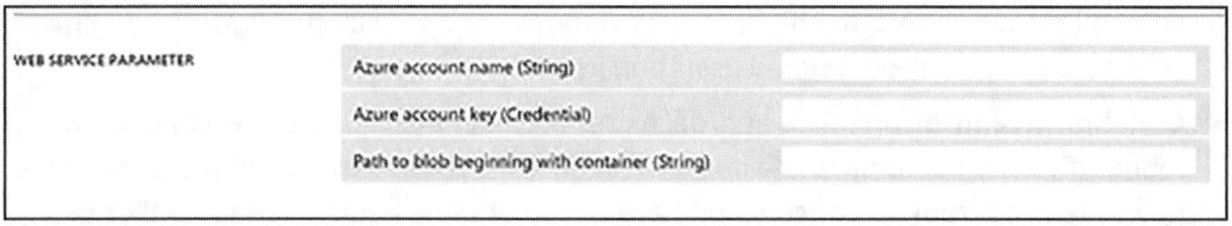

**FIGURE 3-17** Web service parameters

Because it is possible to use parameters in almost every single configuration item of Azure Machine Learning, they can be used in many scenarios. Automatic re-training experiments point to different data sources, and parallel re-trainings with a different number of parameter hyper-tuning sweeps to discover the ideal amount of iterations (especially for Boosted Decision Trees or Forests). Even the R or Python script injections with no need for manual modification of the experiment itself are some examples.

> **NEED MORE REVIEW?** **USING AZURE MACHINE LEARNING WEB SERVICE PARAMETERS**
>
> For a complete step-by-step guide on how to use the parameters you have set up you can check the Azure Machine Learning TechNet blogs at: *https://blogs.technet.microsoft.com/machinelearning/2014/11/25/azureml-web-service-parameters/.*

## Create and publish a recommendation model

Users and companies are overloaded with information coming from multiple sources, from advertisements in the streets to Internet clips. That situation results in too many options for users to choose among, and usually they face difficulties finding a product or service that meets their expectations. Sometimes, companies want to maximize their users' services and product consumption. To achieve both goals, companies must offer their products in a more personalized way. Traditionally this has been implemented using methods like Internet browser cookies, polls, or web clicking analysis. This is still relevant, but the ability to relate all that data with users' opinions and ratings to provide such recommendations comes from machine learning.

A recommendation system is used to solve this problem prioritizing and delivering information relevant to users based on their characteristics, either historical data or attributes related to the final recommendation. Recommendation systems have become very popular in recent years and are used in many different areas such as movies, music, news, books, research articles, search queries, social labels, and products in general. They are even the company business core, providing the main cash source and customer loyalty mechanism.

There are two principal approaches to recommender systems:

- **Content-based** This approach uses features for both users and items. These features are properties of your users or items to recommend. The more similar these features are among items and users, the higher the similitude considered by the algorithm to create recommendations about related users and items.

- **Collaborative filtering**   This approach uses only identifiers of the users or items and ratings given by the users to the items. This can learn about a user from the items they have rated and from other users who have rated the same items. Consequently, the algorithm will consider such ratings as the common points in the relationship and will base its recommendations on those.

In Azure Machine Learning, you can use the Matchbox recommender, a Microsoft Research implementation for recommenders that combines collaborative filtering with a content-based approach. It is a *hybrid recommendation*. When the entity is new to the system, it uses the features of the entity to improve predictions. Alternatively, when you have enough ratings of the entity, it is possible to make personalized predictions based on the ratings.

To create an experiment using the Matchbox recommender, from Azure ML Studio create a new experiment using the Recommender: Restaurant Ratings sample (see Figure 3-18).

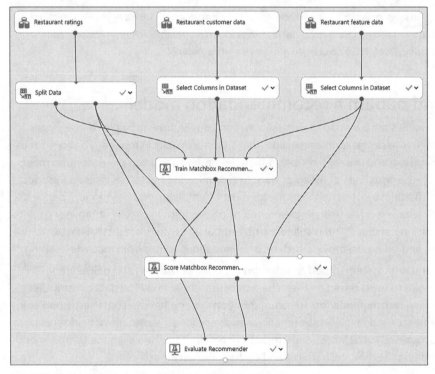

**FIGURE 3-18**  Recommender: Restaurant Ratings sample

The first dataset (and the only one that is required for the algorithm to run) needs to be a user-item-rating triple containing the user ID, the item ID (in this case, restaurant identifiers), and the ratings. Note that ratings can be numeric or categorical, therefore the rating data may be a discrete set of opinions from the users that you have collected in your rating app or website. However, if numeric, the difference between the minimum and the maximum rating values must be less than 100, and ideally not greater than 20. You can find an example in Figure 3-19.

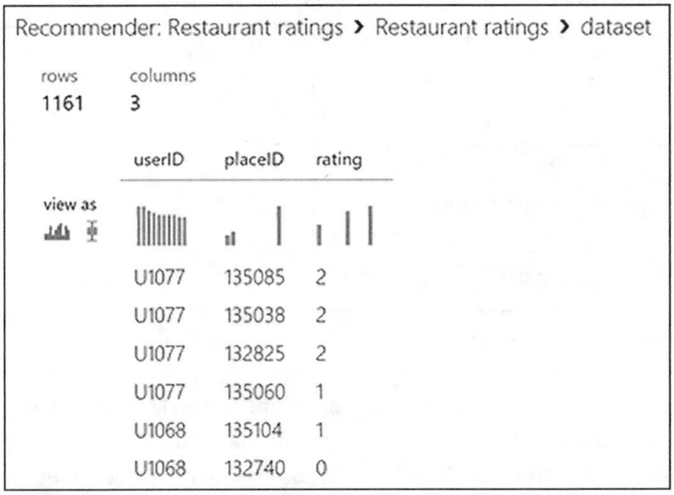

Recommender: Restaurant ratings > Restaurant ratings > dataset

| rows | columns | | |
|------|---------|---|---|
| 1161 | 3 | | |
| | userID | placeID | rating |
| view as | U1077 | 135085 | 2 |
| | U1077 | 135038 | 2 |
| | U1077 | 132825 | 2 |
| | U1077 | 135060 | 1 |
| | U1068 | 135104 | 1 |
| | U1068 | 132740 | 0 |

**FIGURE 3-19** Restaurants Ratings dataset

The second data input is the user features. This dataset must contain the identifiers for users that you provided in the first column of the users-items-ratings triple. The remaining columns can contain any number of features that describe the users. These features help the algorithm to understand the profile of the users, and consequently, to create rules that link such profiles with the items (and their features), and the ratings.

In the example, some columns from the user features are filtered using a Select Columns In Dataset module, selecting only the UserID, Latitude, Longitude, Interest, and Personality features (see Figure 3-20) to pass to the Train Matchbox Recommender.

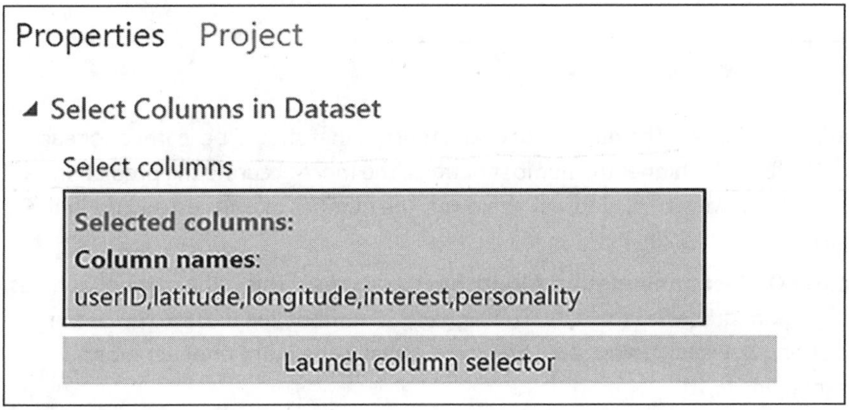

Properties    Project

◢ Select Columns in Dataset

Select columns

Selected columns:
Column names:
userID,latitude,longitude,interest,personality

Launch column selector

**FIGURE 3-20** Select Columns In Dataset

The third data input is the item features. Following the same pattern as the user features, this input needs to contain the item identifiers used in the first users-items-ratings triple. The remaining columns can contain any number of features that describe the Items. In the example, a Select Columns In Dataset module is used to select only the placeID, latitude, longitude, and price columns as features, as seen in Figure 3-21.

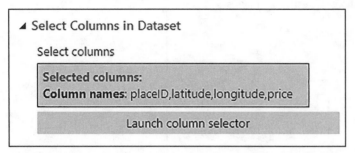

**FIGURE 3-21** Select Columns In Dataset for the restaurants dataset

The next step is to train a recommendation model with the data inputs. The Matchbox Recommender has a special trainer called Train Matchbox Recommender that you will find under the Train section in the main menu. Select the Train Matchbox Recommender Module to see the configuration options (see Figure 3-22).

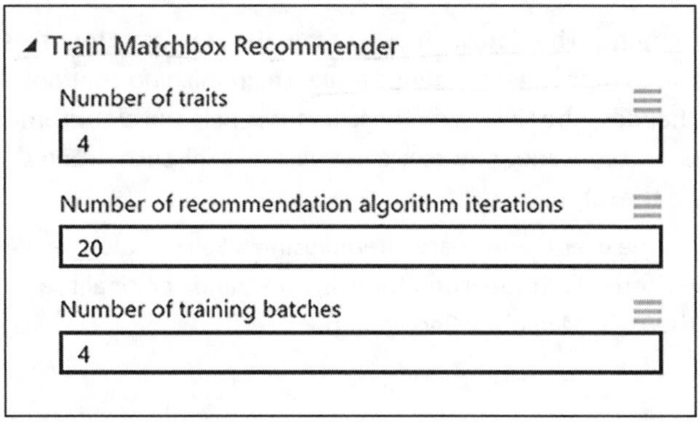

**FIGURE 3-22** Train Matchbox Recommender

- **Number Of Traits** The number of characteristics that should be learned for each user and item. The higher the number of traits, the more accurate the predictions will typically be; however, training will be slower. The number of traits usually fits in the range between 2 to 20.

- **Number Of Recommendation Algorithm Iterations** This is the number of times the algorithm processes the data. The higher this number, the more accurate the predictions; however, training will be slower. Usually, the number of iterations is in the range one to 10.

- **Number Of Training Batches**   This is the number of batches for dividing the data during training because the Train Matchbox Recommender runs batches in parallel. If your dataset fits in memory, it is recommended that you align the training batches with the number of available cores. However, for its implementation in Azure Machine Learning, it is important to understand that there is no specific way to assign resources to our training experiments. Therefore, the only rule of thumb here is the 10GB inner limit present in Azure Machine Learning. You must test your specific dataset to validate that the memory footprint does not cause problems in your executions.

> **NEED MORE REVIEW?**  **AZURE MACHINE LEARNING MEMORY LIMITATIONS**
>
> Knowing if a dataset will fit in memory is important, and in Azure Machine Learning, not straightforward. As a rule of thumb, you may multiply the number of rows by the width of the row (using each data type approximate size), but at the time of writing this book, there is no way to determine exactly the memory usage. For more information about Azure Machine Learning limitations, visit: *https://docs.microsoft.com/ azure/machine-learning/studio/ faq#scalability*.

Once the model has been trained, predictions can be made using the Score Matchbox Recommender module. This module supports different types of predictions, depending on your recommendation goal (see Figure 3-23).

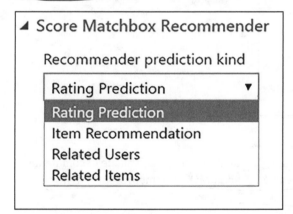

FIGURE 3-23 Score Matchbox Recommender options

- **Rating Prediction**   The model uses training data to calculate the value of a user's rating score on an item. The input dataset must contain user-item pairs and optionally the user-items features. No further parameters are required.

- **Item Recommendation**   To recommend the model using existing data of users and items to generate a list of items that can satisfy each user. Depending on the option of the recommended item selection, you can customize the number of recommendations returned for each user and set minimum number of previous recommendations to generate a new recommendation (see Figure 3-23).

- **Related Users**   The algorithm returns a list of users related to the ones provided. The similitude will be based in the available information: just the ratings (similar preferences about the rated items) or both ratings and features included.

- **Related Items**   The model provides a list of items that are related to the ones provided, based on either just the users who rated them, or both the users who rated them and the item's features, depending on the information provided during the training phase.

*Some sort of clustering*

For rating prediction, you only need to select Rating Prediction in the recommender prediction kind. The input dataset must be in a form of user-item pairs. If a rating column is included, the module will ignore it.

The results will be in the form of three columns, showing the user, the item, and the rating for each pair (see Figure 3-24).

| | User | Item | Rating |
|---|---|---|---|
| view as | | | |
| | U1048 | 135026 | 2 |
| | U1048 | 132723 | 2 |
| | U1048 | 135065 | 2 |
| | U1048 | 135049 | 2 |
| | U1048 | 135034 | 2 |
| | U1117 | 135088 | 2 |
| | U1117 | 135018 | 2 |
| | U1049 | 132862 | 2 |
| | U1049 | 135042 | 0 |

**FIGURE 3-24**  Rating predictions

You can evaluate the precision of your rating predictions using the Evaluate Recommender module. Because the values here are numeric, MAE and RMSE error metrics apply as if you were evaluating a regressor (as described in Skill 2.3).

For item recommendations, select Item Recommendation and you will have the following options to configure the output:

- **Rated Items (for model evaluation)**   The recommendations are provided from the user-item pairs rated dataset that have already been rated and seen by the algorithm (see Figure 3-25).

- **From All Items (for production)** The model creates recommendations from all items seen during training the dataset. The data input should consist of the user identifier.
- **From Unrated Items** The model will return recommendations from the user-item pairs that have not been rated. Thus, the algorithm will suggest new items to users.

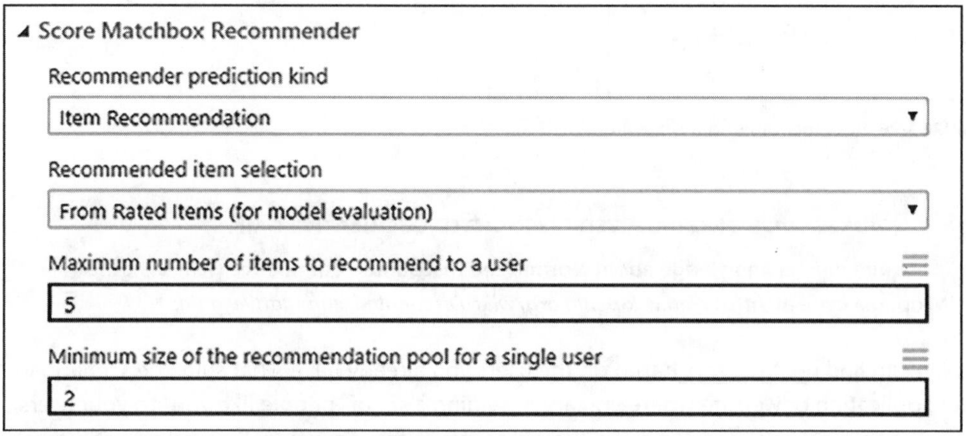

▲ Score Matchbox Recommender

Recommender prediction kind

| Item Recommendation | ▼ |

Recommended item selection

| From Rated Items (for model evaluation) | ▼ |

Maximum number of items to recommend to a user

| 5 |

Minimum size of the recommendation pool for a single user

| 2 |

**FIGURE 3-25** Score Matchbox Recommender

If you want to evaluate the precision of your item predictions using the Evaluate Recommender module you will find a new error measure: NDCG (Normalized Discounted Cumulative Gain), a measure used when analyzing ranking quality. It is generally used to measure how effective web search engines are, or, in your case, how good the list of suggestions your recommender retrieved is.

It is based on the concept stating that most relevant items or recommendations are more useful when appearing earlier in the recommender results. Thus, you may say that they have "higher ranks." The earlier the recommendations appear and the more relevant for the user, the better. The computation of NDCG in the recommender is performed against items in the test dataset to be able to compare an actual set of recommended items (also known as "ground truth"). Otherwise, the initial computation to establish the relevance of the recommendation would not be possible. Because it is a normalized measure, its values vary from zero to one. The closer to one, the more accurate the recommendations (see Figure 3-26).

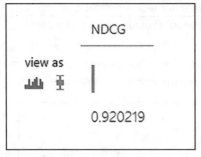

**FIGURE 3-26** Item recommendation evaluation

*NEED MORE REVIEW?* **NORMALIZED DISCOUNTED CUMULATIVE GAIN**

To acquire deeper knowledge about Normalized Discounted Cumulative Gain, visit the Wikipedia page at: *https://en.wikipedia.org/wiki/Discounted_cumulative_gain*.

You can find related users based on the users you already have. That suits the scenario in your application or website where you are providing a set of "people like you" to your users, based on their ratings over items and their user attributes, if existing. You can adjust the results of the recommendations setting the parameters of the Score Matchbox Recommender accordingly:

- **Maximum Number Of Related Users To Find For A User** Sets the length of the list containing the recommended users by the model.

- **Minimum Number Of Items That The Query User And The Related User Must Have Rated In Common** Because you are suggesting similar people to your users, you might want to establish a limit on "how similar" these recommended users are. The more rated items in common, the more similar both users tastes are.

- **Minimum Size Of The Related User Pool For A Single User** The minimum user pool support to establish a relationship. By default it is two, meaning that the algorithm will need at least two users having reviewed the same items to consider that they are related. You might want to increase this parameter if your user base is relatively high and want to consider only strong user pools.

See Figure 3-27 for a detailed view of the configuration menu.

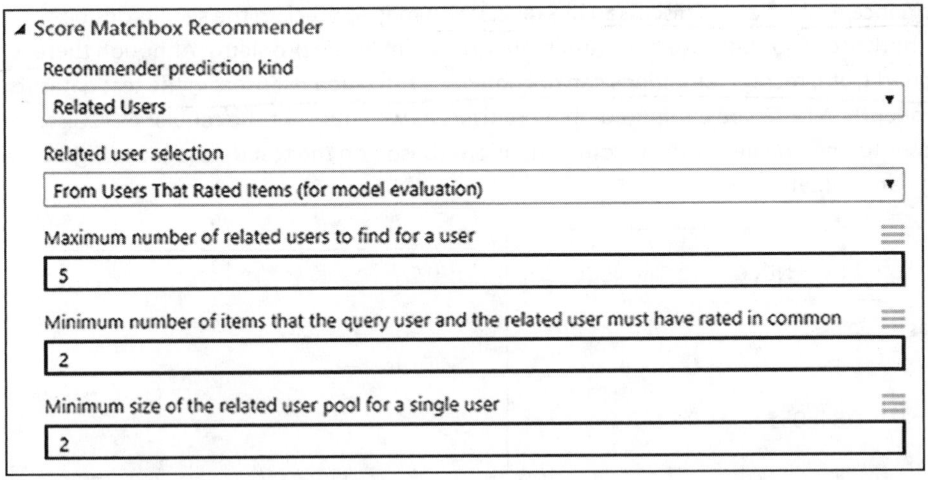

**FIGURE 3-27** Related users configuration

As a result, you will obtain a list of recommended users identified by their unique IDs, as provided in the source datasets. The maximum number of recommendations has been specified in the Score Matchbox Recommender menu, as seen in Figure 3-27. However, the number of actual recommendations may be lesser if the algorithm does not obtain a sufficiently long list of related user (see Figure 3-28).

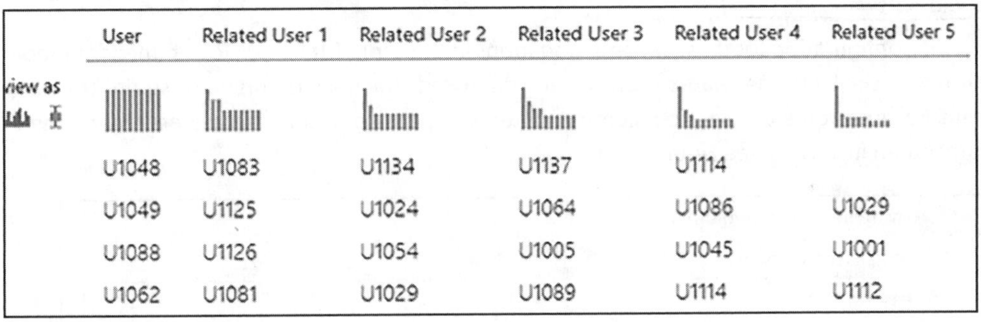

| | User | Related User 1 | Related User 2 | Related User 3 | Related User 4 | Related User 5 |
|---|---|---|---|---|---|---|
| view as | U1048 | U1083 | U1134 | U1137 | U1114 | |
| | U1049 | U1125 | U1024 | U1064 | U1086 | U1029 |
| | U1088 | U1126 | U1054 | U1005 | U1045 | U1001 |
| | U1062 | U1081 | U1029 | U1089 | U1114 | U1112 |

**FIGURE 3-28** Related users results

The evaluation of the related users results is slightly different from the recommended items (see Figure 3-26). It uses the NDCG score as well, but because there is no actual ground truth for a concept as "related users" (you have no occurrences to compare against), the NDCG is computed based on Manhattan (L1 Sim NDCG) and Euclidean (L2 Sim NDCG) distances. These distance-based scores derive from the ones used in clustering algorithms performance evaluation, as discussed in Skill 2.3. You may appreciate the similitudes between both scenarios because both result into group similitude problems. Although there is no ground truth, recommendations can only be performed against users in the test dataset. Consequently, NDCGs are computed on these users as well. Just like the regular NDCG score, the closer to one, the better the recommendations (based on the test dataset). See Figure 3-29 for an evaluation example.

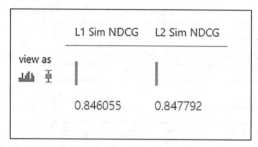

**FIGURE 3-29** Evaluate Recommender module results showing L1 (Manhattan) and L2 (Euclidean) NDCG scores for related users recommendations

Finally, the Matchbox Recommender can perform recommendations about related items as well. This fits a very common scenario in modern e-commerce of any type, recommending items related to items your users already bought, rated, or just visited. Note that the items may be physical objects if the scenario is retail-like, or even services or multimedia items (video, audio, software, etc.).

The configuration for these recommendations in the Score Matchbox Recommender module is very similar to the related users already discussed. The main difference is straightforward here. Because you are trying to recommend items, the configuration parameters regard items rather than just users (see Figure 3-30).

▲ Score Matchbox Recommender

Recommender prediction kind

| Related Items | ▼ |

Related item selection

| From Rated Items (for model evaluation) | ▼ |

Maximum number of related items to find for an item

| 5 |

Minimum number of users that the query item and the related item must have been rated by in c...

| 2 |

Minimum size of the related item pool for a single item

| 2 |

**FIGURE 3-30** Score Matchbox Recommender module configuration for related item recommendations

You will find the results in the same format as they were presented in the related users version of the recommender, as a list of item ID recommendations per each item ID received as input (see Figure 3-31).

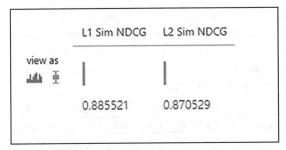

| | Item | Related Item 1 | Related Item 2 | Related Item 3 | Related Item 4 | Related Item 5 |
|---|---|---|---|---|---|---|
| | 135026 | 132954 | 135079 | 135065 | 135075 | 135046 |
| | 132723 | 135072 | 135085 | 135034 | 135049 | 132951 |
| | 135065 | 135026 | 132723 | 132754 | | |
| | 135049 | 132723 | 135034 | | | |
| | 135034 | 132723 | 135049 | | | |
| | 135042 | 135043 | 135076 | 135062 | 135032 | 135081 |

FIGURE 3-31 Score Matchbox Recommender results for related items

As in the related users version of the recommender, and because of the same reasons (no ground truth available), the results are evaluated using L1 and L2 NCDG scores. See Figure 3-32 for an example.

| | L1 Sim NDCG | L2 Sim NDCG |
|---|---|---|
| view as | | |
| | 0.885521 | 0.870529 |

FIGURE 3-32 Evaluate Recommender module results showing L1 (Manhattan) and L2 (Euclidean) NDCG scores for related items recommendations

Note that you can obtain all these versions of the recommender and consume them in different web services from your applications without having to re-train your model. That brings you great flexibility adjusting your recommendations with the same model you trained once. In production scenarios, with real data coming in, re-training is usually an expensive process (especially time wise). Therefore, having the option to adjust recommendations only modifying your scorer is very valuable.

Item and user recommendations fit extremely well in a wide range of businesses, and it is implanted in hundreds of websites and applications. Taking advantage of the Matchbox Recommender is easy, flexible, and powerful.

# Create and publish a language understanding model

Natural language understanding is a problem that Artificial Intelligence (AI) has been facing for a long time. Humans are good at this due to its massive capabilities to understand emotions, intentions, and subtle aspects of language like irony or references. However, algorithms have a much harder time understanding humans beyond a basic and fixed conversation. Building a general model that understands human intentions and associates such intentions to automatic answers or actions is usually a heavy and time-consuming task.

To ease that task, Microsoft offers the Language Understanding Intelligent Service (LUIS), a service that allows applications to understand its interlocutor intentions, using machine learning to extract keywords and semantic structures and their meaning. Thus, a client application, like a website, a bot, or other application able to call and consume a web service can use LUIS to receive information about the text it has received from a user.

LUIS is presented in the form of apps. A LUIS app is a domain-specific language model designed by you, similar to the recommender systems you train and use in Skill 3.4. You can start with a pre-configured domain model, build one of your own from scratch, or add your own pieces to a pre-built domain. Pre-built domains for LUIS are a good way to start with a basic model and keep developing from there.

There are three essential concepts within LUIS:

- **Utterances**   An utterance is a text input from the user. It may be a complete sentence, or a fragment of it. Because it represents what the user wants to say, they are not always well-formed and the model may receive different utterances with the same intent.

- **Intents**   An intent is an action that the user wants to perform. Intents are derived from utterances, being actions or goals like finding news on an article, obtaining any type of information from the company's wiki page, or paying a bill. Depending on your domain, you can define intents that are achievable in such a domain.

- **Entities**  An entity represents some piece of important information in one utterance. For instance, if you receive an utterance like "Pay my rent bill," "rent" would be an entity.

A LUIS sample process is shown in Figure 3-33.

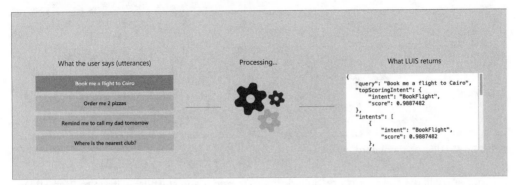

**FIGURE 3-33** LUIS high-level processing sequence

To create a LUIS app that you can use for language understanding model, you first need to have an Azure account, and you need to sign in at *https://www.luis.ai*.

Once you are logged in, you can manage your apps on the My Apps page. Click the New App button, and in the dialog box, name your application "Events Management," and click Create (see Figure 3-34).

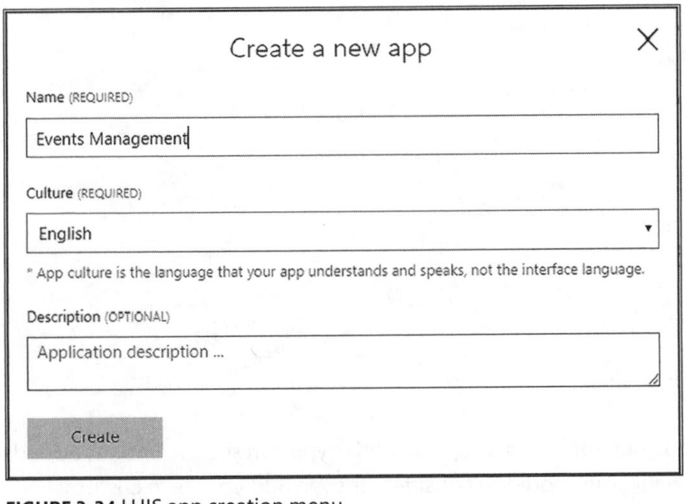

**FIGURE 3-34** LUIS app creation menu

You will see the dashboard for your application. You can explore the different parts of your application using the leftmost menu (see Figure 3-35).

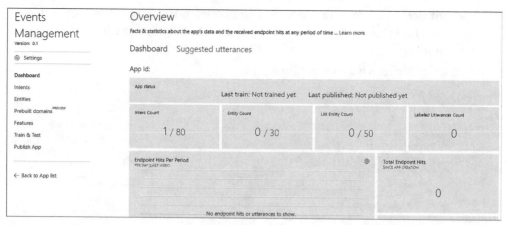

**FIGURE 3-35** LUIS app dashboard

Your app will use the events pre-built domain. To add it and start using it, go to Prebuilt Domains, and click the Not Added button under the Events prebuilt domain. In the pop-up menu, click Yes (see Figure 3-36).

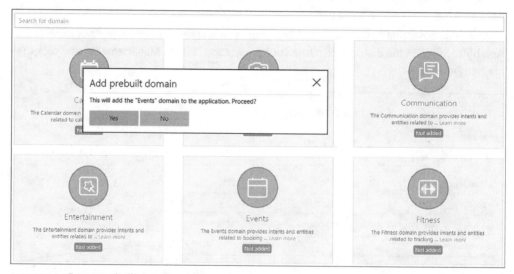

**FIGURE 3-36** Events prebuilt domain addition

The domain will be added to your app. Now, clicking Entities you can see the Entities added, add new prebuilt entities you want your model to consider, or even add your own custom entity to complete the model (see Figure 3-37).

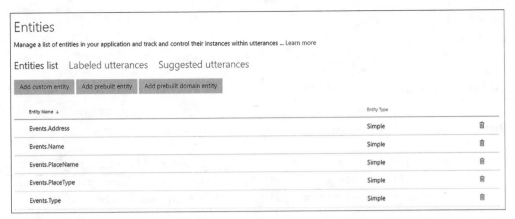

FIGURE 3-37 Events prebuilt domain entities in the Entities menu

To test your model with the prebuild domain already added, first you have to train your model. You need to train your model every time you add or modify the entities, add prebuilt models, or perform any change that may alter the model's behavior. Click Train & Test in the menu, and then click Train Application. After a few seconds, your LUIS app is trained and ready to be tested (see Figure 3-38).

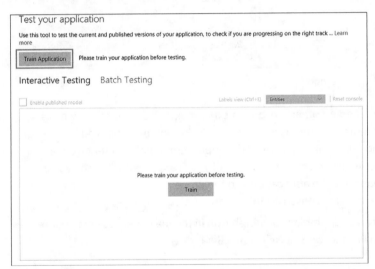

FIGURE 3-38 LUIS app initial training

Once the app is trained, you can write your own sentences to check how the model recognizes the intents that both them and the entities present, for example, some tests against the model recognizing the tokens in the sentences written by the user (see Figure 3-39).

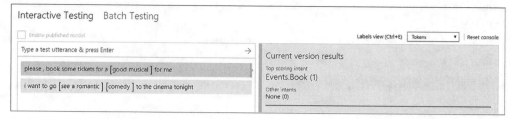

**FIGURE 3-39** LUIS token and intent recognition

It is recognizing correctly that the intention is to book an event, and it is capturing correctly the tokens that are fundamental for this intent. If you change the Labels View option to Entities it will show the type of entities the model has recognized in each token (see Figure 3-40).

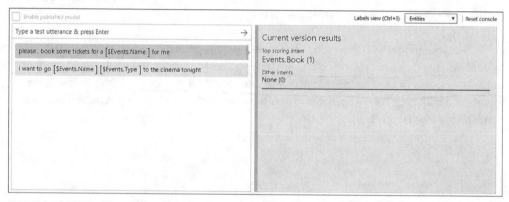

**FIGURE 3-40** LUIS entity and intent recognition

You might want keep on adding other pre-built models to enrich the model, as well as adding custom entities, intents, or utterances for personalized sentences that you know your users will be asking the model. The life cycle of a LUIS application is not different from a typical machine learning experiment: you train the app until you are satisfied with the evaluation results, you publish and consume the application and the process starts again, enriching the application with new data and cases based on the production experience.

To publish your app as an endpoint, go to Publish App in the main menu, select your regions, and click Publish To Production Slot (see Figure 3-41).

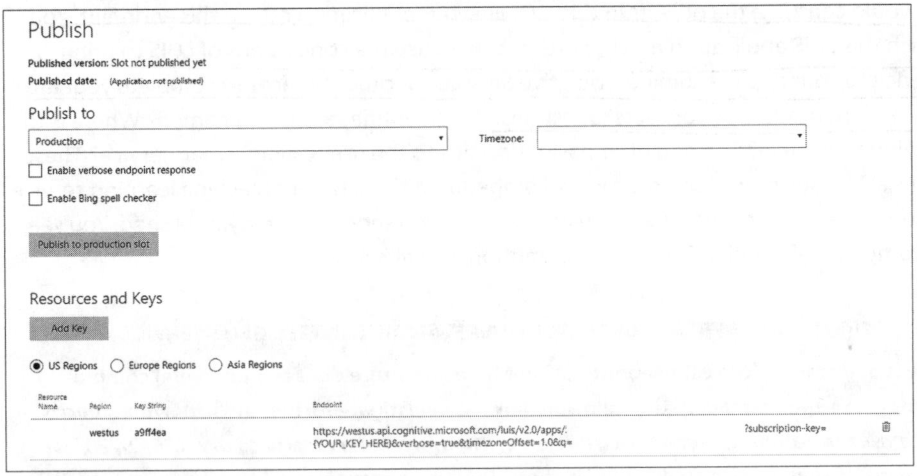

**FIGURE 3-41** LUIS app publishing menu

The publishing process takes a few seconds. Once it is completed, for a brief test of your published endpoint, copy the endpoint URL shown in Figure 3-41, paste it in your browser bar, replace the {YOUR_KEY_HERE} placeholder for the key string you received in the same menu, and append a phrase after the endpoint URL. For example, if you append "&q=get me tickets for the Giants match tonight" (without the double quotes), as a response you will get a JSON document with the items identified by your LUIS app (see Figure 3-42).

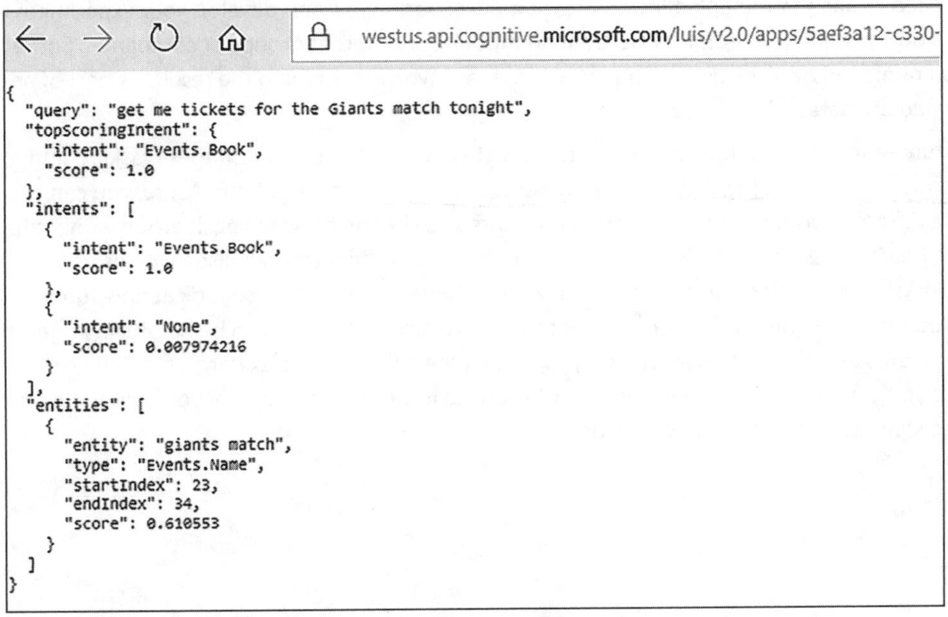

```
{
  "query": "get me tickets for the Giants match tonight",
  "topScoringIntent": {
    "intent": "Events.Book",
    "score": 1.0
  },
  "intents": [
    {
      "intent": "Events.Book",
      "score": 1.0
    },
    {
      "intent": "None",
      "score": 0.007974216
    }
  ],
  "entities": [
    {
      "entity": "giants match",
      "type": "Events.Name",
      "startIndex": 23,
      "endIndex": 34,
      "score": 0.610553
    }
  ]
}
```

**FIGURE 3-42** LUIS app endpoint browser call

You would consume the objects in this JSON in your application calling this endpoint. You can enrich this LUIS application much more, and even use the conclusions of LUIS to bring intelligence to your app consuming Cognitive Services or other services to complete your answers or actions based on your users' questions. Which entities are being named? Where is the event going to be held? Can you offer navigation tips to the user calling a map service? These questions and many more can be answered embedding the different machine learning services available, or even your own Azure Machine Learning web services already published. You see more examples of Cognitive Services consumption in Skill 3.4.

> **NEED MORE INFORMATION?** **NATURAL UNDERSTANDING INTELLIGENT SERVICE**
>
> There is abundant information about LUIS in Microsoft Azure docs and in several community blogs. You can start with the following links to investigate further at: *https://docs.microsoft.com/azure/cognitive-services/LUIS/Home, http://www.garypretty.co.uk/2016/07/20/using-microsoft-luis-service-understand-natural-language-input/ ,* and *https://docs.microsoft.com/azure/cognitive-services/luis/luis-csharp-tutorial-build-bot-framework-sample.*

# Skill 3.2: Manage Azure Machine Learning projects and workspaces

Often times a project contains a number of different machine learning models because you may need to analyze multiple files, create multiple experiments, and develop your experiments with a group of people. You may be creating models for different groups or companies. Some experiments can become quite complex, which may involve examining the results as part of an intermediate dataset.

Azure Machine Learning contains features that allow you to accomplish these tasks. Using the projects will help organize your experiments into logical groups. Within Azure, you can create different workgroups for different accounts and change between each group within the Azure Machine Learning Studio. To share your work with others you can also invite users to the workspace, allowing you to share work with multiple people. We also look at how Jupyter Notebooks can be used to reference intermediate datasets, which can be helpful in large experiments as well as for investigating your data, especially in complex datasets. With notebooks you can extract knowledge and conclusions to improve the design of your experiments, and to share such conclusions with your team.

## Creating experiments, projects, and add assets to a project

Creating experiments, which we have talked about earlier in the book, could not be easier. From within the Azure Machine Learning Studio, when the experiment tab on the left side is selected, click the new button that looks like a plus in the bottom left-hand corner of the screen. All of the experiments you have created are listed in the Experiments tab in date order. If you have many experiments, or are working on groups of experiments for different purposes, you may want to start storing them in folders, as you would if you were creating code on your local machine. Azure Machine Learning provides this same functionality by using projects, which is the top tab on the left side (see Figure 3-43).

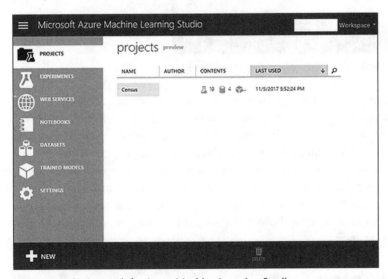

**FIGURE 3-43** Projects tab for Azure Machine Learning Studio

From within the projects window, not only do you have the ability to save the experiments, but also the datasets, modules, notebooks, trained modules, transforms, and web services related to the experiment. When a new project is created by clicking the New button on the bottom left side of the screen, a black screen pops up from the bottom with Project selected on the left, and one option available, Empty project. When you select Empty Project, a new popup window appears, which allows you to enter a name and a description. After you enter a name, the screen shows a single option to add assets. Once that option is selected, a popup window appears, which allows you to add assets to the project (see Figure 3-44).

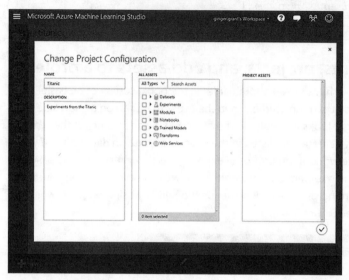

**FIGURE 3-44** Adding items options available to a project called Titanic

Clicking the triangles on the left of any of the menu option displays a list of items, which can be selected by clicking the box to the left of the name. Once items are selected, an arrow appears, and you have the ability to move the items to the window labeled Project Assets. When you have selected the items you wish to place in this project, click the check icon on the bottom left of the window. A new project is then created. To edit the project, click the project name. The window then changes to the same window shown earlier with all of the items previously added. To edit the project, click the icon that looks like a pencil on the bottom center of the screen labeled Edit. The same window shown in Figure 3-44 appears and you will have the ability to add or remove any item.

## Create new workspaces

There are two ways to create an Azure Machine Learning workspace. The first method is to create an account in Azure Machine Learning at *https://studio.azureml.net/* and the second is to create a workspace using an Azure account. To create a free workspace, click the button labeled Sign Up, and select one of the first two of the three options shown in Figure 3-45.

**FIGURE 3-45** Window showing the three different methods for creating an Azure Machine Learning workspace

The first option creates temporary workspaces, which is available for 8 hours. The second option for creating an Azure Machine Learning workspace is free and does not require an Azure account or a credit card to create an account. You need to have a Microsoft email account, which can be created free at *outlook.com* or *live.com*. You need to have a Microsoft email account prior to creating the Azure Machine Learning account. The third method is to use a paid account that requires that you already have an Azure account established prior to creating the standard workspace. If you select the standard workspace, you will be directed to a set of directions at *https://docs.microsoft.com/azure/machine-learning/studio/create-workspace*.

To create a standard account, you need to create an Azure account or login to your existing account at **portal.azure.com.** If you are not already logged in to your Microsoft account, you will be prompted to login. Within Azure, click the +New menu option at the top-left part of the screen. Within the search window, type **Machine Learning Studio workspace** (see Figure 3-46).

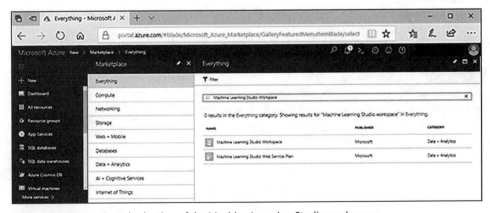

**FIGURE 3-46** Azure Portal selection of the Machine Learning Studio workspace

Select the icon for the Machine Learning Studio Workspace. The screen changes and the next screen contains a button labeled create. Click that button and a screen appears with the information needed by Azure to create a new workspace. You need to give the workspace a name, select a subscription, create or pick from an existing resource group, select a location, create or use an existing storage account, select a Workspace pricing tier, create a Web service Plan, and select a web service plan pricing tier (see Figure 3-47).

**FIGURE 3-47** Displays the menu options for a Machine Learning Studio workspace

Once all of the fields in the menu have been completed, click the Create button shown on the bottom of Figure 3-47, and the new workspace will be created. The process may take a few minutes to complete. Once the process is complete, you see a window indicating that the new workspace has been created (see Figure 3-48).

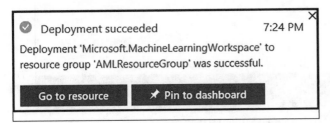

**FIGURE 3-48** Deployment succeeded indicator

Clicking the Go To Resource button allows you to launch Machine Learning Studio with the new workspace. From within Azure Machine Learning, the workspace in use is shown in the top left hand corner of the screen.

## Invite users to a workspace

When you are collaborating with others on a project where you are creating Azure Machine Learning experiments, you may need to add others to your workspace. To add new users, se-lect the last menu item on the list on the left side of the screen next to the gear, Settings. From within the Settings window, select the Users option on the far right of the screen. From there you have the ability to add other users because the Invite More Users button on the bottom of the screen is visible (see Figure 3-49).

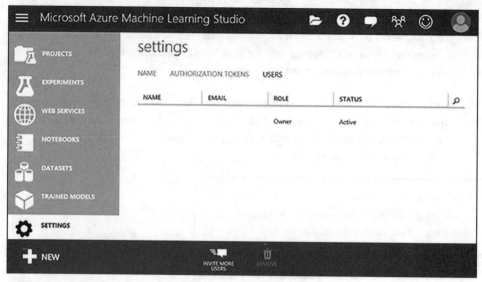

**FIGURE 3-49** Displays Azure Machine Learning Studio Settings screen

When the button Invite More Users is selected, it is possible to add one or more email addresses if you are the owner of the account. The people selected need to have a valid Microsoft account, or an organizational account from Azure Active Directory (see Figure 3-50).

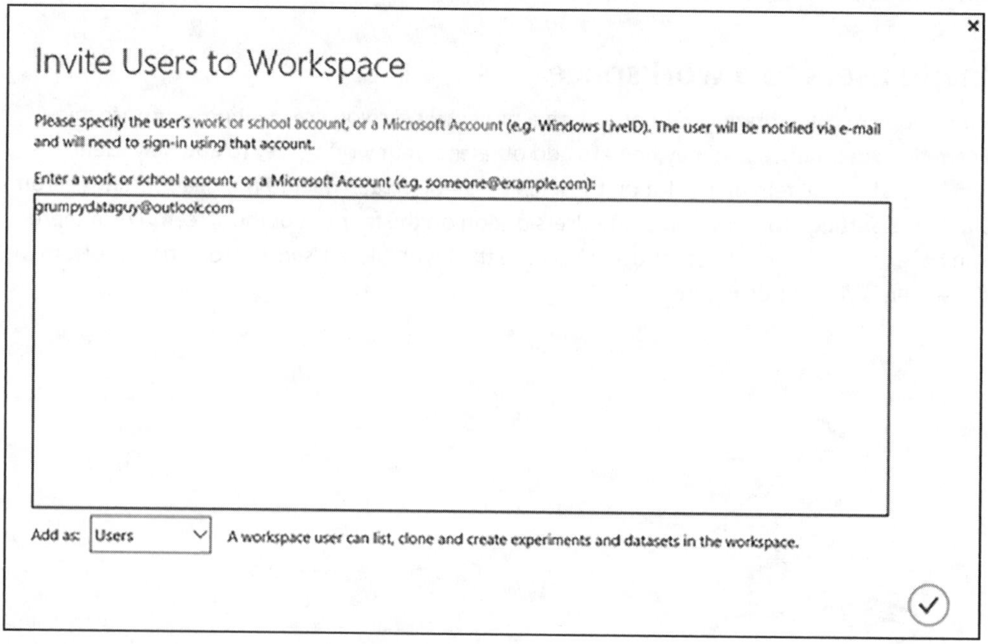

## Invite Users to Workspace

Please specify the user's work or school account, or a Microsoft Account (e.g. Windows LiveID). The user will be notified via e-mail and will need to sign-in using that account.

Enter a work or school account, or a Microsoft Account (e.g. someone@example.com):

grumpydataguy@outlook.com

Add as:  Users ▾    A workspace user can list, clone and create experiments and datasets in the workspace.

**FIGURE 3-50** The Invite Users To Workspace window

There are two different access rights available, users or owners. A user does not have rights to deploy or manage web services. In order to be an owner, the user must have contributor or administer rights within the Azure subscription. If the user is not part of the Azure subscription, they can only have user rights. To invite a user to the account, enter an email address and click the check on the bottom of Figure 3-50. The user will be sent an email with instructions on how to sign into the shared workspace. Until they sign into the shared workspaces, their status is listed as invited.

## Switch between different workspaces

Once you have different workspaces created, you may need to switch between them. As long as all of the workspaces are created with the same Azure account, you can select different workspaces from within Microsoft Azure Machine Learning Studio. If you have two different Azure accounts, it is not possible to switch between multiple workspaces. All of the workspaces are grouped based upon the location that they were created. For example, if you have one workspace in West US, and one workspace in South Central US, to see the workspace in the West US you will first need to change the region to West US to access the account (see Figure 3-51).

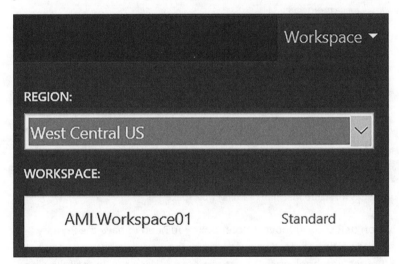

**FIGURE 3-51** The screen that is used to access the workspace AMLWorkspace01, located in the West Central US Region

Selecting the account listed in the drop-down box loads the new workspace, and the Machine Learning Studio then shows all of the experiments in the new workspace.

> **NEED MORE INFORMATION? COPYING EXPERIMENTS BETWEEN WORKSPACES**
>
> It is possible to copy one of more experiments from one workspace to another. You can find the steps at: *http://blogs.solidq.com/en/businessanalytics/bulk-copy-azure-ml-experiments-workspace-another-backup-physical-files*.

# Create a Jupyter Notebook that references an intermediate dataset

If you are using Python or R, you can reference the data generated in an Azure Machine Learning experiment from within your Python or R code as long as you are designated as an owner of the workspace. Using azureml libraries with Python has been tested on Python 2.7, 3.3, and 3.4 under Windows, Mac, and Linux and is dependent upon the packages requests, Python-dateutil and pandas. If you are using Anaconda, these packages are already installed. The azureml needs to be loaded into your Python environment.

To access Azure Machine Learning from your local Jupyter Notebook, you need to obtain authorization tokens from within the settings of the workspace. These tokens are referenced within the code to be able to access intermediate datasets. The tokens can be found in the Settings option on the left hand side of the screen under Authorization Tokens (see Figure 3-52).

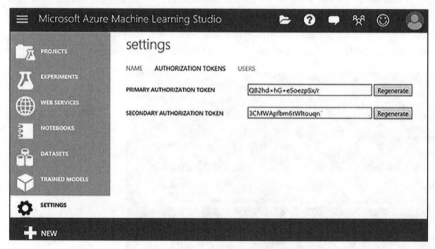

**FIGURE 3-52** Authorization tokens for Azure Machine Learning workspace

From within your Python or R code in Jupyter Notebooks you need to have the Primary Authorization Token and the Workspace id. You can then create an experiment and access the data from within a Jupyter Notebook once the experiment has been run. In the following experiment there is a sample dataset, which has been split and converted to a CSV. By clicking the menu dot on the bottom of the Convert to CSV module, the data access codes needed for a Python Jupyter Notebook are available (see Figure 3-53).

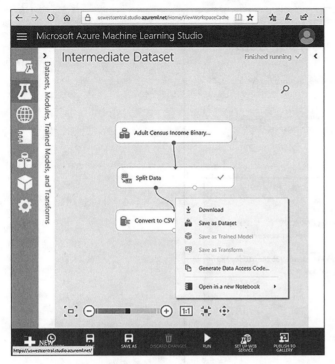

**FIGURE 3-53** Intermediate dataset

From within the experiment, once the option Generate Access Code is selected you have the ability to generate code that can be used within a local Jupyter Notebook in R or Python. Both versions are available in the generated code, which includes the workspace id and the authorization token for this dataset (see Figure 3-54).

**FIGURE 3-54** Code generated through the menu option in your experiment that can be used within a local Jupyter Notebook

The code listed here can be used within your local Jupyter Notebook to access intermediate datasets generated within an Azure Machine Learning experiment. As shown in Figure 3-55, you can also open a session-bound Jupyter Notebook from the menu where you obtained your data access code.

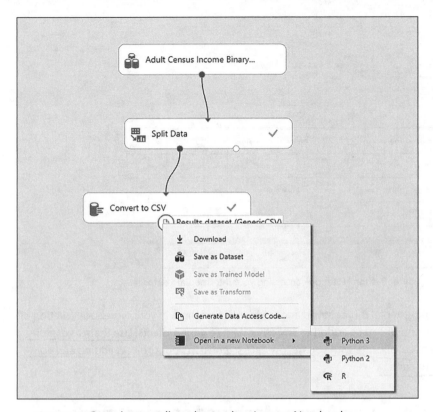

**FIGURE 3-55** Open intermediate dataset in a Jupyter Notebook

If you open a new Notebook you obtain a Notebook with all the code you need to reference the intermediate dataset and start exploring, visualizing, and creating machine learning models using Python or R libraries on top of it. If you are familiar with Python and R languages, this might be a fast way to obtain conclusions out of the dataset to continue your Azure Machine Learning experiment, or to re-use the most of the code you generated in the Notebook in a Python or R module within your Azure Machine Learning experiment (see Figure 3-56).

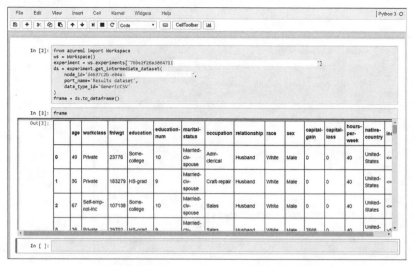

**FIGURE 3-56** Run Jupyter Python Notebook accessing your intermediate dataset

All of these notebooks can be saved and you might find them in your Notebooks section of the main menu, and of course added as any other item to your projects. Use them as exploratory analyses or collaborate with your fellow data scientist in your projects adding and commenting on your code.

# Skill 3.3: Consume Azure Machine Learning models

In Skill 3.1, you have seen how to create web services, and now you see how to consume them in three different ways. The Machine Learning web service is based on REST, a popular web architecture that works through simple HTTP requests. To make a Machine Learning web service call you only need an API key and the URI of the server.

> **This skill covers how to:**
> - Connect to a published Machine Learning web service
> - Consume a published Machine Learning model programmatically using a batch execution service
> - Consume a published Machine Learning model programmatically using a request response service
> - Interact with a published Machine Learning model using Microsoft Excel

Before starting, you should prepare the web service that will be used as an example throughout the skill. The proposed example is an experiment using the breast cancer data (available among example datasets). It is assumed that you have saved a model and built a predictive experiment, as in Figure 3-57.

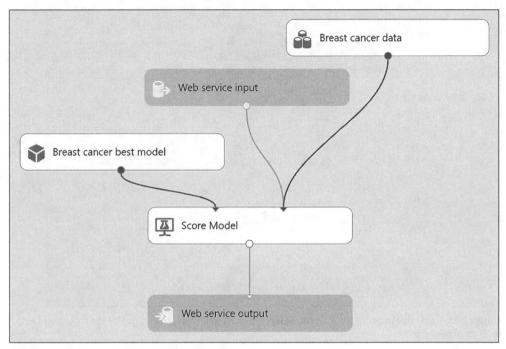

**FIGURE 3-57** Sample predictive experiment using the breast cancer dataset

That experiment is fully functional, but you are going to change a couple of things in order to facilitate the use. You are going to add two *Select Columns In Dataset* modules. The first one deletes the column "Class" of the original dataset because new samples do not have that column (the column that you want to predict). The Score Model module ignores that column, so it does not make sense to send a dummy value for that column in all the requests. The second Select Columns In Dataset module is placed before the web service output element. This time you include only the columns "Scored Labels" and "Scored Probabilities" in order to avoid sending back all of the sample data when we only need the predictions. Figure 3-58 shows how the predictive experiment should be before deploying.

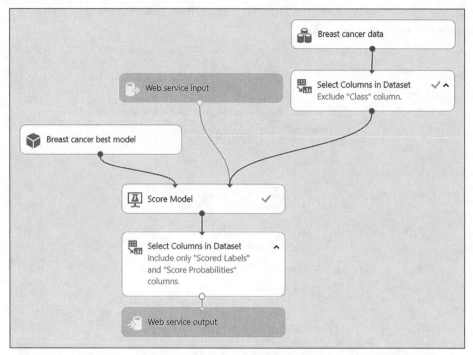

**FIGURE 3-58** Predictive experiment with two Select Columns in Dataset that organize the inputs and outputs of the system

Deploy it as Deploy Web Service [New]. To review how to deploy a web service in Azure Machine Learning, review Skill 3.1.

## Connect to a published machine learning web service

There are three different ways of consuming models:

- **Web Services UI** Web page that allows you to run the model with the data inserted in a form. It is good only for testing the system manually.
- **Excel add-in** This complement allows you to make predictions using data from an Excel spreadsheet as input.
- **Direct API calls** Using a programming language, you can call the API and get predictions.

Behind the scenes, both the Web Services UI and the Excel add-in calls the API, but in a more convenient way. The API allows you to consume the model in two different ways:

- **Request-Response Service (RRS)** Input data is sent in the request and predictions are sent in the response. This service provides a low latency and highly scalable service.
- **Batch Execution Service (BES)** Asynchronous predictions on batches of samples. Input and output files are located in an Azure Blob Storage element.

You study both in detail in this skill. First, you test the model using the web interface, and then you make calls from C# to the API in batch and request-response mode.

Go to the Microsoft Azure Machine Learning Web Services Portal (*https://services.azureml. net/*), open the newly deployed web service, and go to the tab Consume (see Figure 3-59).

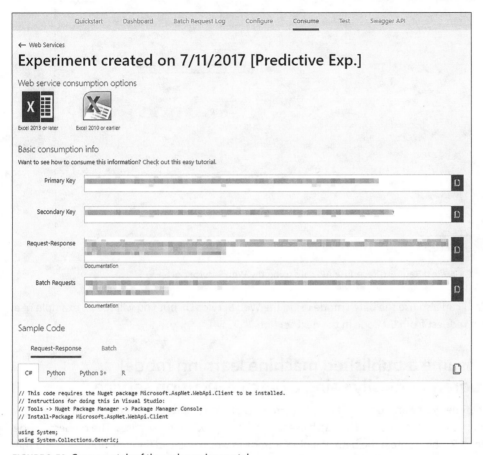

**FIGURE 3-59** Consume tab of the web service portal

There you have all the information you need to consume this model: Excel files connected to the service, keys, endpoints, and sample code that make calls to the API.

Go to the next tab: Test. There you see a form in which you have to enter the input data that you want to pass to the model. The values entered in the fields must match the metadata associated with each input in the predictive experiment. In this case, all values must be numbers. Type the numbers you want and test the model by clicking Test Request-Response (see Figure 3-60). For the example used in the figure, if the model is good, you get a scored label of 0 and a scored probability close to 0.

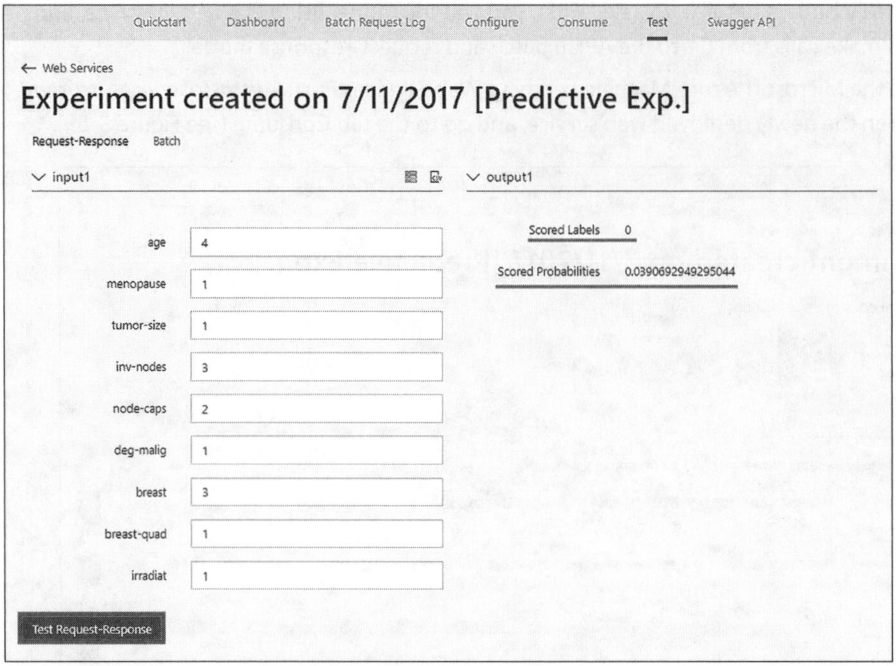

**FIGURE 3-60** Test Request-Response API calls using the Web Service portal

You can also use the batch mode using the Web Service UI, but you will see an example of a batch request from C# code in the next section.

## Consume a published machine learning model programmatically using a batch execution service

Sometimes you want to predict over big amounts of data and do not need an immediate response from the system. The Batch Execution API is good for these cases. The requests made to the API only contain the path of a blob storage in which you can find the input data and the path where it should store the output data. A job is executed asynchronously and performs predictions. In this example you create a text file with the input data, upload it to blob storage, and write a C# code with what you need to call and monitor the job.

Create a file called *breast_cancer_data.csv* with the following content:

```
age,menopause,tumor-size,inv-nodes,node-caps,deg-malig,breast,breast-quad,irradiat
8,10,10,8,7,10,9,7,1
4,1,1,3,2,1,3,1,1
```

The next step is to upload that file to blob storage (see Figure 3-61). When the API is called, those two samples from the file are processed and the predictions saved in another blob storage file.

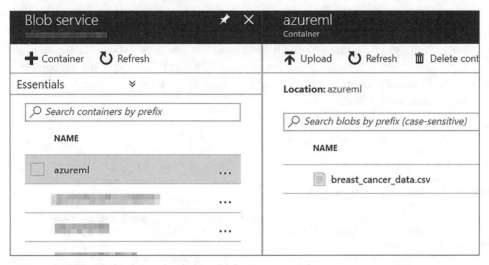

**FIGURE 3-61** CSV with the data uploaded to a blob storage container

For this example you make the API call using C#. In the next skill, you see other examples of API calls with other languages. Create a new C# Console Application project in Visual Studio (see Figure 3-62).

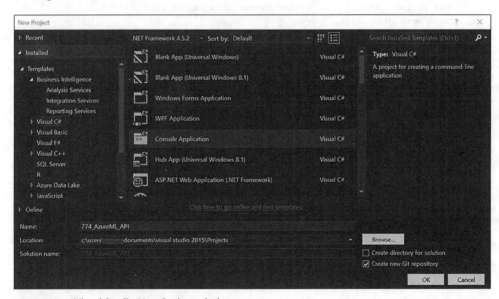

**FIGURE 3-62** Visual Studio New Project window

Once the project is created, you can get an example code in the Consume tab of the Web Service portal (see Figure 3-59). The sample code looks for a local file, uploads it to the blob storage, makes the call that launches the job, polls the system once per second to check when it finishes processing, and downloads the results to local.

The code proposed here is very similar to the script provided in the Consume tab of the Web Service portal, but slightly simplified in order not to deflect attention from the most important part. For example, error control is something that you have to take into account when implementing your application, but the example does not take it much into account. In addition, the code does not include the upload/download to the local file system and the polls to the service until the job ends.

```
using System;
using System.Collections.Generic;
using System.Net.Http;
using System.Net.Http.Headers;
using System.Threading.Tasks;
namespace CallBatchExecutionService {
    class BatchAPI {
        const string BaseUrl = "****"; // Replace this with your API batch endpoint.
        const string StorageAccountName = "****"; /* Replace this with your Azure
  Storage Account name*/
        const string StorageAccountKey = "****"; // Replace this with your Azure Storage
  Key
        const string StorageContainerName = "****"; /* Replace this with your Azure
  Storage container name*/
        const string apiKey = "****"; // Replace this with the API key for the web
  service
        const string inputFile = "breast_cancer_data.csv";
        const string outputFile = "breast_cancer_data_output.csv";
        static void Main(string[] args) {
            InvokeBatchExecutionService().Wait();
        }
        static async Task InvokeBatchExecutionService() {
            string storageConnectionString =
String.Format("DefaultEndpointsProtocol=https;AccountName={0};AccountKey={1}",
StorageAccountName, StorageAccountKey);
            using (HttpClient client = new HttpClient()) {
                var request = new {
                    Inputs = new Dictionary<string, Object>() {
                        {
                            "input1",
                            new {
                                ConnectionString = storageConnectionString,
                                RelativeLocation = string.Format("{0}/{1}",
StorageContainerName, inputFile)
                            }
                        },
                    },
                    Outputs = new Dictionary<string, Object>() {
                        {
                            "output1",
                            new {
                                ConnectionString = storageConnectionString,
                                RelativeLocation = string.Format("{0}/{1}",
StorageContainerName, outputFile)
                            }
                        },
                    },
```

```
            GlobalParameters = new Dictionary<string, string>() {}
        };
            client.DefaultRequestHeaders.Authorization = new
AuthenticationHeaderValue("Bearer", apiKey);

            Console.WriteLine("Submitting the job...");
            var response = await client.PostAsJsonAsync(BaseUrl + "?api-
version=2.0", request);                string jobId = await
response.Content.ReadAsAsync<string>();
            Console.WriteLine(string.Format("Job ID: {0}", jobId));
            Console.WriteLine("Starting the job...");
            response = await client.PostAsync(BaseUrl + "/" + jobId + "/start?api-
version=2.0", null);
        }
    }
  }
}
```

You need to replace the first five lines of the BatchAPI class (lines marked with comments at the end that say "replace this with..."). Those lines contain the blob storage connection settings, and the API key and its endpoint. On the Consume tab several endpoints appear; take the URL from the Batch Execution Service API. Notice that the breast_cancer_data.csv file is specified in the inputFile variable and the name of the output file is the one assigned to the variable outputFile; in this case, *breast_cancer_data_output.csv* file.

Before running the code, you must add the *Microsoft.AspNet.WebApi.Client* package in order to compile your project. You can do that using the *NuGet Package Manager* (in the solution explorer, right-click *References,* and click *Manage NuGet Packages*). The output of the program must be similar to the one shown in figure 3-63.

```
Submitting the job...
Job ID: 9abc0e873a2142408d7b3b5e463fdafc
Starting the job...
```

**FIGURE 3-63** Output of the batch execution API call

The job execution should take only a few seconds. Go to the Azure Blob Storage and download the output file. This is what the breast_cancer_data_output.csv file should have:

```
Scored Labels,Scored Probabilities
1,0.999286234378815
0,0.0390692949295044
```

In a production scenario you would have thousands or millions of predicted rows. At this point, you may want to save these predictions to a database or integrate them as part of a data warehouse. In the next skill, you will see another example of the C# API call, but using the Request-Response Service.

# Consume a published machine learning model programmatically using a request response service

Instead of batches and asynchronously, other times you require an immediate response that gives predictions to all samples. For this we use the Request-Response Service. This mode requires the HTTPS request to pass the input data and not the path to the input file located in the blob storage. In addition, predictions are returned in the body of the HTTPS service response.

You use your breast cancer model again. Create a new project or use the same one from the previous skill and enter the following code:

```
using System;
using System.Collections.Generic;
using System.Net.Http;
using System.Net.Http.Headers;
using System.Threading.Tasks;
namespace _774_AzureML_API {
    class Program {
        // Replace this with your API key and URI.
        const string apiKey = "*****";
        const string apiUri = "*****";
        static void Main(string[] args) {
            InvokeRequestResponseService().Wait();
        }
        static async Task InvokeRequestResponseService() {
            using (var client = new HttpClient()) {
                var scoreRequest = new {
                    Inputs = new Dictionary<string, List<Dictionary<string, string>>>()
{
                        {
                            "input1",
                            new List<Dictionary<string, string>>() {
                                new Dictionary<string, string>() {
                                            {"age", "4"},
                                            {"menopause", "1"},
                                            {"tumor-size", "1"},
                                            {"inv-nodes", "3"},
                                            {"node-caps", "2"},
                                            {"deg-malig", "1"},
                                            {"breast", "3"},
                                            {"breast-quad", "1"},
                                            {"irradiat", "1"},
                                } //, new Dictionary<string, string>() {… add more
samples here
                            }
                        },
                    },
                    GlobalParameters = new Dictionary<string, string>() {}
                };
                client.DefaultRequestHeaders.Authorization = new
AuthenticationHeaderValue("Bearer", apiKey);
                client.BaseAddress = new Uri(apiUri);
                HttpResponseMessage response = await client.PostAsJsonAsync("",
scoreRequest);
```

```
                    string result = await response.Content.ReadAsStringAsync();
                    Console.WriteLine(result);
                }
            }
        }
}
```

As before, you must add the Microsoft.AspNet.WebApi.Client package in order to compile your project. If you are using the same project as the Batch Execution Services example you can skip this step.

As in the previous section, this code is a simpler version of the sample code. Besides not having an appropriate error control, the code only reads the answer, so it needs to be interpreted as JSON and make proper use of the predictions.

The output correctly formatted should be:

```
{
"Results": {
    "output1": [
      {
        "Scored Labels": "0",
        "Scored Probabilities": "0.0390692949295044"
      }
    ]
  }
}
```

Notice that *output1* is an array. This array has the same number of elements as the API received; in this case, a single prediction. You can make calls with more than one sample and all the predictions are returned at the same time. To add more samples on the call, in the code, the only thing you have to do is add more Dictionary objects within the object List<Dictionary<string, string>> (marked in the code with an "add more samples here" comment). In a way, it can be considered a batch request, but it should not be confused with the Batch Execution Service (BES) seen in the previous section.

Two columns are returned: Scored Labels and Scored Probabilities. The meaning of these columns is exactly the same as described when the service was tested using the Web Services UI or tested using the BES API.

## Interact with a published Machine Learning model using Microsoft Excel

Excel is a very widespread tool in the data analysis community. An Excel add-in allows you to make calls to the service in a convenient way using the data contained in an Excel spreadsheet. This is a great advantage if your data is in Excel: you can make predictions with them without writing a more complex solution. In this example, you make predictions using the same data that you used in the Batch Execution Service API call, but instead of using a CSV, you directly use the data introduced in Excel.

Open the Consume tab again (see Figure 3-59) and download the Excel file that best suits your version. When you open the file, you find an empty sheet and a panel on the right that shows something similar to Figure 3-64. If this is your first time using it, you are asked if you want to trust it.

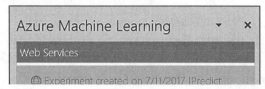

**FIGURE 3-64** Azure Machine Learning panel on the right side of the Excel window

This panel lists all the web services to which Excel can be connected. In this case, it is only connected to one service, but more could be added. The endpoint and service key are already configured because we have downloaded it from the Web Services portal. Click the name of the Web Service to open the predict form.

The next step is to insert the values that will be sent to the web service. To do this, you can create a table with as many columns as the service expects to receive (age, menopause, tumor-size...). Under the headers, add as many rows as you want to be processed. Before calling the service, we must indicate what data will be used. In the *input1* field, select the range of cells contained in the table. In the example, the range is A1: I3. Do not forget to check the box that reads *My Data Has Headers*. You must also select from which cell you want the results to be written. Indicate cell J1 as *output1* and make sure the check box *Include Headers* is checked. Figure 3-65 shows what you should have up to this point.

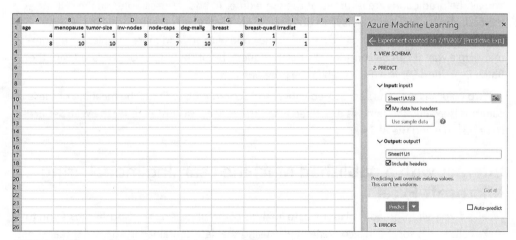

**FIGURE 3-65** Spreadsheet before making the predictions

Click Predict and wait for the response. The results columns are inserted starting from cell J1 (indicated at the time of making the call). See the results in the Figure 3-66.

| | A | B | C | D | E | F | G | H | I | J | K |
|---|---|---|---|---|---|---|---|---|---|---|---|
| 1 | age | menopause | tumor-size | inv-nodes | node-caps | deg-malig | breast | breast-quad | irradiat | Scored Labels | Scored Probabilities |
| 2 | 4 | 1 | 1 | 3 | 2 | 1 | 3 | 1 | 1 | 0 | 0.039069295 |
| 3 | 8 | 10 | 10 | 8 | 7 | 10 | 9 | 7 | 1 | 1 | 0.999286234 |
| 4 | | | | | | | | | | | |

**FIGURE 3-66** Excel spreadsheet with the outputs returned by the model

On the right of the Predict button there is a check box called Auto-predict. If you check it, any changes in the cells range marked as input will trigger a call to the service and the predictions will be updated. This is useful to see how the model reacts to changes in inputs. You can easily come up with what-if scenarios to comprehend how the model works and the effects of such changes. For example, with these options you could easily check what happens if in the first example the tumor-size value goes from 1 to 5. Is it more likely to be a malignant tumor? What if it grows up to 10?

With this, you have enough to start using your prediction services from Excel. You only have to keep in mind that if you save the Excel workbook, the API key is saved with it. Share the workbook only with individuals you trust.

# Skill 3.4: Consume exemplar Cognitive Services APIs

There are certain recurrent problems in the world of machine learning: face recognition, object recognition, translation, speech recognition, sentiment analysis, etc. Would not it be great if there were models already trained to use them for these general purposes? This (and much more) is what Cognitive Services brings to you.

Cognitive Services are a complete suite of tools (APIs, SDKs, and other services) that Microsoft offers to bring intelligence to applications. It provides many different ways to apply intelligence on text, photos, videos, and it is even able to make recommendations and help you in your decision-making processes. Best of all, all of these complex machine learning models are within reach of an API call.

> **This skill covers how to:**
> - Consume Vision APIs to process images
> - Consume Language APIs to process text
> - Consume Knowledge APIs to create recommendations

Cognitive Services give you access to complex machine learning models trained for general purposes. Creating these models from scratch can be very expensive. It requires a lot of data, great computing power, good model design, days of training, and putting into production and, more importantly, highly trained data science specialists.

In addition to those general models, you can create specific models for your environment. For example, apart from offering speech recognition, Cognitive Services allows you to tweak the speech recognition model to a special accent or to a particular vocabulary. Another example is the recommender system that you create in a section of this skill. You need the model to recommend your company's products based on the tastes of your users. For these cases, you need data. In Skill 3.1 you have already seen how to create a recommendation but with Azure Machine Learning.

The way in which these models are made is transparent to the user; you simply have to call an API. In the future, when these models are improved, the API remains the same but returns results that are more accurate. Therefore, the ease and low cost of deploying a machine learning solution with Cognitive Services makes it an alternative to Azure Machine Learning that you might want to consider.

> **NEED MORE INFORMATION?  COGNITIVE SERVICES DOCUMENTATION**
>
> If you want to learn more about all of the possibilities that Cognitive Services offers, visit *https://docs.microsoft.com/azure/#pivot=products&panel=cognitive*.

## Consume Vision APIs to process images

Regarding images, you can use Cognitive Services to detect faces in a photo, recognize a specific individual in a photo, extract text from an image, or even recognize emblematic places.

To use the Vision API, and in general any of the Cognitive Services APIs, you must get a key. There is the possibility of getting a free trial key that allows you to test any API feature. Go to *https://azure.microsoft.com/try/cognitive-services/* to get your trial key. In Figure 3-67 you see a screen shot of that web page. As you can see, there is a different key per set of services. For example, there is a key to control the access to the Computer Vision API and a different one to get access to the Emotion API (although the two are closely related to each other).

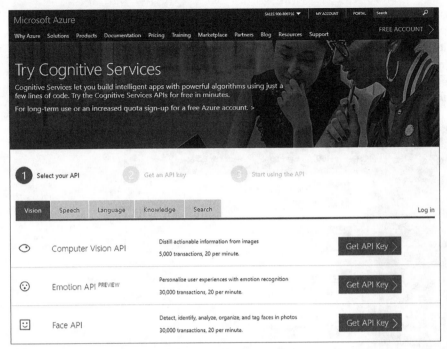

**FIGURE 3-67** Website from which you can obtain the Cognitive Services trial keys

Press Get API Key, accept the conditions, and login with your account. After that, you will see a page similar to the one shown in Figure 3-68 with your API endpoint and your API key. Remember these values for later. Naturally, the value of your keys will be different. You can use either of the two keys.

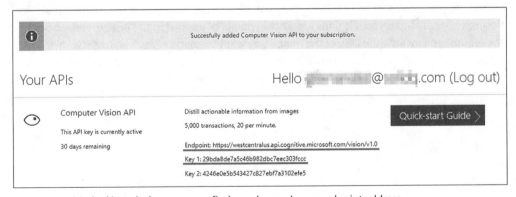

**FIGURE 3-68** Marked in red where you can find your key and your endpoint address

Test keys are restricted, for instance, the vision key is limited to 5,000 calls and a maximum of 20 calls per minute. For development it is more than enough, but when it comes to putting a service into production the number of calls may be too small. If you want to obtain a paid key you must create the specific element in your Azure subscription. In the *Marketplace*, go to *AI + Cognitive Services,* and after that go to *Cognitive Service.* For this case, you need to create a *Computer Vision API* element (see Figure 3-69).

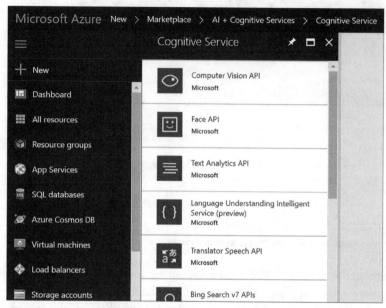

**FIGURE 3-69** Azure elements related to Cognitive Services

You are going to build an example where you make a call to the landmarks detector service. Cognitive Services tells you if it finds any known points of interest in the image. In the body of the request you include the URL of the image you want to analyze. You can test it with an image of the Statue of Liberty (see figure 3-70). You can also send the image binary data instead of the URL, but for simplicity of example, you will do it using the URL.

**FIGURE 3-70** The Statue of Liberty borrowed from Wikipedia at *https://upload.wikimedia.org/wikipedia/commons/3/37/Liberty-statue-from-below.jpg*

If you already have a key and an endpoint, whether it is trial or paid, you can proceed to create the Python script that will be used to make the API call. The following Python script works under Python 3.5.2. You may need to make some modifications to run it on other versions.

```
# Works with Python 3.5.2
import http.client, urllib.parse, json
subscription_key = "29bda8de7a5c46b982dbc7eec303fccc"  # YOUR KEY HERE!
uri_base = "westcentralus.api.cognitive.microsoft.com" # YOUR ENDPOINT HERE!
# Request headers.
headers = {
    'Content-Type': 'application/json',
    'Ocp-Apim-Subscription-Key': subscription_key,}
    # The URL of a JEPG image containing text.
body = "{'url':'https://upload.wikimedia.org/wikipedia/commons/3/37/Liberty-
statue-from-below.jpg'}"
try:
    # Execute the REST API call and get the response.
    conn = http.client.HTTPSConnection(uri_base)
    # Landmarks detector.
    conn.request("POST", "/vision/v1.0/models/landmarks/analyze?model=landmarks",
body, headers)
    json_str = conn.getresponse().read().decode('utf8')
    json_obj = json.loads(json_str)
    print("Response:", json.dumps(json_obj, indent=4, sort_keys=True))
except Exception as e:
    print("Error:", e)
```

After replacing the key and the endpoint with yours, you are able to execute the script and get a result, as shown in Figure 3-71. The script prints the JSON response of the API. In this case, you see that Cognitive Services detects with high confidence that the Statue of Liberty appears in the picture.

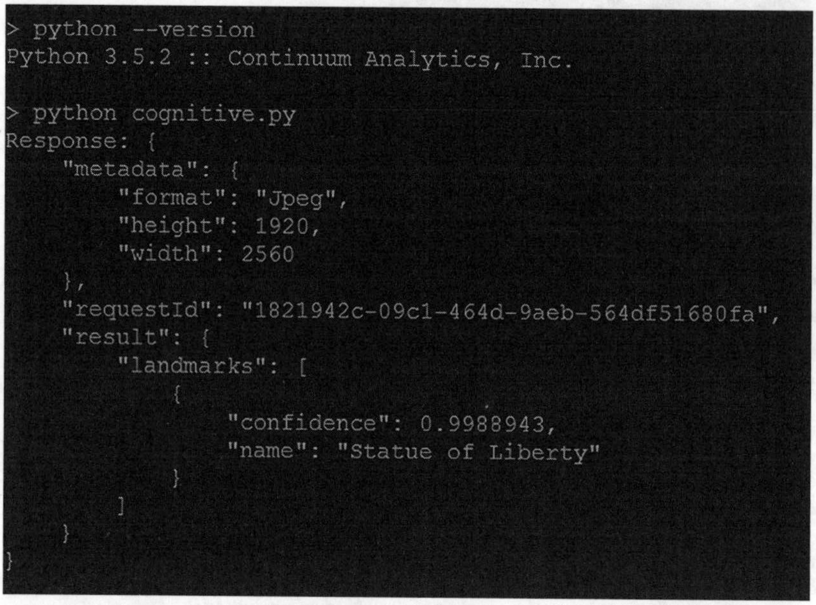

```
> python --version
Python 3.5.2 :: Continuum Analytics, Inc.

> python cognitive.py
Response: {
    "metadata": {
        "format": "Jpeg",
        "height": 1920,
        "width": 2560
    },
    "requestId": "1821942c-09c1-464d-9aeb-564df51680fa",
    "result": {
        "landmarks": [
            {
                "confidence": 0.9988943,
                "name": "Statue of Liberty"
            }
        ]
    }
}
```

**FIGURE 3-71** JSON response from the landmark detection Cognitive Service using Python

One of the key parts of the script is the line:

```
conn.request("POST", "/vision/v1.0/models/landmarks/analyze?model=landmarks", body,
 headers)
```

This line shows the URL of the service we want to consume. You can change this line to the next one in order to find the tags that best match what is in the image and a text description:

```
conn.request("POST", "/vision/v1.0/analyze ?visualFeatures=description", body,
 headers)
```

Run the code again without changing anything else. You get a result like the one shown in figure 3-72. Cognitive Services says that the image contains "a green statue on a cloudy day." It also provides a list of tags.

```
> python cognitive.py
Response: {
    "description": {
        "captions": [
            {
                "confidence": 0.8097484040190992,
                "text": "a green statue on a cloudy day"
            }
        ],
        "tags": [
            "outdoor",
            "green",
            "flying",
            "blue",
            "cloudy",
            "building",
            "looking",
            "clock",
            "clouds",
            "front",
            "air",
            "statue",
            "hanging",
            "large",
            "holding",
            "standing",
            "tall",
            "yellow",
            "street",
            "kite",
            "white",
            "tower",
            "city"
        ]
    },
    "metadata": {
        "format": "Jpeg",
        "height": 1920,
        "width": 2560
    },
    "requestId": "373106c3-7dd4-4b15-b2a4-752e5f8675d7"
}
```

**FIGURE 3-72** Output of the analyze API with visualFeatures=description

Try another API call, this time to find out if there are famous people in the picture. Use the following request:

```
conn.request("POST", "/vision/v1.0/models/landmarks/analyze?model=celebrities", body,
 headers)
```

To test its effectiveness, we must replace the URL of the Statue of Liberty with an image in which a celebrity appears. Use the following image taken again from Wikipedia. Figure 3-73 shows the API call result.

```
body = "{'url':'https://upload.wikimedia.org/wikipedia/commons/thumb/9/96/
Kobe_Bryant_8.jpg/1200px-Kobe_Bryant_8.jpg'}"
```

```
> python cognitive.py
Response: {
    "metadata": {
        "format": "Jpeg",
        "height": 1792,
        "width": 1200
    },
    "requestId": "dcdf0661-9476-4057-937f-488db9d98ed9",
    "result": {
        "celebrities": [
            {
                "confidence": 0.9991092,
                "faceRectangle": {
                    "height": 240,
                    "left": 510,
                    "top": 168,
                    "width": 240
                },
                "name": "Kobe Bryant"
            }
        ]
    }
}
```

**FIGURE 3-73** Results of the celebrity detector

In addition to the services tried in this example (landmarks detector, celebrities detector, and image analysis) there are many others. You can find the exact URLs for each service in the official documentation.

> ***NEED MORE INFORMATION?*** **DOCUMENTATION**
>
> The following page contains all Vision APIs with the parameters described and sample code (in seven different languages). It also has a web interface from which calls can be made without writing a single line of code. Visit: *https://westcentralus.dev.cognitive.microsoft.com/docs/services/56f91f2d778daf23d8ec6739/operations/56f91f2e778daf14a499e1ff.*
>
> You can find pre-built examples to learn how to integrate Cognitive Services in more complete and complex applications such The Intelligent Kiosk at Microsoft's GitHub page *https://github.com/Microsoft/Cognitive-Samples-IntelligentKiosk.*

## Consume Language APIs to process text

Now that you have played with different options of the Vision API, you are going to test some of the functions that the Text Analytics API offers. This time, instead of Python, you use Power BI to make the API calls.

As you have done before for the Vision API, get a trial or paid key for the Text Analytics API. In this example we perform a sentiment analysis on some tweets about Azure (100 tweets containing the hashtag #azure). We assume that you have a text dataset loaded in a Power BI model. Actually, the text can be anything; it does not have to be tweets. It could be comments from a website, for example.

The fields the sentiment analysis API expects are an ID, a text field, and a language. The text field is the text from which we want to get the sentiment. The ID is probably in your application because there is always something that unambiguously identifies the text you want to analyze. An index is used in the source table of the example, but the tweet id could also be used. This example assumes that the language is English because the tweets have been collected with a language filter. Your data may have text in different languages. To identify the language of a text you can also use the Text Analytics API. If you know the language beforehand, you can add a constant column with the value "en" (standing for English) for all rows. The table should look similar to the one shown in Figure 3-74.

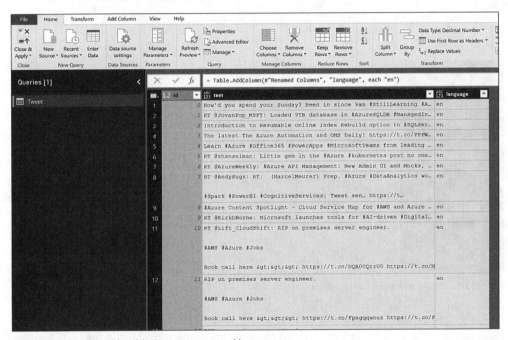

**FIGURE 3-74** Tweet table with ID, tweet text, and language

The next step is to create a new blank query with a function in M language. That function calls the sentiment analysis API and returns the sentiment score, that is, a value between 0 (negative text) and 1 (positive text). Here is the code:

```
(id, text, lang) => let
    apikey      = "38ad09b51ede40f38dd1bcf518419de9",
    endpoint    = "https://westcentralus.api.cognitive.microsoft.com/text/analytics/
```

```
v2.0/sentiment?",
    jsontext    = Text.FromBinary(Json.FromValue(Text.Start(Text.Trim(text), 5000)))),
    jsonbody    = "{ documents: [ { language: """ & lang & """, id: """ & Text.From(id)
 & """, text: " & jsontext & " } ] }",
    bytesbody   = Text.ToBinary(jsonbody),
    headers     = [#"Ocp-Apim-Subscription-Key" = apikey],
    bytesresp   = Web.Contents(endpoint, [Headers=headers, Content=bytesbody]),
    jsonresp    = Json.Document(bytesresp),
    sentiment   = jsonresp[documents]{0}[score]
in  sentiment
```

The API specifies that the maximum text length is 5,000 characters, so the first 5,000 are taken using Text.Start. Do not forget to replace the key and endpoint with your own values in the first and second line of the function.

To apply this function, go to the tweets table and go to the ribbon option Add column > Invoke Custom Function. Select the correct columns as input (see Figure 3-75).

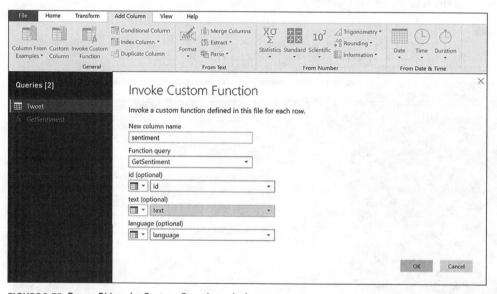

**FIGURE 3-75** Power BI Invoke Custom Function window

At this point you are asked about dataset security and API call authentication. Select the value you want for security and anonymous authentication (this is because in the code you already provide the key). Now you must have a new column in your tweet table that contains the sentiment value between 0 and 1. You can add a column containing a Positive, Negative, or Neutral tag depending on the value of the sentiment column. Make a simple report to verify the performance, as shown in Figure 3-76.

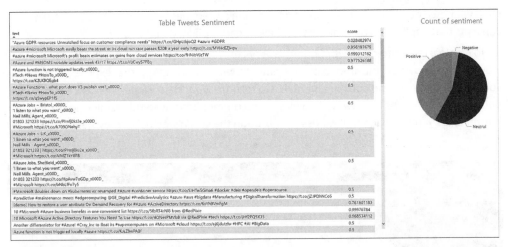

| Table Tweets Sentiment | |
|---|---|
| text | score |
| "Azure GDPR resources: Unmatched focus on customer compliance needs" https://t.co/GHpLtbjoQ2 #azure #GDPR | 0.028482974 |
| #azure #microsoft Microsoft easily beats the street as its cloud run rate passes $20B a year early https://t.co/MVHcEZJvqw | 0.956197679 |
| #azure #microsoft Microsoft's profit beats estimates on gains from cloud services https://t.co/fHNibVJzTW | 0.999312182 |
| #Azure and #MSOMS notable updates week 43/17 https://t.co/rbCwyS7FEq | 0.977526188 |
| #Azure function is not triggered locally_x000D_<br>#Tech #News #HowTo_x000D_<br>https://t.co/k2LKBOEgb4 | 0.5 |
| #Azure Functions - what port does VS publish use?_x000D_<br>#Tech #News #HowTo_x000D_<br>https://t.co/qSwypEP1f5 | 0.5 |
| #Azure Jobs ~ Bristol_x000D_<br>'I listen to what you want'_x000D_<br>Neil Mills Agent_x000D_<br>01803 321233 https://t.co/PlmfJ0kJ2e_x000D_<br>#Microsoft https://t.co/k709ONehyT | 0.5 |
| #Azure Jobs ~ UK_x000D_<br>'I listen to what you want'_x000D_<br>Neil Mills - Agent_x000D_<br>01803 321233 | https://t.co/PlmfJ0kJ2e_x000D_<br>#Microsoft https://t.co/AiMZ1kY8F8 | 0.5 |
| #Azure Jobs, Sheffield_x000D_<br>'I listen to what you want'_x000D_<br>Neil Mills Agent_x000D_<br>01803 321233 https://t.co/HpAvw7oGDp_x000D_<br>#Microsoft https://t.co/bNbLfFo7y5 | 0.5 |
| #Microsoft doubles down on #kubernetes w/ revamped #Azure #container service https://t.co/SIHTw5Gma6 #docker #deis #opendeis #opensource | 0.5 |
| #predictive #maintenance meets #edgecomputing @GE_Digital #PredictiveAnalytics #azure #aws #bigdata #Manufacturing #DigitalTransformation https://t.co/jZJPDhNCe5 | 0.5 |
| [demo] How to restore a user attribute On Demand Recovery for #Azure #ActiveDirectory https://t.co/6xYh9VmFgM | 0.761801183 |
| 10 #Microsoft #Azure business benefits in one convenient list https://t.co/5fbRT4zNl6 from @RedPixie | 0.99976784 |
| 10 Microsoft #Azure Active Directory Features You Need To Use https://t.co/4ONesPMVbB via @RedPixie #tech https://t.co/jHf2PQ5X35 | 0.968534112 |
| Another differentiator for #Azure! #Cray_inc to float its #supercomputers on #Microsoft #cloud https://t.co/ej6Jdutzfw #HPC #AI #BigData | 0.5 |
| Azure function is not triggered locally #azure https://t.co/RJsZ9wPA8f | 0.5 |

Count of sentiment

**FIGURE 3-76** Power BI report using the results of the API calls

A drawback of this implementation is that one call per row is made. Making batch calls can optimize it (up to a maximum of 1,000 texts per call).

> **NEED MORE INFORMATION? BATCH CALLS FROM POWER BI**
>
> Doing the API calls row by row is quite slow; learn how to do it in batch mode in this article at: *https://community.powerbi.com/t5/Community-Blog/Sentiment-Analysis-in-Power-BI/ba-p/55898.*

You can try adding another column with the key phrases of each tweet extracted using the Key Phrases API. This way you can make a word cloud without noisy words, only containing the most significant words.

> **NEED MORE INFORMATION? API DOCUMENTATION**
>
> Find out what URLs and parameters are needed to make other Text Analytics API calls at: *https://westcentralus.dev.cognitive.microsoft.com/docs/services/TextAnalytics.V2.0/operations/56f30ceeeda5650db055a3c7.*

# Consume Knowledge APIs to create recommendations

In this section you learn how to use the Cognitive Services solution to build a recommendation system. In contrast to what has been done in this skill up to now, for this example we need data and training a new model. There is no general-purpose recommendation model that does not need your own data.  A restaurant recommendation system has been built in Skill 3.1. Many concepts that apply to recommenders have also been explained in that Skill.

To create a recommender with Cognitive Services, you need to deploy a solution template in Azure that provides you, among other elements, with an Azure App that exposes an API that you will use to create and consume models. Go to: *https://gallery.cortanaintelligence.com/Tutorial/Recommendations-Solution* to deploy your recommendations solution. Clicking the Deploy button takes you to a page that guides you through the seven steps of deployment (see Figure 3-77).

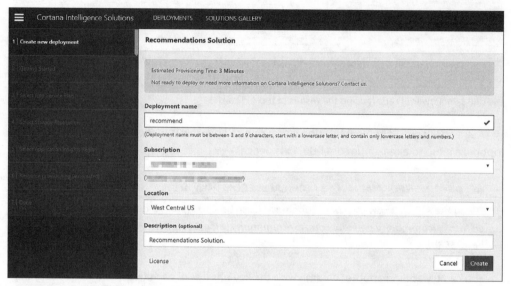

**FIGURE 3-77** Deployment assistant of the Recommendation solution

In step 1, you have to specify basic deployment information such as subscription and resource group name.

Step 2 tells you which elements will be deployed:

- An Azure App Service to host the recommendations service
- An Azure Storage account to store training data and models
- An Application Insights app to collect traces and telemetry

In the next three steps you select the characteristics of each of the created elements. In step 3 select a tier B1 (more than enough to test) for the Azure App, in step 4 choose a replication strategy for the Azure Storage, and in step 5 select the Application Insights app region.

After a few minutes of deployment in step 6, you reach step 7 where the information needed to access the system is shown. In addition to the exposed API, this solution has a web interface that allows you to train models and test them easier than having to make the calls "by hand." See Figure 3-78. Save the endpoint URL, the admin and recommender key, and the recommendations UI URL for later.

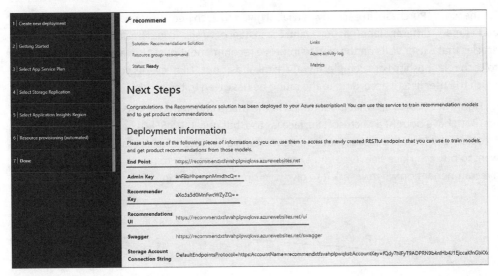

**FIGURE 3-78** Last step of the deployment

Check that the elements have been created in Azure (see Figure 3-79). If after closing step 7 you want to recover the keys and URLs again, you must do it from the Azure portal.

| NAME | TYPE | LOCATION | |
|------|------|----------|---|
| recommendxtfsvahplpwqkappInsights | Application Insights | South Central US | ••• |
| recommendxtfsvahplpwqkhostingplan | App Service plan | West Central US | ••• |
| recommendxtfsvahplpwqkst | Storage account | West Central US | ••• |
| recommendxtfsvahplpwqkws | App Service | West Central US | ••• |

4 items

**FIGURE 3-79** Azure elements deployed by the template

Once the solution is deployed you need to define your catalog file (a list of items) and a usage file (relationships between users and objects). Create an items.csv file with the following content:

```
ITEM01,Optical mouse,Accessories
ITEM02,Surface sleeve,Accessories
ITEM03,Microsoft Surface Laptop,PC
```

Those are the items of an imaginary shop. The file format is "id, name, category." You can also add features to each item to enhance model recommendations (not used in this example).

Create a usage.csv file with the following content:

```
USER01,ITEM03,2017-10-30T11:00:02,Purchase
USER01,ITEM02,2017-10-30T11:01:50,Purchase
USER02,ITEM03,2017-10-30T11:03:20,Purchase
```

The word "Purchase" in each row is a label given to each item-user relationship. You can add as many different labels as you want. For instance, "Visits" could be added to represent the articles that a user visits on the web to improve recommendations. Also, a weight can be added to each relationship. For example, if you are talking about "Like" events you could indicate how much the user likes it according to the rating he has given to the article.

Figure 3-80 sums up what is contained in the usage and items files. Your system has two users. Both have bought a Microsoft Surface laptop, but only the USER01 has also bought a Surface sleeve. It is quite obvious that if someone buys a Microsoft Surface laptop they may also want to buy a Surface sleeve, so you expect your recommender to return the Surface sleeve as a recommendation when we ask it to give items related to the laptop.

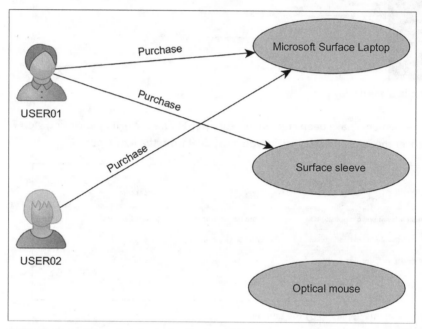

**FIGURE 3-80** An illustration shows the files from which our recommended system learns

Go to the Azure Portal and open the Azure Storage element of the template. Upload both files (items.csv and usage.csv) to a new container named data (see Figure 3-81).

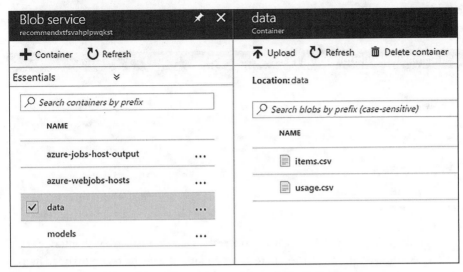

**FIGURE 3-81** A data container with the items.csv and usage.csv files

Go to the recommendation UI using the URL you receive in the last step of the deployment. You are asked to enter the admin key. Once you have accessed the page, click Train New Model and set the three options that refer to where the data is located (see Figure 3-82). Click Train and wait for the model to train. If necessary, the API has an option that allows you to know the status each model at any time, so you can monitor the trainings. For this case, with a very small amount of data, it is not necessary.

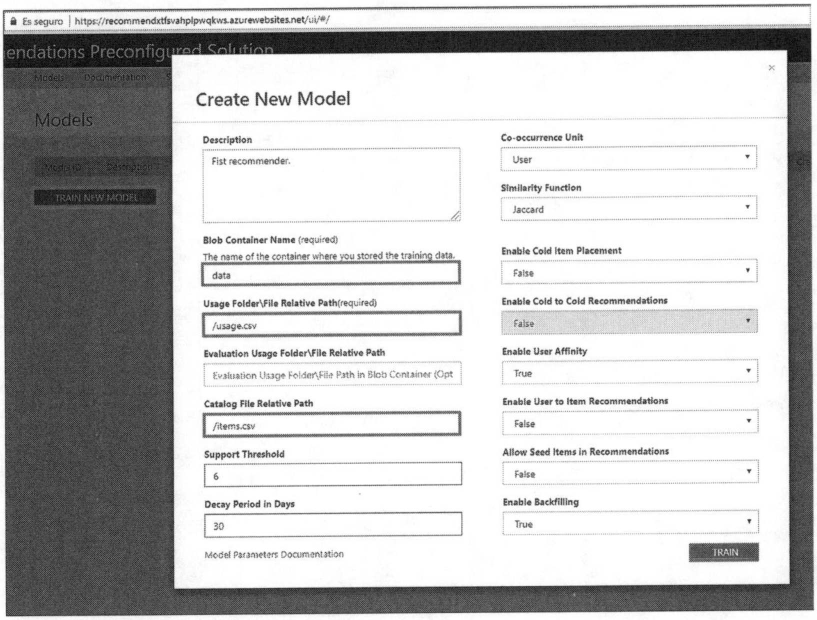

**FIGURE 3-82** Create New Model form

Go to the home page of the recommendation UI to see a list of models (see Figure 3-83). Save the ID of the model for later.

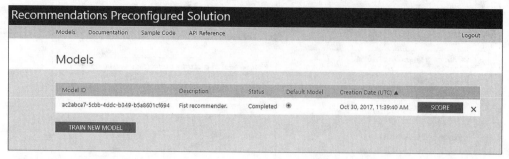

**FIGURE 3-83** A list of models

In the list of models (Figure 3-83), click Score to test the system. You see a web interface that allows you to make requests for item-to-item recommendations. See the recommended items for ITEM03 (laptop) in figure 3-84. ITEM02 (laptop sleeve) is returned, just as expected. Because the system has little data, scores are always at 0 and ITEM01 does not even appear. The higher the score, the more likely it is that a user who bought ITEM02 will buy ITEM03.

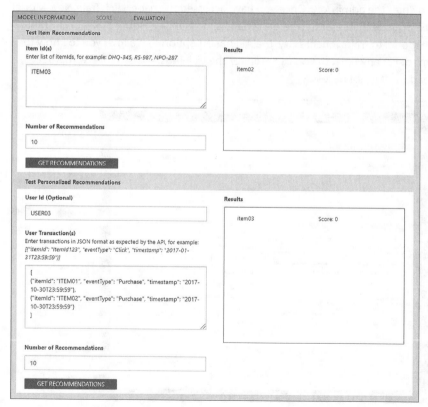

**FIGURE 3-84** Score form

You can test your model manually using the UI, but to integrate recommendations into applications you need to use the API. Below you find a Python script that contains what you need to make a call and get recommendations. The script is very similar to those used to call the Vision API. The main difference lies in the URL you call. Do not forget to replace the key, URI, and model ID with your own.

```
# Works with Python 3.5.2
import http.client, urllib.parse, json
api_key = "aXo3a3d0MnFwcWZyZQ==" # YOUR RECOMMENDER KEY HERE!
uri_base = "recommendxtfsvahplpwqkws.azurewebsites.net" # YOUR URI HERE!
model_id = "d7d5fd26-a97e-4d04-9dd5-7417248821bd" # YOUR MODEL ID HERE!
item_id = "ITEM03" # YOUR ITEM ID HERE!
headers = {
    'x-api-key': api_key,}
try:
    # Make API call.
    conn = http.client.HTTPSConnection(uri_base)
    conn.request("GET", "/api/models/%s/recommend?itemId=%s" % (model_id, item_id), {},
 headers)
    # Read and print response.
    json_str = conn.getresponse().read().decode('utf8')
    json_obj = json.loads(json_str)
    print("Response:", json.dumps(json_obj, indent=4))
except Exception as e:
    print("Error:", e)
```

Run the script, and as with using the user interface, you will receive that the ITEM02 is recommended for ITEM03 (see Figure 3-85).

```
> python "Skill 3.4 Recommender API.py"
Response: [
    {
        "score": 0.0,
        "recommendedItemId": "item02"
    }
]
```

**FIGURE 3-85** Item-to-item recommendation

What you have done so far is a toy example. After a little bit of preprocessing (convert *.dat files to *.csv) you can use the data in *https://github.com/sidooms/MovieTweetings* to build a movie recommender engine. The process would be exactly the same as the previous one, but with the data taken from the repository. You do not need to deploy the template again; you can create a new model that uses the new data. Figure 3-86 shows the output of a script requesting recommendations for the first Toy Story film. Among the results, it recommends more confidently the second and third part of the film. Other recommendations are Monsters, Inc., Up, WALL-E and more animation movies. For convenience, the executed script converts returned movie IDs to the title using a reference table.

```
> python "Skill 3.4 Recommendation.py"
Film: Toy Story (1995)
0.40287014842033386 Toy Story 2 (1999)
0.3068525791168213 Toy Story 3 (2010)
0.16526944935321808 Monsters, Inc. (2001)
0.1465817242860794 Up (2009)
0.1291583776473999 WALL·E (2008)
0.1161978468298912 The Lion King (1994)
0.111064612865448 Finding Nemo (2003)
0.10367929190397263 Cars (2006)
0.09754881262779236 A Bug's Life (1998)
0.09173513948917389 Titanic (1997)
0.08751609921455383 The Incredible Hulk (2008)
0.08230680972337723 Indiana Jones and the Last Crusade (1989)
0.07773420214653015 Spider-Man (2002)
0.07763436436653137 The Incredibles (2004)
0.07597551494836807 Shrek (2001)
```

FIGURE 3-86 Movies similar to the first Toy Story film returned by the recommender

---

*NEED MORE INFORMATION?* **RECOMMENDATION SOLUTION DOCUMENTATION**

All of the documentation of the recommendations solution can be found in the following Github repository at: *https://github.com/Microsoft/Product-Recommendations*.

---

Besides the three different APIs studied in this skill, there are others such as:

- **Speech APIs**   Allows you to translate, recognize a speaker's voice in an audio, recognize the content of an audio clip, convert text to speech and other features such as creating systems that best suit your application's vocabulary or the speech style of your users.

- **Search APIs**   Adds the power of Bing to your apps: web, image, video, and news search; autosuggest queries; entity search and custom search.

In addition to these different APIs, you can still explore many other options of the APIs. For example, there are many more possibilities to explore in the Vision APIs, like working with videos. There are also, apart from item-to-item recommendations shown, recommendations based on a user's history. An entire book could be written about Cognitive Services. Browse the documentation for help and more examples.

As discussed throughout the chapter, the use of APIs facilitates the use and future deployment of machine learning models. Regardless of what is behind the API, an Azure Machine Learning model or a Cognitive Services model, the calls are the same and make development easier. Cognitive Services enriches your applications embedding them with AI without the need to develop a complicated machine learning model if you do not need to. Consider using Azure Machine Learning if you have a very specialized problem that requires personalized pre-processing and training to increase the performance. After this chapter you are able to use your machine learning models from any programming language that can make web requests, that is, all the modern ones.

# Thought experiment

This thought experiment allows you to demonstrate the skills and knowledge gained by re-viewing the topics covered in the chapter. The answers are included in the next section.

Publish and consume machine learning models as well as cognitive services already in place is a very common task that has to be addressed and included in the development pipeline of any data science solution. Having a clear idea of the different scenarios that you can cover, how to leverage pre-built solutions and even how to troubleshoot your publishing or consumption processes is a key part of the success of your implementation.

This thought experiments allows you to demonstrate the skills and knowledge gained by reviewing the topics covered in the chapter. Now you will go through several scenarios that will require you to use the knowledge that you have obtained during this Chapter.

1. Once you have developed your Azure Machine Learning Model and published it as a web service so your team is able to consume its predictions. However, they do not know the web service APIs, and you need to advise them on the best method to consume. To retrieve more than one prediction from the web service, would you use a single request to the Request-Response Service API?

   A. No, to do that you have to use the Batch Execution Service API.

   B. Yes, you can send more than one sample in the request body.

2. After building or retraining your model to improve its performance or made some needed adjustments, you might want to publish it. Nevertheless, when you try to do so, the options to either publish it as a 'Predictive Web Service' or 'Retraining Web Service' are greyed out.  This could be due to:

   A. Error during a previous execution.

   B. Experiment has not been executed at least once.

   C. There is a missing input to one of the modules.

   D. All of the above.

   E. Answers A and C.

   F. Answers A and B.

3. While developing a solution proposal for a potential client you are required to provide a mixture of on-premises and cloud machine learning solution that does not upload the client's data but allows you to use a predictive web for other applications. What do you do?

4. In order to publish a model as a web service you will have to estimate a consumption rate to choose the pricing tier you want to use. There might be the case when you get it incorrectly because the model gets very popular and the number of API calls associated to the pricing tier you chose is exceeded. What happens in that case?

5. You and a collaborating data scientist on a different company are tasked with the de-velopment of a predictive application on Azure Machine Learning. As both of you start

developing independent experiments and models, you decide to unify your solutions and collaborate on a single development. What would be the steps in order to unify the work already done?

- **A.** Compare model performances through notebooks and decide which models and datasets will be the used.
- **B.** Decide which workspace will hold the final solution / model.
- **C.** Invite users to final workspace.
- **D.** Develop final machine learning experiment by combining datasets, models and other developed modules.
- **E.** Migrate models and datasets to the final workspace.

6. One of the most powerful features of Azure Machine Learning is the fact that its modules are published as web services. The immense majority of modern programming languages are able to consume web services. That combination creates a scenario where you can easily consume your machine learning models from a multitude of platforms, devices and tools. If you are asked to make an API call to the Request-Response Service of your Azure Machine Learning Model using Python instead of C#, would it be possible? If so, which would be the easiest way?

## Thought experiment answers

This section contains the answers to the thought experiment in this chapter.

1. The correct answer is B.
2. The correct answer is D.
3. Develop and train a predictive model on-premises with Python or R and upload the trained model as a scoring function to an Azure Machine Learning experiment.
4. Nothing, the API is still running normally, but you will be charged for blocks of 1000 transactions and computing hours.
5. The correct order is ( B ) – ( C ) – ( E ) – ( A ) – ( D ).
6. Yes, it is possible. Open the Microsoft Azure Machine Learning Web Services portal (*https://services.azureml.net/webservices/*) of your web service and copy and paste the sample code of the Python version that best fits your local installation. Replace the key value with the correct key for your service (the key and the code are located under the Consume tab).

# Chapter summary

Operationalize and consume machine learning models has been a pain point in the industry for years. Luckily, in the recent years the expansion of more advanced machine learning platforms has eased the process of publishing and consuming these models. One of the major trends in the industry, the transformation of software to services, has not been ignored by these platforms and now leveraging web services and RESTful APIs is not uncommon within the data science community.

In this chapter:

- You have reviewed how to publish your experiments in Azure Machine Learning as web services to easily consume them from multiple platforms.

- You learnt how to manage your data science projects in the cloud to collaborate with your colleagues to explore your data and enrich your machine learning models.

- More advanced machine learning usages have been reviewed too, like building and consuming, through multiple methods, languages and platforms, of complex, pre-trained machine learning models.

- You have been able to leverage the power of deep learning models such as the ones present in the Vision Cognitive Services or configure your own personalized Language Understanding services without the hassle of building them from scratch. Thus, you are able to integrate advanced machine learning models in your applications and data process pipelines, saving time and money.

# CHAPTER 4

# Use other services for machine learning

You have been learning about Azure Machine Learning as a powerful tool to solve the vast majority of common machine learning problems, but it is important to consider that it is not the only tool provided by Microsoft for that purpose. A previously seen alternative is Cognitive Services, and in this chapter, we look at other systems capable of dealing with large amounts of unstructured data (HDInsight clusters), data science tools integrated with SQL Server (R Services), and preconfigured workspaces in powerful Azure Virtual Machines (Deep Learning Virtual Machines and Data Science Virtual Machines).

## Skills in this chapter:

- Skill 4.1: Build and use neural networks with the Microsoft Cognitive Toolkit
- Skill 4.2: Streamline development by using existing resources
- Skill 4.3: Perform data sciences at scale by using HDInsights
- Skill 4.4: Perform database analytics by using SQL Server R Services on Azure

## Skill 4.1: Build and use neural networks with the Microsoft Cognitive Toolkit

Microsoft Cognitive Toolkit (CNTK) is behind many of the Cognitive Services models you learned to use in Skill 3.4: Consume exemplar Cognitive Services APIs. You can find CNTK in Cortana, the Bing recommendation system, the HoloLens object recognition algorithm, the Skype translator, and it is even used by Microsoft Research to build state-of-the-art models.

But what exactly is CNTK? It is a Microsoft open source deep learning toolkit. Like other deep learning tools, CNTK is based on the construction of computational graphs and their optimization using automatic differentiation. The toolkit is highly optimized and scales efficiently (from CPU, to GPU, to multiple machines). CNTK is also very portable and flexible; you can use it with programming languages like Python, C#, or C++, but you can also use a model description language called BrainScript.

## Simple linear regression with CNTK

With CNTK you can define many different types of neural networks based on building block composition. You can build feed forward neural networks (you review how to implement one in this skill), Convolutional Neural Networks (CNN), Recurrent Neural Networks (RNN), Long Short-Term Memory (LSTM), Gated Recurrent Unit (GRU), and others. You can actually define almost any type of neural network, including your own modifications. The set of variables, parameters, operations, and their connections to each other are called are called computational graphs or computational networks.

As a first contact with the library, you create a Jupyter Notebook in which you adjust a linear regression to synthetic data. Although it is a very simple model and may not be as attractive as building a neural network, this example provides you an easier understanding of the concept of computational graphs. That concept applies equally to any type of neural network (including deep ones).

> *NOTE*  **INSTALL CNTK**
>
> To follow the next example you need to install CNTK from *https://docs.microsoft.com/en-us/cognitive-toolkit/Setup-CNTK-on-your-machine*. If you already have Python installed in your environment you only need to install CNTK using *pip* and the URL of the wheel package that you can find in a given website. Also, you can use an Azure Deep Learning Virtual Machine, a virtual machine with pre-installed deep learning tools. You review how to create one in the next sections.

The first thing you must include in your notebook is an import section. Import *cntk, matplotlib* for visualizations, and *numpy* for matrices. Note that the fist line is a special Jupyter Notebook syntax to indicate that the matplotlib plots must be shown without calling the *plt.show* method.

```
%matplotlib inline
import matplotlib.pyplot as plt

import cntk as C

import numpy as np
```

For this example, you use synthetic data. Generate a dataset following a defined line plus noise y_data = x_data * w_data + b_data + noise where the variable w_data is the slope of the line, b_data the intercept or bias term and noise is a random gaussian noise with standard deviation given by the noise_stddev variable. Each row in x_data and y_data is a sample, and n_samples samples are generated between 0 and scale.

```
np.random.seed(0)

def generate_data(n_samples, w_data, b_data, scale, noise_stddev):
    x_data = np.random.rand(n_samples, 1).astype(np.float32) * scale
    noise = np.random.normal(0, noise_stddev, (n_samples, 1)).astype(np.float32)
    y_data = x_data * w_data + b_data + noise
    return x_data, y_data

n_samples = 50
scale = 10
w_data, b_data = 0.5, 2
noise_stddev = 0.1
x_data, y_data = generate_data(n_samples, w_data, b_data, scale, noise_stddev)

plt.scatter(x_data, y_data)
```

The last line of the code fragment shows the dataset (see Figure 4-1).

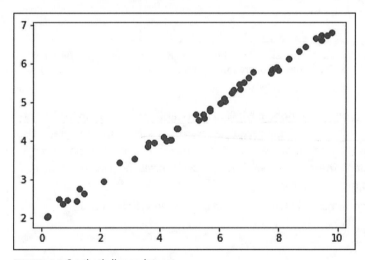

**FIGURE 4-1** Synthetic linear dataset

You implement linear regression, so you would try to find an estimation of y, normally written as y_hat, using a straight line: y_hat = w*x + b. The goal of this process would be to find w and b values that make the difference between y and y_hat minimal. For this purpose, you can use the least square error $(y - y\_hat)^2$ as your loss function (also called target / cost / objective function), the function you are going to minimize.

In order to find these values using CNTK, you must create a computational graph, that is, define which are the system's inputs, which parameters you want to be optimized, and what is the order of the operations. With all of this information CNTK, making use of automatic differentiation, optimizes the values of w and b iteration after iteration. After several iterations, the final values of the parameters approach the original values: w_data and b_data. In Figure 4-2 you can find a graphical representation of what the computational network looks like.

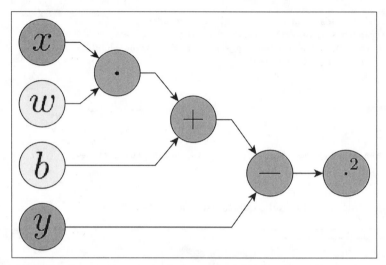

**FIGURE 4-2** Computation graph of a linear regression algorithm. The x and y nodes are inputs, w and b nodes are parameters and the remaining nodes are operations. The rightmost node '·2' performs the squaring operation

If you execute operations from left to right, it is called a forward pass. If you run the derivatives of each operation from right to left, it is a called backwards pass. Note that the graph also includes the loss calculation. The outputs of the '+' node are the predictions y_hat and, from then on, the graph is computing the loss. The backward pass optimizes the parameter values (w and b) in such a way as to minimize the loss.

To define your computational graph in CNTK, just use the following lines of code.

```
x = C.input_variable(1)
y = C.input_variable(1)

w = C.parameter(1)
b = C.parameter(1)

y_hat = x * w + b
loss = C.square(y - y_hat)
```

Notice that everything here is a placeholder, no computation is done. This code only creates the computational graph. You can see it as a circuit, so you are connecting the different elements but no electricity is flowing. Notice that the '*', '-' and '+' operators are overloaded by

CNTK, so in those cases the operators have a behavior different from the one they have in standard Python. In this case, they create nodes in the computational graph and do not perform any calculations.

Now paint the predictions of the model and the data on a plot. Of course, getting good predictions is not expected, since you are only preparing a visualization function that will be used later. The way in which the visualization is done is by evaluating the model at point x=0 and point x=10 (10 is the value of the scale defined when creating the dataset). After evaluating the model at these points, only one line is drawn between the two values.

```
def plot():
    plt.scatter(x_data, y_data)  # plot dataset
    x_line = np.array([[0], [scale]], dtype=np.float32)
    y_line = y_hat.eval({x: x_line})
    plt.plot(x_line.flatten(), y_line.flatten())  # plot predictions

plot()
```

The result of calling the plot function is shown in Figure 4-3. The initial values of w and b are 0, which is why a constant line is painted in 0.

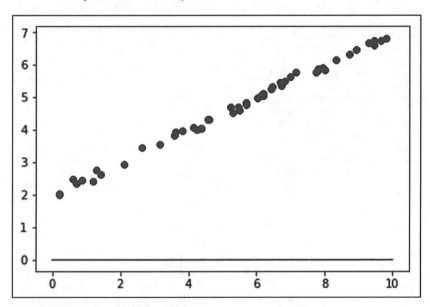

**FIGURE 4-3** Dataset and initial predictions

Train the model using *batch gradient descent* (all samples are used in each iteration). You can do that because there is little data. The following script performs 600 iterations and every 50 iterations shows the model loss on the training data (it actually performs 601 iterations in order to show the loss in the last iteration). The learner used is Stochastic Gradient Descent (*C.sgd*) and uses a learning rate of 0.01.

Note that a test set is not being used and performance is being measured only on the training set. Even if it is not the most correct way to do it, it is a simple experiment that only aims to show how to create and optimize computational networks with CNTK.

```
learner = C.sgd(y_hat.parameters, lr=0.01)  # learning rate = 0.01
trainer = C.Trainer(y_hat, loss, learner)

for i in range(601):
    trainer.train_minibatch({
        x: x_data,
        y: y_data
    })
    if i % 50 == 0:
        print("{0} - Loss: {1}".format(i, trainer.previous_minibatch_loss_
average))
```

Figure 4-4 shows the training output and the plot of the predictions. Now the prediction line is no longer zero and is correctly adjusted to the data.

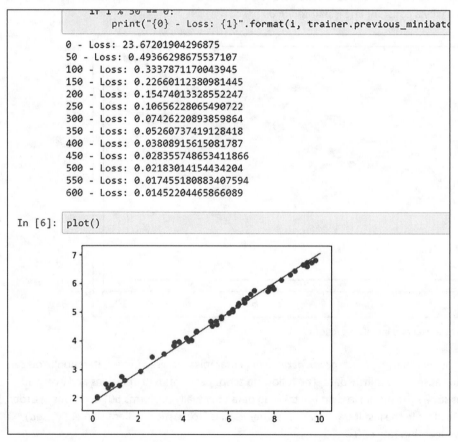

**FIGURE 4-4** Training log and prediction results

Print the values of w and b and you will obtain some values near the original ones, w ≈ 0.5 and b ≈ 2. Notice that you need to use the property *value* to access the current value of the parameters:

```
print("w = {:.3}, b = {:.3}".format(np.asscalar(w.value), np.asscalar(b.value)))
```

This example is a very simple one, used to explain the key concepts of CNTK. There are a lot of operations (nodes in the computation graph) that can be used in CNTK; indeed there are losses already defined so you do not need to explicitly write the least square error manually ('-' and '·2' nodes), you can use a pre-defined operation that implements that loss. For example, you can replace loss = C.square(y – y_hat) with loss = C.squared_loss(y, y_hat). Defining the least squared error manually is trivial, but for complex ones is not so trivial. You see more examples in the next sections.

## Use N-series VMs for GPU acceleration

Although GPUs were initially created to perform computer graphics related tasks, they are now widely used for general-purpose computation (commonly known as general-purpose computing on Graphics Processing Units or GPGPU). This is because the number of cores that a graphics card has is much higher than a typical CPU, allowing parallel operations. Linear algebra is one of the cornerstones of deep learning and the parallelization of operations such as matrix multiplications greatly speeds up training and predictions.

Despite the fact that GPUs are cheaper than other computing hardware (clusters or supercomputers), it is true that buying a GPU can mean a large initial investment and may become outdated after a few years. Azure, the Microsoft cloud, provides solutions to these problems. It enables you to create virtual machines with GPUs, the N-Series virtual machines. Among the N-Series we find two types: the computation-oriented NC-Series and the visualization-oriented NV-Series. Over time, newer versions of graphics cards are appearing and you can make use of them as easily as scaling the machine.

Those machines are great for using the GPU but they need a previous configuration: installing NVIDIA drivers and installing common tools for data science (Python, R, Power BI...).

> ***NEED MORE INFORMATION?*** **INSTALL NVIDIA DRIVERS**
>
> **Visit the documentation to learn how to install NVIDIA drivers for GPUs on N-Series VMs at:** *https://docs.microsoft.com/en-us/azure/virtual-machines/linux/n-series-driver-setup*.

In this section you create a Deep Learning Virtual Machine (DLVM). This machine comes with pre-installed tools for deep learning. Go to Azure and search for it in the Azure Marketplace (see Figure 4-5).

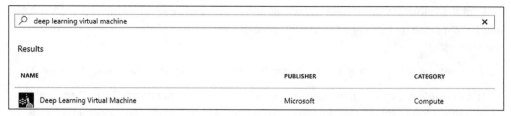

**FIGURE 4-5** DLVM in the Azure Marketplace

The procedure is quite similar to creating any other VM. The only difference is when you have to select the size of the machine, which is restricted to NC-Series sizes (see Figure 4-6). For testing purposes select the NC6, which is the cheaper one.

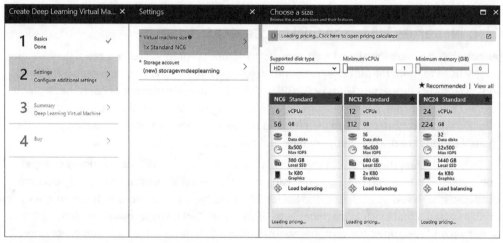

Figure 4-6 In the second step of the Create Deep Learning Virtual Machine you must select the NC-Series sizes

> **NEED MORE INFORMATION? MACHINE SIZES AND PRICES**
>
> Learn about the different GPU machines available in Azure at: *https://docs.microsoft.com/en-us/azure/virtual-machines/windows/sizes-gpu*. Check the prices at: *https://azure.microsoft.com/en-us/pricing/details/virtual-machines*.

Once the machine is created you can connect to it by remote desktop and discover that it comes with a lot of tools installed. Figure 4-7 shows a screenshot of the desktop showing some of the pre-installed tools. This allows you to start development quickly without having to worry about installing tools. The Skill 4.2 lists most of the pre-installed applications that a Windows machine has.

**FIGURE 4-7** Desktop of the DLVM with a lot of pre-installed tools

Open a command window and check that the virtual machine has all the NVIDIA drivers installed and detects that the machine has a GPU connected. Use the command nvidia-smi to do this (see Figure 4-8).

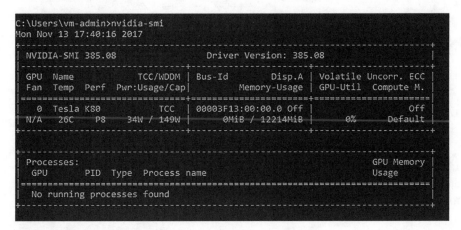

**FIGURE 4-8** Output of the nvidia-smi

# Build and train a three-layer feed forward neural network

After building a simple example of computation graph at the beginning of this skill, it is time to build a deep model using the same principles exposed there: create a differentiable computational graph and optimize it by minimizing a cost function. This time you use a famous handwritten digits dataset: MNIST (introduced in LeCun et al., 1998a). The MNIST dataset contains 70000 images of digits from 0 to 9. Images are black and white and have 28x28 pixels. It is common in the machine learning community to use this dataset for tutorials or to test the effectiveness of new models.

The Figure 4-9 shows the implemented architecture: a three-layer feed forward network. This type of networks is characterized by the fact that neurons between contiguous layers are all connected together (dense or fully connected layers). As has been said before, data are black and white 28x28 images, 784 inputs if the images are unrolled in a single-dimensional array. The neural network has two hidden layers of 400 and 200 neurons and an output layer of 10 neurons, one for each class to predict. In order to convert the neural network output into probabilities, softmax is applied to the output of the last layer.

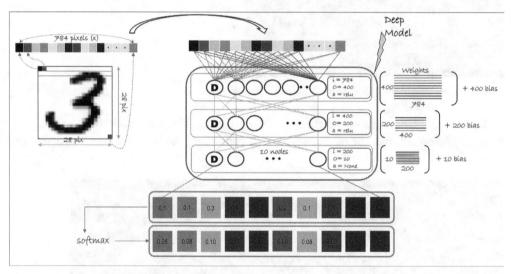

**FIGURE 4-9** Diagram of the implemented architecture

> **NOTE  NCNTK EURAL NETWORKS**
>
> This example is a modified version of the one located at: *https://cntk.ai/pythondocs/CNTK_103C_MNIST_MultiLayerPerceptron.html*.

Each of the neurons in the first layer are connected to all input pixels (784). This means that there is a weight associated with this connection, so in the first layer there are 400 neurons x 784 inputs weights. As in linear regression, each neuron has an intercept term. In machine learning this is also known as bias term. So, the total number of parameters of the first layer are 400 x 784 + 400 bias terms. To obtain the output value of a neuron, what is done internally is to multiply each input by its associated weight, add the results together with the bias and apply the ReLU activation function.

The neurons of the second layer are connected, rather than to the input pixels, to the outputs of the first layer. There are 400 output values from the fist layer and 200 neurons on the second. Each neuron of the second layer is connected to all the neurons of the fist layer (fully connected as before). Following the same calculations as before, the number of parameters of this second layer is 200 x 400 + 200. ReLU is also used as activation function in this layer.

The third and last layer has 10 x 200 + 10 weights. This layer does not use ReLU, but uses softmax to obtain the probability that a given input image is one digit or another. The first neuron in this layer corresponds to the probability of the image being a zero, the second corresponds to the probability of being a one and so on.

The number of neurons and the number of layers are actually hyperparameters of the model. As the number of neurons or layers increases, the expressiveness of the network increases, being able to generate more complex decision boundaries. This is good to some extent, when the number of neurons or layers is very large, in addition to performance problems it is easy to overfit (memorize the training set making the error of generalization very high). More about overfitting has been said in Chapter 2, "Develop machine learning models."

> ***NEED MORE INFORMATION?*** **NEURAL NETWORKS**
>
> A great resource for learning about neural networks is the Geoffrey Hinton course at Coursera: *https://www.coursera.org/learn/neural-networks*. Another good resource is CS231n Convolutional Neural Networks for Visual Recognition at: *http://cs231n.stanford.edu/*.

Create a new Notebook for this exercise. If you are using a Deep Learning Virtual Machine you can run the Jupyter Notebook by clicking the desktop icon (see Figure 4-7).

First write all the necessary imports. Apart from numpy, matplotlib and cntk, you use sklearn to easily load the MNIST dataset.

```
%matplotlib inline
import matplotlib.pyplot as plt

import cntk as C

import numpy as np

from sklearn.datasets import fetch_mldata
```

Fetch the data, preprocess it and split it for training and test. The values of each pixel range from 0 to 255 in grayscale. In order to improve the performance of neural networks, always consider normalizing the inputs, which is why each pixel is divided between 255.

```python
# Get the data and save it in your home directory.
mnist = fetch_mldata('MNIST original', data_home='~')
# Rescale the data
X = mnist.data.astype(np.float32) / 255

# One hot encoding
y = np.zeros((70000, 10), dtype=np.float32)
y[np.arange(0, 70000), mnist.target.astype(int)] = 1

# Shuffle samples.
np.random.seed(0)
p = np.random.permutation(len(X))
X, y = X[p], y[p]

# Split train and test.
X_train, X_test = X[:60000], X[60000:]   # 60000 for training
y_train, y_test = y[:60000], y[60000:]   # 10000 for testing
```

Now that the data is loaded you can create the computational graph.

```python
input_dim = 784
hidden_layers = [400, 200]
num_output_classes = 10

input = C.input_variable((input_dim))
label = C.input_variable((num_output_classes))

def create_model(features):
    with C.layers.default_options(init=C.layers.glorot_uniform(), activation=C.ops.
relu):
        h = features
        for i in hidden_layers:  # for each hidden layer it creates a Dense layer
            h = C.layers.Dense(i)(h)
        return C.layers.Dense(num_output_classes, activation=None)(h)

label_pred = create_model(input)
loss = C.cross_entropy_with_softmax(label_pred, label)
label_error = C.classification_error(label_pred, label)
```

The variable hidden_layers is a list with the number of hidden neurons of each layer. If you add more numbers to the list, more layers are added to the final neural network. Those layers are initialized using Xavier Glorot uniform initialization (C.layers.glorot_uniform) and are using ReLU (C.ops.relu) as activation function. Xavier's initialization is a way to set the initial weights of a network with the objective of increasing gradients to speed up training. ReLU activations are commonly used in deep nets because does not suffer from the vanishing gradient problem. The vanishing gradient problem refers to the fact that using sigmoids or hyperbolic tangents (tanh) as activation functions causes the backpropagation signal to degrade as the number of layers increases. This occurs because the derivatives of these functions are between 0 and 1, so consecutive multiplications of small gradients make the gradient of the first layers close to 0. A gradient close to zero means that the weights are practically not updated after each iteration. ReLU activation implements the function max(0, x), so the derivative when x is positive is always 1, avoiding the vanishing gradient problem.

Notice that this time you have used "multi-operation" nodes like the cross entropy and the dense layer. In this way there is no need to manually implement the Softmax function, or implement the matrix multiplication and bias addition that takes place under the wood in a Dense layer. Most of the time, CNTK manages the optimization of these nodes in an even more efficient way than implementing operation by operation.

Once the computational network has been built, all that remains is to feed it with data, execute forward passes, and optimize the value of the parameters with backward passes.

```python
num_minibatches_to_train = 6001
minibatch_size = 64

learner = C.sgd(label_pred.parameters, 0.2)  # constant learning rate -> 0.2
trainer = C.Trainer(label_pred, (loss, label_error), [learner])

# Create a generator
def minibatch_generator(batch_size):
    i = 0
    while True:
        idx = range(i, i + batch_size)
        yield X_train[idx], y_train[idx]
        i = (i + batch_size) % (len(X_train) - batch_size)
# Get an infinite iterator that returns minibatches of size minibatch_size
get_minibatch = minibatch_generator(minibatch_size)


for i in range(0, num_minibatches_to_train):  # for each minibatch
    # Get minibatch using the iterator get_minibatch
    batch_x, batch_y = next(get_minibatch)
    # Train minibatch
    trainer.train_minibatch({
        input: batch_x,
        label: batch_y
    })
    # Show training loss and test accuracy each 500 minibatches
    if i % 500 == 0:
        training_loss = trainer.previous_minibatch_loss_average
        accuracy = 1 - trainer.test_minibatch({
            input: X_test,
            label: y_test
        })
        print("{} - Train Loss: {:.3f}, Test Accuracy: {:.3f}".format(i, training_
loss, accuracy))
```

Probably the trickiest part of this script is the function minibatch_generator. This function is a Python generator and the variable get_minibatch contains an iterator that returns a different batch each time next(get_minibatch) is called. That part really has nothing to do with CNTK, it's just a way to get different samples in each batch.

During the training, every 500 minibatches, information is printed on screen about the state of the training: number of minibatches, training loss, and the result of the model evaluation on a test set.

The output of the code fragment above is shown in Figure 4-10.

```
0 - Train Loss: 2.403, Test Accuracy: 0.197
500 - Train Loss: 0.230, Test Accuracy: 0.949
1000 - Train Loss: 0.058, Test Accuracy: 0.966
1500 - Train Loss: 0.037, Test Accuracy: 0.968
2000 - Train Loss: 0.072, Test Accuracy: 0.972
2500 - Train Loss: 0.064, Test Accuracy: 0.972
3000 - Train Loss: 0.058, Test Accuracy: 0.976
3500 - Train Loss: 0.036, Test Accuracy: 0.977
4000 - Train Loss: 0.034, Test Accuracy: 0.975
4500 - Train Loss: 0.004, Test Accuracy: 0.976
5000 - Train Loss: 0.059, Test Accuracy: 0.975
5500 - Train Loss: 0.010, Test Accuracy: 0.980
6000 - Train Loss: 0.018, Test Accuracy: 0.981
```

FIGURE 4-10 Training output log, in 6000 minibatches the network reaches 98.1 percent accuracy

It is always convenient to display some examples of the test set and check the performance of the model. The following script creates a grid of plots in which random samples are painted. The title of each plot is the value of its label and the value predicted by the algorithm. If these values do not match, the title will be painted in red to indicate an error.

```python
def plotSample(ax, n):
    ax.imshow(X_test[n].reshape(28,28), cmap="gray_r")
    ax.axis('off')
    # The next two lines use argmax to pass from one-hot encoding to number.
    label = y_test[n].argmax()
    predicted = label_pred.eval({input: [X_test[n]]}).argmax()
    # If correct: black title, if error: red
    title_prop = {"color": "black" if label == predicted else "red"}
    ax.set_title("Label: {}, Predicted: {}".format(label, predicted), title_prop)

np.random.seed(2)  # for reproducibility
fig, ax = plt.subplots(nrows=4, ncols=4, figsize=(10, 6))
for row in ax:
    for col in row:
        plotSample(col, np.random.randint(len(X_test)))
```

Execute the code. If you use the same random seed, the samples should be like those in Figure 4-11. The value 2 has been chosen as seed because it offers samples in which errors have been made; other random seed values give fewer or no errors. A very interesting way to evaluate neural networks is to look at the errors. In the Figure 4-11 you can see that both misclassifications occur in numbers that are cut below. This kind of visualization can help you to discover bugs in data acquisition or preprocessing. Other common bugs that can be discovered visualizing errors are bad labeled examples, where the algorithm fails because it is actually detecting the correct class but the label is not correct.

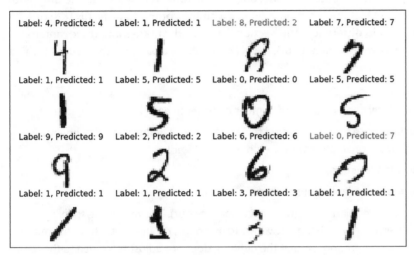

**FIGURE 4-11** Showing examples of predictions, errors are in red

The model is already properly trained and has been proven to work. The example ends here, but consider playing with some hyperparameters like the number of hidden layers/neurons, minibatch size, learning rate, or even other learners different to SGD.

In addition to what you have seen, CNTK offers you many options that have not been discussed: a lot of different operations and losses, data readers, saving trained models to disk, and loading them to later executions.

---

***NEED MORE INFORMATION?* DEPLOY MODELS**

Visit the documentation to learn how to deploy your training models in different environments at: *https://docs.microsoft.com/en-us/cognitive-toolkit/CNTK-Evaluation-Overview.*

---

***NEED MORE INFORMATION?* CNTK PYTHON API DOCUMENTATION**

Get a complete description of each of the methods offered by the CNTK Python API at: *https://www.cntk.ai/pythondocs/cntk.html.*

# Determine when to implement a neural network

You have seen something about neural nets on Azure Machine Learning in Skill 2.1. One section of that skill discussed how to create and train neural networks using the Azure Machine Learning module. It was mentioned that, in order to define the structure of the network, it was necessary to write a Net# script. An example was shown on how to construct a neural network with two hidden layers and an output of 10 neurons with Softmax activation. In fact, that example addressed the same problem as in the previous section: classification using the MNIST dataset. If we compare the four Net# lines and the dragging and dropping of Azure Machine Learning modules with the complexity of a CNTK script, you see that there is a big difference. This section lists the advantages and disadvantages of implementing your own neural network in CNTK as opposed to using the Azure Machine Learning module.

With Net# you can:

- Create hidden layers and control the number of nodes in each layer.
- Specify how layers are to be connected to each other and define special connectivity structures, such as convolutions and weight sharing bundles.
- Specify activation functions.

But it has other important limitations such as:

- It does not accept regularization (neither L2 nor dropout). This makes the training more difficult, especially with big networks. To avoid this problem, you have to limit the number of training iterations so that the network does not adjust too much to the data (overfitting).
- The number of activation functions that you can use are limited and you cannot define your own activation functions either. For example, there is no ReLU activation that are commonly used in deep learning due to their benefits in backpropagation.
- There are certain aspects that you cannot modify, such as the batch size of the Stochastic Gradient Descent (SGD). Besides that, you cannot use other optimization algorithms; you can use SGD with momentum, but not others like Adam, or RMSprop.
- You cannot define recurrent or recursive neural networks.

Apart from the Net# limitations, the information provided during training in the output log is quite limited and cannot be changed (see Figure 4-12).

```
[ModuleOutput]
[ModuleOutput] ***** Net definition *****
[ModuleOutput]   input Data [784];
[ModuleOutput]   hidden H_1 [300] sigmoid from Data all;
[ModuleOutput]   output Result [10] sigmoid from H_1 all;
[ModuleOutput] ***** Reduced *****
[ModuleOutput]   input Data 784;
[ModuleOutput]   hidden H_1 300 sigmoid from Data all;
[ModuleOutput]   output Result 10 sigmoid from H_1 all;
[ModuleOutput] ***** End net definition *****
[ModuleOutput] Input count: 784
[ModuleOutput] Output count: 10
[ModuleOutput] Output Function: Sigmoid
[ModuleOutput] Loss Function: CrossEntropyLoss
[ModuleOutput] PreTrainer: NoPreTrainer
[ModuleOutput] Input normalization: MinMaxNormalizer
[ModuleOutput] Normalizing training data...
[ModuleOutput] _____
[ModuleOutput] Starting training...
[ModuleOutput] Learning rate: 0.100000
[ModuleOutput] Momentum: 0.000000
[ModuleOutput] InitWtsDiameter: 0.100000
[ModuleOutput] _____
[ModuleOutput] Initializing 1 Hidden Layers, 238510 Weights...
[ModuleOutput] Estimated Pre-training MeanError = 7.421581
[ModuleOutput] Iter:1/50, MeanErr=0.397516(-94.64%), 2564.17M WeightUpdates/sec
[ModuleOutput] Iter:2/50, MeanErr=0.189279(-52.38%), 2595.72M WeightUpdates/sec
[ModuleOutput] Iter:3/50, MeanErr=0.134265(-29.07%), 2580.32M WeightUpdates/sec
[ModuleOutput] Iter:4/50, MeanErr=0.099158(-26.15%), 2439.03M WeightUpdates/sec
[ModuleOutput] Iter:5/50, MeanErr=0.074416(-24.95%), 1973.67M WeightUpdates/sec
[ModuleOutput] Iter:6/50, MeanErr=0.056943(-23.48%), 2509.95M WeightUpdates/sec
[ModuleOutput] Iter:7/50, MeanErr=0.043253(-24.04%), 2597.97M WeightUpdates/sec
[ModuleOutput] Iter:8/50, MeanErr=0.031837(-26.39%), 2632.62M WeightUpdates/sec
```

**FIGURE 4-12** Azure Machine Learning output log of a neural network module

With all these shortcomings it is difficult to build a deep neural network that can be successfully trained. But apart from that Net# and log limitations, for deep architectures and to handle a high volume of data (MNIST is actually a small dataset), training a neural network in Azure Machine Learning can be very slow. For all those cases it is preferable to use a GPU-enabled machine. Another drawback of Azure Machine Learning is that it does not allow you to manage the resources dedicated to each experiment. Using an Azure virtual machine you can change the size of the machine whenever you need it.

In CNTK we have all the control during training. For instance, you can stop training when loss goes under a certain threshold. Something as simple as that cannot be done in Azure Machine Learning. All that control comes from the freedom you get from using a programming language.

Programming can become more difficult than managing a graphical interface such as in Azure Machine Learning, but sometimes building a neural network with CNTK is not that much more complicated than writing a complex Net# script. On the other hand, CNTK has a Python API, which is a programming language that is very common in data science and easy to learn. If programming is difficult for you, you should consider using tools like *Keras*. This tool is a high level deep learning library that uses other libraries like *Tensorflow* or CNTK for the computational graph implementation. You can implement a digit classifier with far fewer lines than those shown in the example in the previous section and with exactly the same benefits as using CNTK. Also, CNTK is an open source project, so there is a community that offers support for the tool and a lot of examples are available on the Internet.

> **NEED MORE INFORMATION? BRAINSCRIPT**
>
> Quite similar to Net#, there is a BrainScript language for CNTK that allows you to define models in a non-programmatic way. To learn more, visit: *https://docs.microsoft.com/en-us/cognitive-toolkit/BrainScript-Network-Builder*.

Deep learning models work very well, especially when working with tons of unstructured data. Those big models are almost impossible to implement in Azure Machine Learning due to the computation limitations, but for simple, small, and structured datasets, the use of Azure Machine Learning can be more convenient and achieve the same results as CNTK.

Figure 4-13 shows a summary table with all the pros and cons listed in this section.

| | Comparative table | |
|---|---|---|
| | Azure Machine Learning and Net# | Custom implemented |
| Positive | • Rapid development<br>• Works well with relatively simple datasets (like MNIST)<br>• Cheap | • Accuracy<br>• Fast (VMs with GPUs and powerful CPUs)<br>• Different optimization methods, activations, architectures, regularization...<br>• Full control during training<br>• Manage computing resources (choose VM size) |
| Negative | • Slow<br>• Limited optimization methods, activations, architectures, regularization...<br>• Less control during training<br>• Fixed computing resources | • Difficult to build (requires programming skills and deeper knowledge of machine learning)<br>• Deeper models need much data and much memory<br>• Expensive VM with GPU |

**FIGURE 4-13** Comparative table showing the pros and cons of implementing a neural network with Azure Machine Learning versus custom implementations with tools like CNTK

# Skill 4.2: Streamline development by using existing resources

As in most jobs, like a data science project, it is likely that many things can be reused: tools installation, data pre-processing, model architectures, the way to store the results, and more. The reutilization of some of these processes saves you time while developing data science solutions.

In this Skill you see how Cortana Intelligence Gallery makes it easier for you to access and publish pre-built machine learning solutions. The gallery offers access to Azure Machine Learning experiments, Jupyter Notebooks, projects (usually links to GitHub projects), complete solutions (solutions may contain other Azure elements beyond Azure Machine Learning experiments), tutorials, and custom Azure Machine Learning modules. In addition, all of these items can be grouped into collections, making it easy to access related resources.

You can upload your work to the gallery, so deploying it in another subscription is trivial. And not only that, you can make them public and share them with other users. Just as you can publish solutions that have worked well for you, you can also benefit from the solutions that other users have uploaded. Cortana Intelligence Gallery is, therefore, a powerful community-driven tool.

In addition, in this Skill you see in detail the main advantages of using Azure virtual machines such as the Data Science Virtual Machine or the Deep Learning Virtual Machine (already used in Skill 4.1).

> **This skill covers how to:**
> - Clone template experiments from Cortana Intelligence Gallery
> - Use Cortana Intelligence Quick Start to deploy resources
> - Use a data science VM for streamlined development

## Clone template experiments from Cortana Intelligence Gallery

Throughout the book, references have been made of example experiments that you can use in your learning process. In this section you see how to clone an experiment in your current subscription. You use an example of a digit recognition experiment using convolutional networks defined with Net#.

In order to do so, go to the Cortana Intelligence Gallery page (*https://gallery.cortanaintelligence.com*). The home page shows you the latest news and the most popular resources (see Figure 4-14).

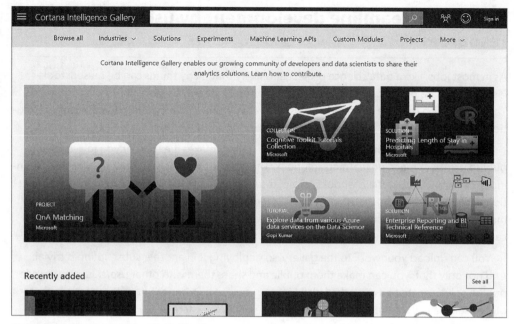

**FIGURE 4-14** Cortana Intelligence Gallery home page

Use the search bar and enter **Neural Networks**, and then press Enter, or click the magnifying glass icon. A list of experiments and some other resources will appear. Note that on the left pane you have a series of filters that allow you to filter results by categories, tags, algorithms used, or programming language used, to name a few examples. Click the Neural Network: Convolution And Pooling Deep Net experiment (see Figure 4-15).

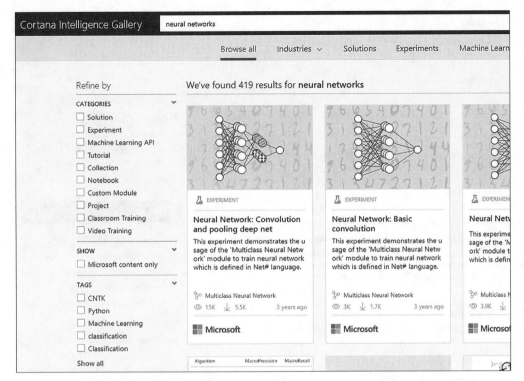

FIGURE 4-15 Neural networks search results

The new page that appears (see Figure 4-16) shows you detailed information about the experiment. The explanation usually includes captures that help you better understand the experiment and show you how to interpret the results correctly.

Related experiments are listed on the right, so it is easy to find similar experiments if you want to try more models. Also on the right you find the button that allows you to clone this experiment in your workspace. Click that button.

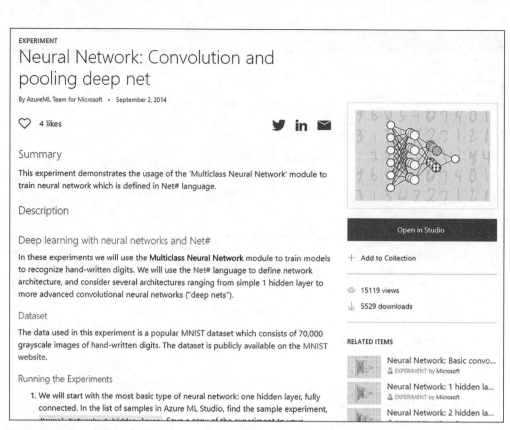

**EXPERIMENT**

# Neural Network: Convolution and pooling deep net

By AzureML Team for Microsoft  •  September 2, 2014

♡  4 likes

## Summary

This experiment demonstrates the usage of the 'Multiclass Neural Network' module to train neural network which is defined in Net# language.

## Description

### Deep learning with neural networks and Net#

In these experiments we will use the **Multiclass Neural Network** module to train models to recognize hand-written digits. We will use the Net# language to define network architecture, and consider several architectures ranging from simple 1 hidden layer to more advanced convolutional neural networks ("deep nets").

### Dataset

The data used in this experiment is a popular MNIST dataset which consists of 70,000 grayscale images of hand-written digits. The dataset is publicly available on the MNIST website.

### Running the Experiments

1. We will start with the most basic type of neural network: one hidden layer, fully connected. In the list of samples in Azure ML Studio, find the sample experiment,

Open in Studio

+ Add to Collection

👁 15119 views

⤓ 5529 downloads

**RELATED ITEMS**

Neural Network: Basic convo...
⚠ EXPERIMENT by Microsoft

Neural Network: 1 hidden la...
⚠ EXPERIMENT by Microsoft

Neural Network: 2 hidden la...

**FIGURE 4-16** Description of a neural network experiment that uses a convolution network with maxpooling

Pressing this button takes you to the Azure Machine Learning Studio. There you can select in which subscription you want to clone the experiment. When you have selected the desired subscription, click the tick button (see Figure 4-17).

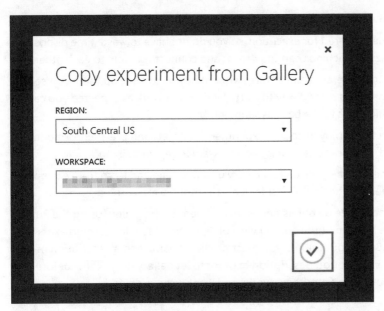

**FIGURE 4-17** Copy experiment from Gallery window that appears in Azure Machine Learning Studio when you open a gallery experiment

After a short charging time, a new experiment opens and you can start working with it.

Another option for cloning the experiment is to do it directly from the Azure Machine Learning Studio. Click the '+ New' in the lower left corner and search again for 'neural networks'. In Figure 4-18 you can find the search result. By placing the cursor over an experiment, you see a green button that reads, Open In Studio. Press to create new experiments directly from the Azure Machine Learning Studio.

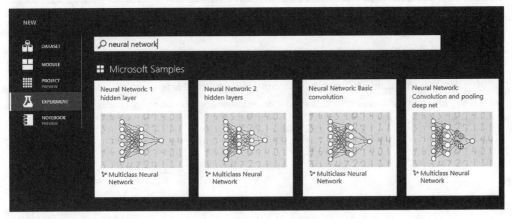

**FIGURE 4-18** Neural networks experiments samples from Azure Machine Learning

Using gallery experiments saves you time in different ways:

- Experiments come prepared for execution, so you do not have to waste time disposing modules in the Azure Machine Learning canvas and connecting them to each other.

- By quickly exploring different architectures without having to develop them yourself. Cloning an experiment is a good way to start; if it does not work as expected you can always add modifications to the base experiment.

- Additionally, with the deployed copied experiments datasets and pre-trained models are also provided, so in some cases it is not necessary to re-run training.

In addition to the time you save, the gallery is very useful to train and learn from examples developed by other experts in the field. Consider it also a resource for learning.

Do not hesitate to contribute by publishing an experiment to the gallery using the Publish To Gallery button at the bottom of the editing view of an Azure Machine Learning experiment (see Figure 4-19). Before publishing, you must provide a name and a description of the experiment. Be sure to write a good description in order to let gallery users know before they clone the experiment how your experiment works and what it can provide.

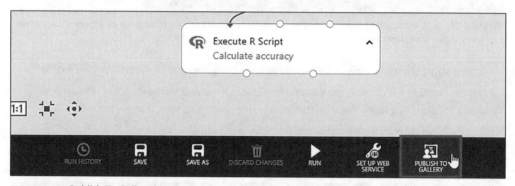

**FIGURE 4-19** Publish To Gallery button

> **NEED MORE INFORMATION? CONTRIBUTE TO THE GALLERY**
>
> Visit the documentation to learn how to contribute to the Cortana Intelligence Gallery at: *https://docs.microsoft.com/en-gbus/azure/machine-learning/studio/gallery-experiments#contribute.*

# Use Cortana Intelligence Quick Start to deploy resources

Cloning experiments is fine when everything you need to implement your solution is within an Azure Machine Learning experiment. It is often necessary to deploy other Azure elements that deal with certain parts of the process, such as data acquisition and pre-processing or saving results in a SQL Database with an added Analysis Services on top of it. Other times it is not necessary to use any Azure Machine Learning experiments, such as the solution that you use in Skill 3.3 where you built a recommendation system. Along those lines, Cortana Intelligence Solution is a prebuilt machine learning solution that you can easily deploy on your subscription.

Go to the front page of the Cortana Intelligence site (see Figure 4-14) and click the tab Solutions. You see a list of solutions that you can easily deploy in your subscription (see Figure 4-20).

**FIGURE 4-20** Cortana Intelligence Solutions

In the ribbon under the header you find a link to the deployed solutions. If you have followed Skill 3.3, you see the recommender solution listed there (see Figure 4-21).

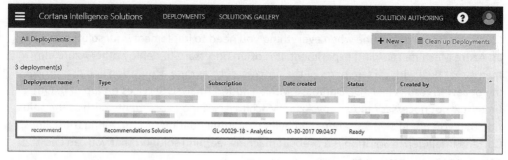

**FIGURE 4-21** List of deployed solutions

Return to the solutions page shown in Figure 4-20, and click the See All button that is on the right side. This takes you to the same page where you searched for experiments with Neural Networks in the previous section, but with the difference that this time the results are filtered by solutions (see Figure 4-22).

**FIGURE 4-22** Searching for solutions in the Cortana Intelligence Gallery

If you are looking for the recommendation solution you deployed in Skill 3-4 you will not find it because it belongs to the Tutorial category and not the Solutions category. Regardless of whether it is a tutorial or a solution, the principle is the same: Azure architecture deploys in just a few clicks.

Scroll down and search for the Demand Forecasting For Shipping And Distribution solution. Click the solution title and you will see a detailed description, similar to the experiments (see Figure 4-23).

SOLUTION
# Demand Forecasting for Shipping and Distribution

By Tomas Singliar for Microsoft  •  June 26, 2017

♡ 4 likes

## Summary

The Demand Forecasting for Shipping and Distribution Solution uses historical demand data to forecast demand in future periods across varios customers, products and destinations. For instance, a shipping or delivery company wants to predict the quantities of the different products its customers want delivered at different locations at future times. A company can use these forecasts as input to an allocation tool that optimizes operations, such as delivery vehicles routing, or to plan capacity in the longer term.

## Description

**Note:** If you have already deployed this solution, click here to view your deployment.

**Estimated Daily Cost:** $4.66

Estimated Provisioning Time: 15 Minutes

Deploy

\+  Add to Collection

👁 2215 views

**FIGURE 4-23**  Demand Forecasting For Shipping And Distribution Solution

Scroll down and, in the right column, you see the list of used elements for that solution. In the Demand Forecasting solution, a lot of Azure elements will be deployed (see Figure 4-24).

SERVICES USED

Azure Data Factory

Azure Machine Learning

Azure Sql

Azure Blob Storage

PowerBI

**FIGURE 4-24**  Services used by the Demand Forecasting For Shipping And Distribution solution

Clicking Deploy takes you to a deployment wizard (see Figure 4-25) very similar to the one seen in Skill 3.4: Consume exemplar Cognitive Services APIs. For a complete deployment example, review the recommendations system deployment carried out in that Skill.

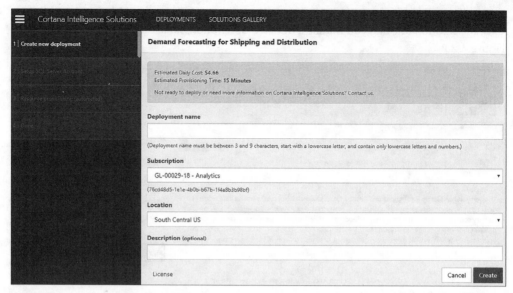

**FIGURE 4-25** Solutions Deployment Wizard

As with the gallery's experiments, Cortana Intelligence Solutions, in addition to saving you time allows you to use architectures designed by experts and ensure you get good predictions, performance, and scalability. They are also good resources for training and education.

## Use a data science VM for streamlined development

The Data Science Virtual Machine (DSVM) is a virtual machine image that aims to save you time by providing a predefined environment for doing data science. The Azure Virtual Machines minimize hardware maintenance and allows you to scale resources easily. DSVMs are currently available on Windows Server, Ubuntu, and Cent OS. A special type of DSVM is the Deep Learning Virtual Machine (DLVM) that, in addition to the data science tools, contains tools specifically designed for deep learning and is configured to use GPUs.

The prerequisite for creating Azure Virtual Machines is a subscription. You should keep in mind that the number of cores of the machine you want to create must not exceed the limit set by your subscription. In Skill 4.1, you have seen how to create and use a DLVM. You also will create a DSVM in the first section of Skill 4.4. Because two examples are given in this book on the creation of virtual machines, in this section you look at different use cases and the preinstalled tools.

You have already seen some of the advantages provided by these machines, but here you find a more detailed list of different scenarios in which a DSVM or a DLVM can be useful:

- **Preconfigured workspace**   With zero configurations, you can get a cloud computer ready to solve data science problems. If you are working in teams, the work is more comfortable because there will not be any problems with versions, as could be the case with personal desktop computers.

- **Training**   If you are giving a course and want to give exercises to the students, the environments of a DSVM are perfect because it leads to predictable results. Very easy to deploy in a lecture or for students. Moreover, the ease with which machines are deployed also makes it convenient to create one machine per student.

- **Scalability**   Usually, while defining the models and performing small tests, a powerful machine is not necessary, but when working with a lot of data, it is normal to increase the size of the machine during preprocessing and model training. Azure virtual machines can be easily scaled, so you do not need to create a new machine with better capabilities for heavy tasks, you can use the same.

- **Quick experiments**   Sometimes you may want to test new tools, make demos, or replicate published experiments. For all of those tasks, a DSVM is useful.

- **Deep learning**   Regarding deep learning, you have already seen the facilities it can provide. In addition to all the pre-installed tools, mounting the images of a DSVM on N-series machines gives you GPU acceleration, a required condition to train deep models in reasonable time. Use DLVMs to write applications capable of performing difficult tasks such as understanding images, videos, or text. Deep learning shines in these kinds of tasks, sometimes even surpassing the performance of a human in many tasks.

As mentioned above, there are three different images of the DSVM depending on the operating system used. Below are some of the applications and tools preinstalled in the Windows version:

- **Microsoft ML Server Developer Edition**   You use this powerful tool in Skill 4.4.

- **Anaconda Python**   Two distributions are available: 2.7 and 3.5 versions. Anaconda is a Python environment in which most of the packages used for data science are pre-installed. Among them are numpy, pandas, and sklearn to name a few. Jupyter Notebooks also come with Anaconda distributions.

- **JuliaPro**  A complete distribution of the Julia programming language, including scientific and data science libraries.

- **Azure Machine Learning Workbench**  It is a desktop application plus command-line tools that allows you to manage machine learning solutions through the entire data science life cycle.

- **Visual Studio**  Community Edition and other IDEs and code editors.

- **Power BI**  Desktop.

- **SQL Server 2017**  Developer Edition.

- **Spark**  Standalone instance for local development and testing (includes a PySpark kernel for Jupyter Notebooks).

- **Git**  Git Bash and Visual Studio Team Services.

- **Other machine learning and data analytics tools**  Such as XGBoost, Tensorflow, Keras, CNTK, mxNet, Weka, Vowpal Wabbit, Apache Drill, and Rattle.

Notice that all of the tools listed here are not available in all of the operating systems. For instance, Power BI is only available in Windows Server. Linux versions of the DSVM are more oriented toward the use of deep learning. The two Linux versions have libraries like Caffe, Caffe2, Torch, Theano, and NVIDIA DIGITS, which the Windows DSVM version does not have.

> ***NEED MORE INFORMATION?*** **WINDOWS AND LINUX PREINSTALLED PROGRAMS**
>
> Check the following comparison table to see the differences between DSVMs in Windows and Linux at: *https://docs.microsoft.com/en-us/azure/machine-learning/data-science-virtual-machine/overview*.

In addition to individual virtual machines, Azure allows you to deploy large clusters (computer groups working in a coordinated way). In the next Skill you review how to manage clusters.

# Skill 4.3: Perform data science at scale by using HDInsight

This skill covers how to perform data science processes when your datasets are too big to fit in your typical development environment (e.g. your laptop) or Azure Machine Learning. On the other hand, maybe the type of data you are dealing with is too complex to be ingested with a regular tabular form and needs to be pre-treated with appropriate languages and storage platforms (e.g. big data technology) before you are able to create models on top of it.

> **This skill covers how to:**
> - Deploy the appropriate type of HDInsight cluster
> - Perform exploratory data analysis by using Spark SQL
> - Build and use Machine Learning models with Spark on HDI
> - Build and use Machine Learning models using MapReduce
> - Build and use Machine Learning models using Microsoft R Server

## Deploy the appropriate type of HDInsight cluster

HDInsight is the Microsoft cloud-based implementation of Hadoop clusters. It is offered as PaaS (Platform as a Service), giving you most of the common Hadoop Data Platform (HDP) services, such as HBase, Storm, or Spark, to name a few. When you create an HDInsight cluster, several VMs (either Windows or Linux) are provisioned and deployed, creating a connected and running cluster in around 20 minutes. The cluster is available worldwide, as any other PaaS resource in Azure.

You can use either Blob Storage Containers or Data Lake Storage accounts as the primary storage for your HDInsight cluster. Consequently, all data that you can access can be unstructured, semi-structured, or fully structured. You can delete the cluster if you are done using it, but the storage is available after the clusters deletion. Having computation (the cluster itself) detached from the storage (Blob Storage / Data Lake) allows you to have your clusters up and running only for the time you need them, destroying them when your data analyses are finished and thus save money. Depending on the services you need to use on top of your data you will create different cluster types, each of them with different price rates.

To create your HDInsight cluster you need to log into your Azure Portal and click New, and search HDInsight, and then Create. A step-by-step form appears. You will provide a cluster name, the type of the cluster, and the basic storage settings. In the example, basic security (user and password, both for administrative user and the secure connection –ssh- user) has been selected, although a private and public key could have been used if you had corporate keys and want to use certificates to connect securely. Note that you need to use a private and public key to connect from a local Visual Studio environment. As seen in Figure 4-26, you can select different cluster types.

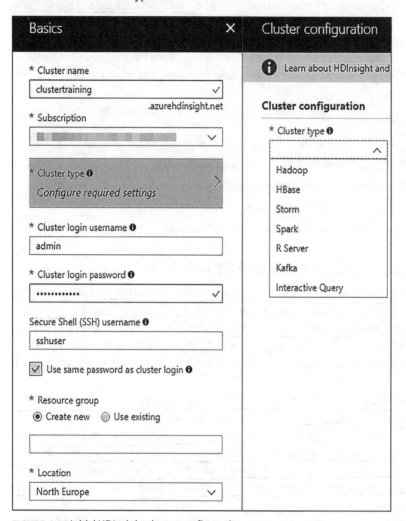

**FIGURE 4-26** Initial HDInsight cluster configuration

The different types of clusters are based in the same structures, as described; supported at the time of writing this book are:

- **Hadoop** The basic option uses HDFS, YARN, and Map Reduce programming models to process and analyze potentially massive and diverse data in a batch, parallel fashion. Tools like Hive for SQL-like queries are available in this mode.

- **HBase**   A NoSQL database on top of a traditional Hadoop cluster, providing strong consistency for large amounts of unstructured and semi-structured data.
- **Storm**   A distributed, real-time computation system for processing large streams of data. It is extremely scalable but requires manual implementation of its main elements, bolts, and spouts in Java or C# programming languages.
- **Spark**   A parallel processing framework that supports in-memory processing to boost big data analysis. Spark includes SQL-like, streaming data or machine learning applications that use the framework.
- **R Server**   A server for hosting and managing parallel, distributed R processes. It offers many improvements from the base R language with the ScaleR and other proprietary packages. It works both with Spark and with classic Hadoop jobs, acting as a "translator" of R scripts into Spark applications or Map Reduce jobs.
- **Kafka**   An open-source platform used for building streaming data pipelines and applications. It provides message-queue functionality, allowing you to publish and subscribe to data streams. It is often used along with Storm in the implementation of real-time event processing systems.
- **Interactive Query**   In-memory caching and improved columnar storage engine for Hive queries.

In this case, an R Server cluster is used so you will see examples and demos with it in the skill. Because R Server sits on top of a Spark cluster, all the features available in a Spark cluster are also available in an R Server cluster. R Server clusters include an extra node called Edge Node where the R Server engine resides, and the rest of the cluster is a normal Spark cluster. The Edge Node appears as "EN0" in Figure 4-27, where you can find the high-level architecture.

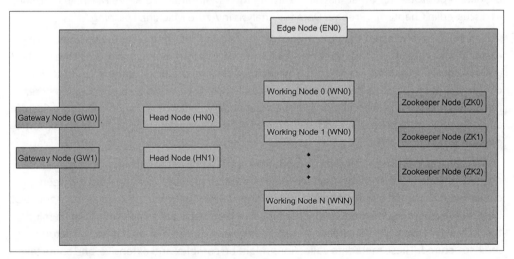

**FIGURE 4-27** HDInsight Spark high-level architecture

The rest of the elements might be defined as follows:

- **HN - Head nodes**   Hadoop services under any HDInsight cluster type are installed and run in the head nodes. There are two head nodes to ensure high availability of these services. Therefore, head nodes control the access to the data and how computations are performed in the worker nodes.

- **WN - Worker nodes**   Worker nodes (also known as data nodes in different documentation) are the nodes that perform the computations on the data. They all can act in parallel to resolve a computation (sent by an application), or just some of them can be running an activity. They provide redundant access to the data.

- **GW - Gateway nodes**   By default each Spark cluster has two Gateway nodes for management and security. These nodes control access and management features as the Ambari Web UI or the SSH connections against the rest of the nodes in the cluster.

- **ZK - Zookeeper nodes**   Zookeeper nodes are used for leader election of master services on head nodes and to ensure that worker nodes and gateways know which head node has which master services running on. They are, in fact, responsible for availability and reliability of Hadoop clusters in HDInsight.

The election of the cluster type depends mainly on the type of workload you intend to perform with it. In this case, because you want to explore and build machine learning models on top of your datasets, either structured or unstructured, the ideal election seems to be R Server on Spark because both engines included have already been discussed. However, you can perform machine learning with other cluster configurations: only Spark using the MLlib, Spark with third-party applications like H2O machine learning, or classic Hadoop with Mahout to name a few. Even further, you might want to use other configurations like Hive on Hadoop to serve as big data repositories for other machine learning tools or libraries like Azure Machine Learning, as discussed in Chapter 1, "Prepare Data for Analysis in Azure Machine Learning."

Once you have selected the type of cluster, you need to set up the storage settings. In the example, an Azure Storage account has been selected. That storage account holds the master and configuration data for you cluster. You can provide a secondary storage account to your cluster in order to access data from many sources. Different combinations are possible here: using an Azure storage account for your main data that you can reuse when creating a cluster on demand for data processing and accessing an Azure Data Lake Store as well as to consume data stored there.

You can also choose your metastore settings in case you want to preserve your metadata defined in Hive or Oozie (a workflow scheduler system to manage Hadoop jobs) between cluster creations when using a creation-processing-deletion schema. You can use an Azure SQL Database (even a very inexpensive one) to preserve that metadata to re-use it. Keep in mind that in Hive, for example, you create metadata to query your data, even if it is unstructured or semi-structured. These metadata collections might be complex and extensive, and some take a lot of time to develop. Consider saving this metadata if you do not want to lose all that development. For a complete example of storage options, see Figure 4-28.

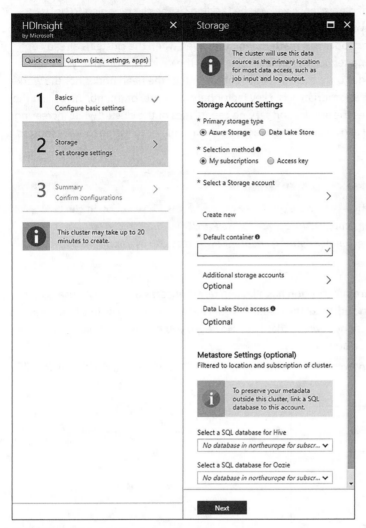

**FIGURE 4-28** HDInsight Spark storage settings

For a detailed cluster creation process, click the Custom (Size, Setting, Apps) button in the main creation blade. In this custom mode you get to choose the third-party apps that you want to pre-install in your cluster, if it applies. In the example, at the moment of writing this book, there are no applications available for an R Server cluster on Linux. However, many applications are ready to pre-install in other types of clusters, easing the process to automatically provision an HDInsight cluster.

The next step is to choose among different sizes for your cluster's nodes. Choosing the right size is not an easy task before you know your requisites: How big is your data? How fast will it grow? Which kinds of data science will you be tackling? Is the cluster going to be used to run other workloads beyond data science? Luckily, having HDInsight in Azure allows you to scale the number of worker nodes in a matter of minutes even when the cluster is already up and running, although some services might be restarted in the process. Note that you cannot change the sizes of the nodes once the cluster is created, neither the head nodes nor the workers. Therefore, sizing them appropriately is a key factor here. As a rule of thumb, increasing the size of head nodes increases the application serving capabilities of the cluster, while increasing the worker nodes sizes will allow us to run more jobs concurrently or to assign more resources to each job or query.

***NEED MORE INFORMATION?*** **CLUSTER SIZING**

**Check the following articles for more guidance on the hardware selection in clusters:**
*https://docs.hortonworks.com/HDPDocuments/HDP2/HDP-2.6.3/bk_cluster-planning/
content/ch_hardware-recommendations_chapter.html, https://0x0fff.com/hadoop-
cluster-sizing/.*

Consider that each Azure subscription has a limit in terms of cores that you can use, so the total number of cores in (including all the nodes in your cluster and other clusters that might exist in your subscription) cannot exceed that limit. However, you can ask for a higher limit contacting your subscription admin.

In the example shown in Figure 4-29, a two-worker node cluster is created with the default node sizes.

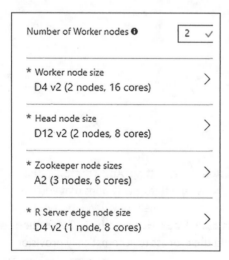

**FIGURE 4-29** Node sizes

The fifth step in the creation process is to establish possible Script Actions and advanced networking options. In this example, this is not necessary, but keep in mind Script Actions if you need to install extra R packages in your nodes for your scripts. You will need to create a Script Action (one of the pre-configured existing ones) to set up such packages in your nodes, both edge and workers. You can also invoke custom bash (remember that you are working with Linux nodes in this case) scripts performing your own actions.

In the last step you see the summary of all your configurations before proceeding to create the cluster. Just click Create to provision your cluster.

## Perform exploratory data analysis by using Spark SQL

As in any data science problem, an initial exploratory data analysis is fundamental to understanding your data and, at least having a basic comprehension of how much data is there, its distribution, and the relationships present between the features. By default, all HDInsight clusters come with sample data that you can use to test your applications or try different features on. In this example the Food Inspections dataset shows public restaurant inspections results from the city of Chicago.

Spark is a framework that allows you to process data and run applications in an in-memory fashion accessing the data stored in your HDInsight clusters. Many applications can run on top of that framework, leveraging the in-memory capabilities and the different programming languages available (natively, Java, Scala, and Python). These applications can be included in regular HDInsight Spark clusters, or are available to install as third-party applications.

One of these applications is Spark SQL, an engine that allows you to write SQL queries on top of in-memory data structures, which may come from many data sources. In the example, you access a CSV file present in the default Azure Storage Blob Container.

Once you have your HDInsight cluster already created you can write Spark SQL queries, for example, using a Jupyter Notebook running on top of Spark. You can access your list of Jupyter Notebooks on your HDInsight cluster clicking R Server Dashboards in your main cluster blade in the Azure Portal (see Figure 4.30).

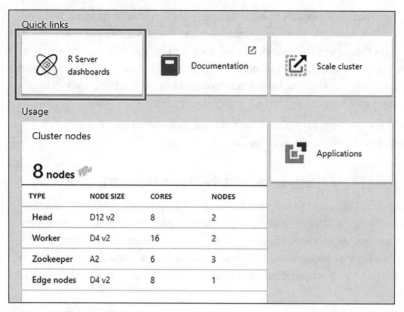

**FIGURE 4-30** R Server dashboards link

Once you have access to the reports, click the Jupyter Notebook button to launch the notebook tree (see Figure 4.31).

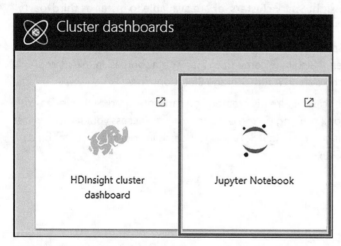

**FIGURE 4-31** Jupyter Notebook trees link

You can access the same web UI using the URL: *https://name_of_your_cluster.azurehdinsight. net/jupyter/tree*. Here you see a list of existing Notebooks. To create a new Notebook, click the upper right button New and PySpark to create a Python notebook, as you did in Skill 1.2.

To start using the notebook and import the needed libraries from Spark SQL, you need a piece of code like the following:

```
from pyspark.sql import Row
from pyspark.sql.functions import UserDefinedFunction
from pyspark.sql.types import *
```

A Spark application is created automatically, as needed in any interaction with the Spark framework. You can use the sqlContext created automatically within the application to perform transformations on structured data as the CSV file that you will access, as well as many other libraries available in Python. See Figure 4-32 to see an example of a Spark application started.

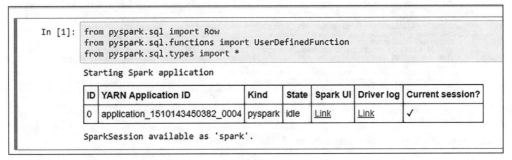

FIGURE 4-32 Spark application started in a Jupyter Notebook

Your source data in this example is a CSV file. Therefore, you need to define a function that parses the data read from the raw text file. The results are stored in a Spark Resilient Distributed Dataset (RDD) because Spark SQL has not yet been invoked, and RDDs are Spark native data structure. You can use the "map" method, which is implemented by RDDs, to apply the function to the RDD returned by the "textFile" raw reader. You can find how in the following code:

```
def csvParser(s):
    import csv
    from StringIO import StringIO
    sio = StringIO(s)
    value = csv.reader(sio).next()
    sio.close()
    return value

# The sc variable is by default the name of the SparkContext, created when the Spark
application is initialized
restaurants = sc.textFile('wasb:///HdiSamples/HdiSamples/FoodInspectionData/Food_
Inspections1.csv').map(csvParse)
restaurants.take(1)
```

The output of this is the first row of the parsed CSV file stored in the RDD. As you can see in Figure 4-33, this row is not a header row because it is sometimes found in text files.

```
In [16]:   def csvParse(s):
               import csv
               from StringIO import StringIO
               sio = StringIO(s)
               value = csv.reader(sio).next()
               sio.close()
               return value

           restaurants = sc.textFile('wasb:///HdiSamples/HdiSamples/FoodInspectionData/Food_Inspections1.csv').map(csvParse)

           restaurants.take(1)

[[['413707', 'LUNA PARK INC', 'LUNA PARK DAY CARE', '2049789', "Children's Services Facility", 'Risk 1 (High)', '3250 W FOSTER
AVE ', 'CHICAGO', 'IL', '60625', '09/21/2010', 'License-Task Force', 'Fail', '24. DISH WASHING FACILITIES: PROPERLY DESIGNED,
CONSTRUCTED, MAINTAINED, INSTALLED, LOCATED AND OPERATED - Comments: All dishwashing machines must be of a type that complies
with all requirements of the plumbing section of the Municipal Code of Chicago and Rules and Regulation of the Board of Healt
h. OBSERVED THE 3 COMPARTMENT SINK BACKING UP INTO THE 1ST AND 2ND COMPARTMENT WITH CLEAR WATER AND SLOWLY DRAINING OUT. INST N
EED HAVE IT REPAIR. CITATION ISSUED, SERIOUS VIOLATION 7-38-030 H000062369-10 COURT DATE 10-28-10 TIME 1 P.M. ROOM 107 400 W. S
URPERIOR. | 36. LIGHTING: REQUIRED MINIMUM FOOT-CANDLES OF LIGHT PROVIDED, FIXTURES SHIELDED - Comments: Shielding to protect a
gainst broken glass falling into food shall be provided for all artificial lighting sources in preparation, service, and displa
y facilities. LIGHT SHIELD ARE MISSING UNDER HOOD OF  COOKING EQUIPMENT AND NEED TO REPLACE LIGHT UNDER UNIT. 4 LIGHTS ARE OUT
 IN THE REAR CHILDREN AREA,IN THE KINDERGARDEN CLASS ROOM. 2 LIGHT ARE OUT EAST REAR, LIGHT FRONT WEST ROOM. NEED TO REPLACE AL
L LIGHT THAT ARE NOT WORKING. | 35. WALLS, CEILINGS, ATTACHED EQUIPMENT CONSTRUCTED PER CODE: GOOD REPAIR, SURFACES CLEAN AND D
UST-LESS CLEANING METHODS - Comments: The walls and ceilings shall be in good repair and easily cleaned. MISSING CEILING TILES
 WITH STAINS IN WEST,EAST, IN FRONT AREA WEST, AND BY THE 15MOS AREA. NEED TO BE REPLACED. | 32. FOOD AND NON-FOOD CONTACT SURF
ACES PROPERLY DESIGNED, CONSTRUCTED AND MAINTAINED - Comments: All food and non-food contact equipment and utensils shall be sm
ooth, easily cleanable, and durable, and shall be in good repair. SPLASH GUARDED ARE NEEDED BY THE EXPOSED HAND SINK IN THE KIT
CHEN AREA | 34. FLOORS: CONSTRUCTED PER CODE, CLEANED, GOOD REPAIR, COVING INSTALLED, DUST-LESS CLEANING METHODS USED - Comment
s: The floors shall be constructed per code, be smooth and easily cleaned, and be kept clean and in good repair. INST NEED TO E
LEVATE ALL FOOD ITEMS 6INCH OFF THE FLOOR 6 INCH AWAY FORM WALL. ', '41.97583445690982', '-87.7107455232781', '(41.97583445690
982, -87.7107455232781)']]
```

FIGURE 4-33 CSV file processed with a Python function in Spark

In order to process data with Spark SQL you need some structure in the dataset. Even when reading data from a CSV file (which is structured, although our data sources might be unstructured or semi-structured) you need to apply a schema to be able to process it with Spark SQL. You can do this in Python in Spark creating a Struct object and applying it using the lambda function. On top of that you can create a Spark SQL DataFrame, another type of object that allows you to write SQL queries using that object with the give schema. In the following code and in Figure 4-34 you see examples of this process.

```
#Define the struct object that will apply the desired schema
schema = StructType([
 StructField("name", StringType(), False),
 StructField("Type", StringType(), False),
 StructField("RiskLevel", StringType(), False),
 StructField("Date", StringType(), False),
 StructField("results", StringType(), False),
 StructField("violations", StringType(), True)])

#apply the lambda function and parse the output object into a Spark SQL dataframe
using the context
# As with the sc variable, sqlContext is created when the Spark session is
initialized
df = sqlContext.createDataFrame(restaurants.map(lambda l: (l[1], l[4], l[5],
l[10], l[12], l[13])) , schema)

#show the first 5 elements of the Spark SQL DataFrame
df.show(5)
```

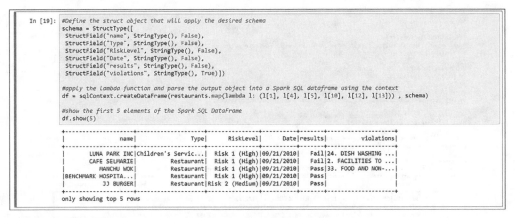

```
In [19]:   #Define the struct object that will apply the desired schema
           schema = StructType([
             StructField("name", StringType(), False),
             StructField("Type", StringType(), False),
             StructField("RiskLevel", StringType(), False),
             StructField("Date", StringType(), False),
             StructField("results", StringType(), False),
             StructField("violations", StringType(), True)])

           #apply the lambda function and parse the output object into a Spark SQL dataframe using the context
           df = sqlContext.createDataFrame(restaurants.map(lambda l: (l[1], l[4], l[5], l[10], l[12], l[13])) , schema)

           #show the first 5 elements of the Spark SQL DataFrame
           df.show(5)

           +---------------+-----------------+-------------+----------+-------+--------------------+
           |           name|             Type|    RiskLevel|      Date|results|          violations|
           +---------------+-----------------+-------------+----------+-------+--------------------+
           | LUNA PARK INC|Children's Servic...| Risk 1 (High)|09/21/2010|   Fail|24. DISH WASHING ...|
           | CAFE SELMARIE|       Restaurant| Risk 1 (High)|09/21/2010|   Fail|2. FACILITIES TO ...|
           |    MANCHU WOK|       Restaurant| Risk 1 (High)|09/21/2010|   Pass|33. FOOD AND NON-...|
           |BENCHMARK HOSPITA...|  Restaurant| Risk 1 (High)|09/21/2010|   Pass|                    |
           |      JJ BURGER|       Restaurant|Risk 2 (Medium)|09/21/2010|   Pass|                    |
           +---------------+-----------------+-------------+----------+-------+--------------------+
           only showing top 5 rows
```

**FIGURE 4-34** Spark SQL DataFrame created and temporal table registered

You can even manipulate the data using other Python libraries like Pandas and custom defined functions. Pandas is a popular data structure manipulation open source library that might ease the manipulation process. In this example you go through a simple example but keep in mind that these custom defined functions might be invoking other more complex algorithms or libraries, enriching your dataset with little effort. Finally, you need to register the Spark SQL DataFrame as a temporary table in order to write SQL queries and visualize the results.

See the following code and Figure 4-35 for an example of this, counting the number of occurrences of the "pipe" character (|), and therefore retrieving the number of items in the text column called "violations" in the DataFrame shown in Figure 4-34.

```
import pandas as pd

def countViolations(st):
    number = len(st.split('|'))-1 #When no | is found, it would retrieve 1, so we
substract 1 by default
    return number

#cast the DataFrame into a Pandas data frame
df_pd = df.toPandas()

#create a new row applying the custom function
df_pd['numberOfViolations'] = df_pd['violations'].apply(countViolations)

#cast the object back into a Spark SQL DataFrame
df = sqlContext.createDataFrame(df_pd)

#register the DataFrame as a temporal table in Spark SQL
df.registerTempTable('restaurantsTable')

df.show(5)
```

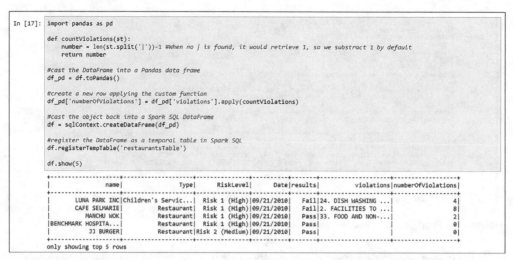

```
In [17]:  import pandas as pd

          def countViolations(st):
              number = len(st.split('|'))-1 #When no | is found, it would retrieve 1, so we substract 1 by default
              return number

          #cast the DataFrame into a Pandas data frame
          df_pd = df.toPandas()

          #create a new row applying the custom function
          df_pd['numberOfViolations'] = df_pd['violations'].apply(countViolations)

          #cast the object back into a Spark SQL DataFrame
          df = sqlContext.createDataFrame(df_pd)

          #register the DataFrame as a temporal table in Spark SQL
          df.registerTempTable('restaurantsTable')

          df.show(5)
```

```
+-------------------+-----------------+---------------+----------+-------+--------------------+------------------+
|               name|             Type|      RiskLevel|      Date|results|          violations|numberOfViolations|
+-------------------+-----------------+---------------+----------+-------+--------------------+------------------+
|     LUNA PARK INC|Children's Servic...|  Risk 1 (High)|09/21/2010|   Fail|24. DISH WASHING ...|                 4|
|      CAFE SELMARIE|       Restaurant|  Risk 1 (High)|09/21/2010|   Fail|2. FACILITIES TO ...|                 8|
|        MANCHU WOK|       Restaurant|  Risk 1 (High)|09/21/2010|   Pass|33. FOOD AND NON-...|                 2|
|BENCHMARK HOSPITA...|       Restaurant|  Risk 1 (High)|09/21/2010|   Pass|                    |                 0|
|          JJ BURGER|       Restaurant|Risk 2 (Medium)|09/21/2010|   Pass|                    |                 0|
+-------------------+-----------------+---------------+----------+-------+--------------------+------------------+
only showing top 5 rows
```

**FIGURE 4-35** Spark SQL DataFrame manipulated to add a column and registered as a temporal table

Now you can start writing SQL queries against the temporal table as if you were using a relational engine. Remember that, in fact, what you will be querying is an in-memory data object with a partial schema you applied in Figure 4-34 from a raw CSV file stored in an Azure Blob Storage account. The power behind that idea is that you are able to leverage your SQL knowledge to analyze data that is not purely structured; you are just applying a view of abstraction on top of it. Later in your analysis, you can apply many other data processing methods to get the most out of that data (a machine learning algorithm, for example).

In the following code and in Figure 4-36 you find how to query your temporal table, using the %%sql magic. Everything that will appear will be treated as SQL code, including the comments syntax.

```
%%sql

select Type, sum(numberOfViolations) as numberOfViolations
from restaurantsTable
group by Type
order by 2 desc
```

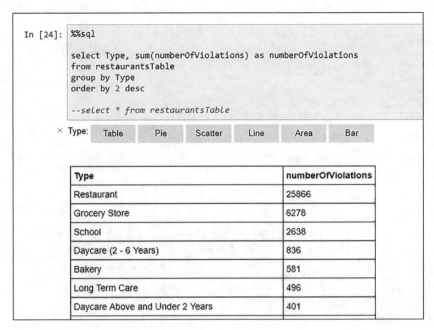

```
In [24]:   %%sql

           select Type, sum(numberOfViolations) as numberOfViolations
           from restaurantsTable
           group by Type
           order by 2 desc

           --select * from restaurantsTable
```

× Type:   Table   Pie   Scatter   Line   Area   Bar

| Type | numberOfViolations |
|---|---|
| Restaurant | 25866 |
| Grocery Store | 6278 |
| School | 2638 |
| Daycare (2 - 6 Years) | 836 |
| Bakery | 581 |
| Long Term Care | 496 |
| Daycare Above and Under 2 Years | 401 |

**FIGURE 4-36** Spark SQL aggregated query

As you are executing this code in a Jupyter Notebook you can even create simple visualizations based on the results of your query. See Figure 4-37 for an example of visualizations using the results of other aggregated query, this time using the date field to see the evolution of the regulation violations over time using an area visualization, with its selector in the menu marked in red. Note that you can choose between aggregation functions, even when the Spark SQL query results already have an aggregation function.

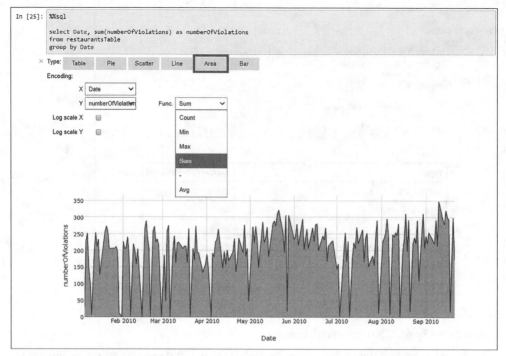

**FIGURE 4-37** Spark SQL query results represented by an area visual in the Jupyter Notebook

The Jupyter Notebook provides this visualization option, and it is useful for quick and easy analyses over data stored in Spark. However, going beyond you may be consuming Spark SQL query results from any data visualization tool with even better visual types and options and create analytic panels directly against your Spark SQL engine.

In this section, you have gone through some simple examples on how to create exploratory analysis over your data using Spark SQL, perhaps to continue creating more advanced analytics on top of such data. In the next section, you reuse the data already explored to learn how to build machine learning models in Spark.

## Build and use machine learning models with Spark on HDI

After having explored and understood the dataset, and following the exact same experiment pipeline you have been following in the previous chapters, you are ready to start creating machine learning models within Spark on HDInsight. You can build them using libraries like MLlib, which is a Spark core library that offers machine learning features such as classification, regression, clustering, or Principal Component Analysis, among others.

In this section you learn how to create a classification model using the DataFrames you obtained up to Figure 4-10. Your goal is to predict the Risk Groups of the Chicago City inspections on different businesses based on their attributes or features. Note that the dataset you have been working on in the previous section has other fields that would fit as a label for a classification problem, even for a regression problem. This example intends to show the process itself, but changing just small pieces of code, you might obtain results for other labels as well.

You start evaluating the label you use, the RiskLevel column from your previously explored dataset. Spark SQL DataFrames (as well as other data manipulation libraries) have methods that you can leverage to get information that you might also obtain with other more classical languages, like any SQL ANSI-compliant one. For example, you subselect certain rows or columns from the DataFrame, apply filters, or transformations. In Figure 4-38 you find a distinct selection of the RiskLevel column.

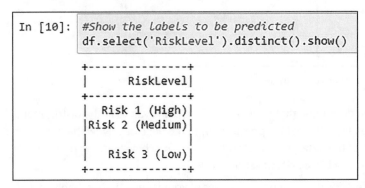

```
In [10]:  #Show the labels to be predicted
          df.select('RiskLevel').distinct().show()

          +---------------+
          |      RiskLevel|
          +---------------+
          |    Risk 1 (High)|
          |Risk 2 (Medium)|
          |               |
          |    Risk 3 (Low)|
          +---------------+
```

FIGURE 4-38 Spark SQL distinct RiskLevel values

Note that methods are used following each other, leveraging the objects retrieved by the previous operation. That is quite common in high-level programming languages like Python, and the concept of "pipeline of operations applied" is present in this example.

You might want to use the %%sql magic from the previously registered restaurantsTable temporal table to better understand how the distinct values are represented in the DataFrame. This is especially important since, as shown in Figure 4-38, there are blank values. The weight of such values in the dataset, as you have learned in Chapter 1, "Prepare Data for Analysis in Azure Machine Learning," can be very important because it might undermine the importance of the useful (from the prediction perspective) values (Risks Low, Medium, and High). See Figure 4-39 for an example of an aggregated query studying the distribution of the RiskLabel values in the DataFrame.

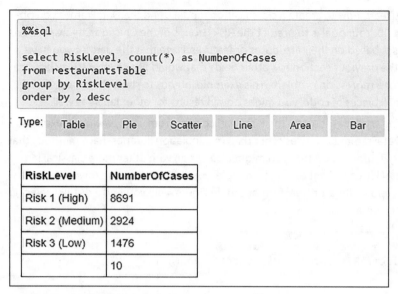

```
%%sql

select RiskLevel, count(*) as NumberOfCases
from restaurantsTable
group by RiskLevel
order by 2 desc
```

Type:  | Table | Pie | Scatter | Line | Area | Bar

| RiskLevel | NumberOfCases |
|---|---|
| Risk 1 (High) | 8691 |
| Risk 2 (Medium) | 2924 |
| Risk 3 (Low) | 1476 |
|  | 10 |

**FIGURE 4-39** Spark SQL RiskLevel values distribution

From Figure 4-39 you can determine that the weight of the blank values in the distribution is not especially relevant. You treat this value appropriately in the next step. Now that you have understood the distribution of the data, you can start building a machine learning model using MLlib. For simplicity, you create a binary classification model.

Because, as seen in Figure 4-39, if the number of values of your label is higher than two, you need to transform these values into a binary form, represented by numbers in this case. You will divide the classes into High (coded as "1") and Medium and Low (coded as 0). In order to do that, you can use the following code that implements a user defined function and creates a new dataset with the new label, the violations list, the type of the business, and the numberOfViolations columns that you created in Figure 4-35. See Figure 4-40 for an example of the execution.

```
# Import the necessary libraries for Spark SQL and Spark MLlib
from pyspark.sql import *
from pyspark.ml.feature import *
# Create a user defined function to code a binary label
def udf_createLabel(st):
    if st == 'Risk 1 (High)':
        return 1.0
    elif st == 'Risk 2 (Medium)' or st == 'Risk 3 (Low)':
        return 0.0
    else: #in case we are facing any other case, like blank spaces
        return 0.0

# Register the function as a UserDefinedFunction (function from the Spark SQL library)
returning a double data type
createLabel = UserDefinedFunction(udf_createLabel, DoubleType())
```

```
# Apply the UserDefinedFunction applying the 'label' alias, as well as the violations,
type and numberOfViolations fields
labeledData = df.select(createLabel(df.RiskLevel).alias('label'), df.violations,
df.Type, df.numberOfViolations)

labeledData.show(5)
```

```
In [74]:  # Import the necessary libraries for Spark SQL and Spark MLlib
          from pyspark.sql import *
          from pyspark.ml.feature import *

          # Create a user defined function to code a binary label
          def udf_createLabel(st):
              if st == 'Risk 1 (High)':
                  return 1.0
              elif st == 'Risk 2 (Medium)' or st == 'Risk 3 (Low)':
                  return 0.0
              else:
                  return 0.0

          # Register the function as a UserDefinedFunction (function from the Spark SQL library) returning a double data type
          createLabel = UserDefinedFunction(udf_createLabel, DoubleType())

          # Apply the UserDefinedFunction applying the 'label' alias, as well as the violations, type and numberOfViolations fields
          labeledData = df.select(createLabel(df.RiskLevel).alias('label'), df.violations, df.Type, df.numberOfViolations)

          labeledData.show(5)

          +-----+--------------------+------------------+----------------+
          |label|          violations|              Type|numberOfViolations|
          +-----+--------------------+------------------+----------------+
          |  1.0|24. DISH WASHING ...|Children's Servic...|               4|
          |  1.0|2. FACILITIES TO ...|        Restaurant|               8|
          |  1.0|33. FOOD AND NON-...|        Restaurant|               2|
          |  1.0|                    |        Restaurant|               0|
          |  0.0|                    |        Restaurant|               0|
          +-----+--------------------+------------------+----------------+
          only showing top 5 rows
```

FIGURE 4-40 Label creation using a user defined function in Spark SQL

You have created your binary risk label and your dataset already contains three feature columns. However, the Logistic Regression model that you use in MLlib only accepts DataFrames with a structure of label–vector of numeric features. Therefore, you need to transform your dataset to fit this structure.

First, you need to separate the violations column in words and apply a hashing function. This retrieves a column with the numeric representation of the text containing the violations committed by that particular business in the inspection. You can look at that representation as a codification of the text data, and therefore you can leverage the correlations between the number and type of violations committed, and the risk level.

You also need to transform the Type column into a numeric column. As mentioned, it is necessary that your feature vector is numeric to be fed to the Logistic Regression model. Luckily, MLlib provides a lot of tools and features, and one of them is a "string indexer" that you can use for this purpose.

Finally, you require the union of all these items you have up to this point: the hashed text feature, the Type column coded as a number, and the numberOfViolations feature that you previously had. Again, MLlib contains functionality for this with the VectorAssembler transformer.

In the following code sample you find all of these steps stored into objects in Spark. The goal of all these items is to use the previously processed data, referencing the new and / or transformed columns. That is why you will find references to columns that were not present yet but will be there when the transformers are invoked. You need all of these objects for the next step.

```
# Import needed MLlib libraries
from pyspark.ml import Pipeline
from pyspark.ml.classification import LogisticRegression
from pyspark.ml.feature import HashingTF, Tokenizer

# Definition of each stage of the pipeline to process the DataFrame
# Tokenizer for the text column dividing the text attribute in a new vector of
words
tokenizer = Tokenizer(inputCol="violations", outputCol="words")

# Hashing stage to create a vector of numeric features representing the text
features from the tokenizer
hashingTF = HashingTF(inputCol=tokenizer.getOutputCol(), outputCol="feats")

# String indexer to convert the Type string column into numeric values. Logistic
regression in MLlib only accepts numeric features
strIndexer = StringIndexer(inputCol="Type", outputCol = "TypeID")
strIndexer.setHandleInvalid("skip")

# Transformation to assemble all the vectors into a final single vector to feed
the Logistic Regressor
assembler = VectorAssembler(inputCols=["feats", "TypeID", "numberOfViolations"],
outputCol = "features")
```

Now that you have all the transformers in place, you are ready to build your Logistic Regression model. In order to do that, you use the MLlib Pipeline object, used to chain multiple transformer objects (as the ones you created in the previous piece of code). At the end of this pipeline you will place your Logistic Regression model, which will consume the processed data (remember, in a form of label – vector of features) and will be trained.

```
# Creation of the Logistic regression model
lr = LogisticRegression(maxIter=10, regParam=0.01)

# Creation of the pipeline with the different stages (from left to right), finally using
the logistic regression model fed with the processed data
pipeline = Pipeline(stages=[tokenizer, hashingTF, strIndexer, assembler, lr])

#Fit the pipeline sequence, retrieving the final model trained with the processed
dataframe
model = pipeline.fit(labeledData)
```

A few seconds after you run this code, your Logistic Regression model is trained and stored in your model object.

Now is time to test its performance. In your HDInsight sample folders there is another Food Inspections CSV file. You need to pre-process it in the same way you did with the first dataset. However, to create the predictions using that data you will not need to re-execute the Pipeline you created for the test data. Instead of this, you only need to call the function *transform* from the model you have trained and it will apply the same transformations that were applied to the original data, which is required for the building of the model. Remember from Chapter 2 that your test dataset should have the same schema as your training dataset for the algorithm to be able to create predictions. See Figure 4-41 for the result of the execution of this code.

```
#Load test data to predict using the model
testData = sc.textFile('wasb:///HdiSamples/HdiSamples/FoodInspectionData/Food_
Inspections2.csv')
.map(csvParse)

# Apply the lambda function and parse the output object into a Spark SQL dataframe
using the context
df_test = sqlContext.createDataFrame(testData.map(lambda l: (l[1], l[4], l[5], l[10],
 l[12], l[13])) , schema)

# Cast the DataFrame into a Pandas data frame
df_test_pd = df_test.toPandas()

# Create a new row applying the custom function
df_test_pd['numberOfViolations'] = df_test_pd['violations'].apply(countViolations)

# Cast the object back into a Spark SQL DataFrame
df_test = sqlContext.createDataFrame(df_test_pd)

# Apply the UserDefinedFunction applying the 'label' alias, as well as the violations,
 type and numberOfViolations fields
df_test = df_test.select(createLabel(df_test.RiskLevel).alias('label'),
df_test.violations, df_test.Type, df_test.numberOfViolations)

# Apply the transformations needed to fit the model's schema and create predictions on
test data
predictionsDF = model.transform(df_test)

predictionsDF.printSchema()
```

```
In [170]: #Load test data to predict using the model
          testData = sc.textFile('wasb:///HdiSamples/HdiSamples/FoodInspectionData/Food_Inspections2.csv').map(csvParse)

          # Apply the Lambda function and parse the output object into a Spark SQL dataframe using the context
          df_test = sqlContext.createDataFrame(testData.map(lambda l: (l[1], l[4], l[5], l[10], l[12], l[13])) , schema)

          # Cast the DataFrame into a Pandas data frame
          df_test_pd = df_test.toPandas()

          # Create a new row applying the custom function
          df_test_pd['numberOfViolations'] = df_test_pd['violations'].apply(countViolations)

          # Cast the object back into a Spark SQL DataFrame
          df_test = sqlContext.createDataFrame(df_test_pd)

          # Apply the UserDefinedFunction applying the 'label' alias, as well as the violations, type and numberOfViolations fields
          df_test = df_test.select(createLabel(df_test.RiskLevel).alias('label'), df_test.violations, df_test.Type, df_test.numberOfViolati

          # Apply the transformations needed to fit the model's schema and create predictions on test data
          predictionsDF = model.transform(df_test)

          predictionsDF.printSchema()

          root
           |-- label: double (nullable = true)
           |-- violations: string (nullable = true)
           |-- Type: string (nullable = true)
           |-- numberOfViolations: long (nullable = true)
           |-- words: array (nullable = true)
           |    |-- element: string (containsNull = true)
           |-- feats: vector (nullable = true)
           |-- TypeID: double (nullable = true)
           |-- features: vector (nullable = true)
           |-- rawPrediction: vector (nullable = true)
           |-- probability: vector (nullable = true)
           |-- prediction: double (nullable = true)
```

**FIGURE 4-41** Test data preprocessing and prediction creation using MLlib

If you want to test the performance of the model on your test dataset, you need to compare the already observed label and the predictions. From the schema in Figure 4-41 you can infer that these columns are called label and prediction. In the following code sample you create a simplified DataFrame. and from it, register a temporal table to analyze the results with familiar SQL code using Spark SQL again.

```
simpleDF = predictionsDF.select(predictionsDF.label, predictionsDF.prediction)
simpleDF.registerTempTable('Preds')
```

Now, you are able to use your existing SQL skills to test the performance of your model. Use the following sample code for that purpose and see Figure 4-42 for the results.

```
%%sql

select
cast(sum(case when (label = 1.0 and prediction = 1.0) or (label = 0.0 and prediction
 = 0.0) then 1 else 0 end) as double) as NumberOfSuccesses,
cast(sum(case when (label = 1.0 and prediction = 1.0) or (label = 0.0 and prediction
 = 0.0) then 0 else 1 end) as double) as NumberOfFailures,
count(*) as TotalCases,
(cast(sum(case when (label = 1.0 and prediction = 1.0) or (label = 0.0 and prediction
 = 0.0) then 1 else 0 end) as double) / count(*)) * 100 as Accuracy
from Preds
```

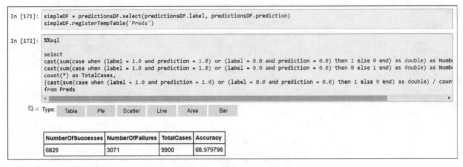

**FIGURE 4-42** Model performance evaluation using Spark SQL

With a measured accuracy of nearly 69 percent your model is showing a good (although improvable) performance. You can even create a more detailed visual analysis adding the True Positive, True Negative, False Positive, and False Negative classification you already learn in Chapter 2 Develop Machine Learning Models. Follow the next sample code and see Figure 4-43 for the detailed performance results.

```
%%sql

Select case
    when label = 1.0 and prediction = 1.0 then 'True Positive'
    when label = 0.0 and prediction = 0.0 then 'True Negative'
    when label = 0.0 and prediction = 1.0 then 'False Positive'
    when label = 1.0 and prediction = 0.0 then 'False Negatives'
    else 'Unknown' end as Cases
from Preds
```

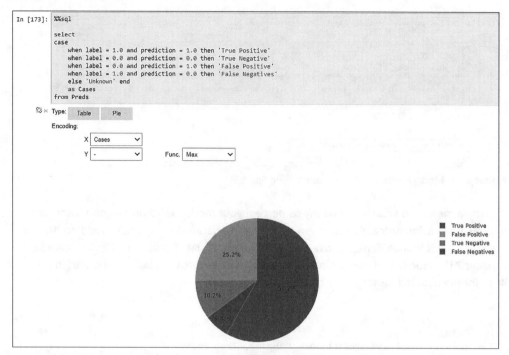

**FIGURE 4-43** Model performance evaluation using Spark SQL and Jupyter visualizations

In this section, you have reviewed how to manipulate Spark SQL DataFrames and the construction of pipelines with Spark MLlib to train and consume machine learning models. The use of an in-memory framework like Spark with support for high-level languages and exploration tools like Jupyter Notebooks allows you to rapidly create an end-to-end machine learning experiment. You could easily transform the code in your Notebooks to create Python or Scala scripts to train and / or consume your machine learning models on a scheduled basis, depending on your business requirements.

> **NEED MORE INFORMATION? SPARK MLLIB**
>
> If you want to investigate and learn on the machine learning capabilities of MLlib on Spark you can start visiting its home website for documentation and examples at: *https://spark. apache.org/mllib*.

# Build and use machine learning models using MapReduce

MapReduce is a data processing technique that allows parallel computations on clusters. Using this programming model it is possible to process large amounts of data in a batch fashion, even reaching petabytes of data. MapReduce breaks down into two phases:

- **Map**    Each working node receives a subset of the data and transforms it into *(key, value)* tuples.

- **Reduce**    Tuples with the same key are sent to the same node and it applies a reduction function.

*NEED MORE INFORMATION*  **MAPREDUCE**

You can find a detailed example of MapReduce at *https://www.guru99.com/introduction-to-mapreduce.html.*

A popular open source implementation of this programming model is the one included in HDInsight clusters. In this section, you learn to create a recommendation system for movies using Mahout (similar to the one created in Chapter 3, "Operationalize and Manage Azure Machine Learning Services"). Mahout is a framework for building scalable machine learning algorithms on top of clusters. To achieve this scalability, Mahout algorithms are implemented using MapReduce to fetch, process, and retrieve the data they use.

For this example you can use the same cluster you have used so far in this chapter. The data used for this example is sample data that is copied to blob storage when the cluster is deployed. We launch the recommendations using SSH, so the first step is to open an SSH connection with the cluster.

*NEED HELP?*  **SSH CLUSTER**

Do you need help connecting to a HDInsight cluster using SSH? Visit the following website for more information at: *https://docs.microsoft.com/en-us/azure/hdinsight/hdinsight-hadoop-linux-use-ssh-unix.*

The files you use are located in the blob storage in the /HdiSamples/HdiSamples/MahoutMovieData/moviedb directory. The moviedb.txt file contains a list of movies in movieID|title|... format. You only use the first two columns (movieID and title) as a lookup table in order to transform the movies IDs returned by the recommender into titles. The file user-ratings.txt has a structure of userID, movieID, userRating, and timestamp. Mahout will use this file as training data. The file contains scores of 100 users, so it is an example file and you cannot expect to get good recommendations with so little data. After executing the recommendation, 10 recommendations per user are obtained.

```
hdfs dfs -text /HdiSamples/HdiSamples/MahoutMovieData/moviedb.txt
hdfs dfs -text /HdiSamples/HdiSamples/MahoutMovieData/user-ratings.txt
```

Run the recommendation with the command below. In addition to specifying the file with the input data (-i option), where to save the output data (-o), and where to save the temporary files (--tempDir), you can provide the similarity function used during model training (-s). With this command, Mahout launches MapReduce jobs that will read input data and train the model in parallel. When the model is trained, it calculates which 10 films are recommended for each user and saves the results in a file. The output file generated can be consumed in many ways, but in this example you will use Spark to transform and display the data.

```
mahout recommenditembased -s SIMILARITY_COOCCURRENCE -i /HdiSamples/HdiSamples/
MahoutMovieData/user-ratings.txt -o /example/data/mahoutout --tempDir /temp/mahouttemp
```

Many log messages appear in the console until the program is finished (see Figure 4-44).

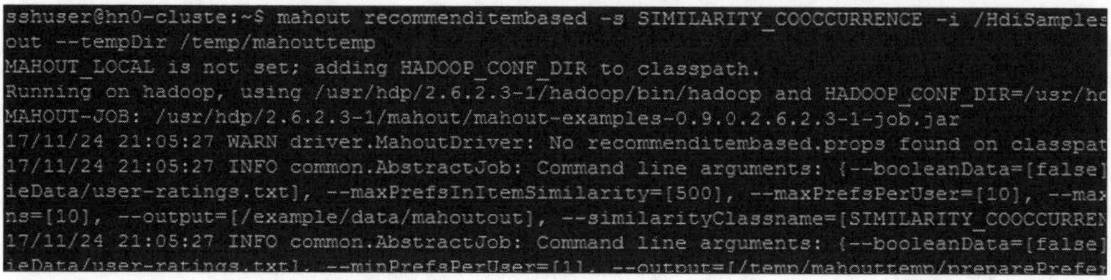

**FIGURE 4-44** Running Mahout item based recommender system

The output is saved on the file /example/data/mahoutout/part-r-00000 (output directory indicated by the option -o of the Mahout command).

```
hdfs dfs -text /example/data/mahoutout/part-r-00000
```

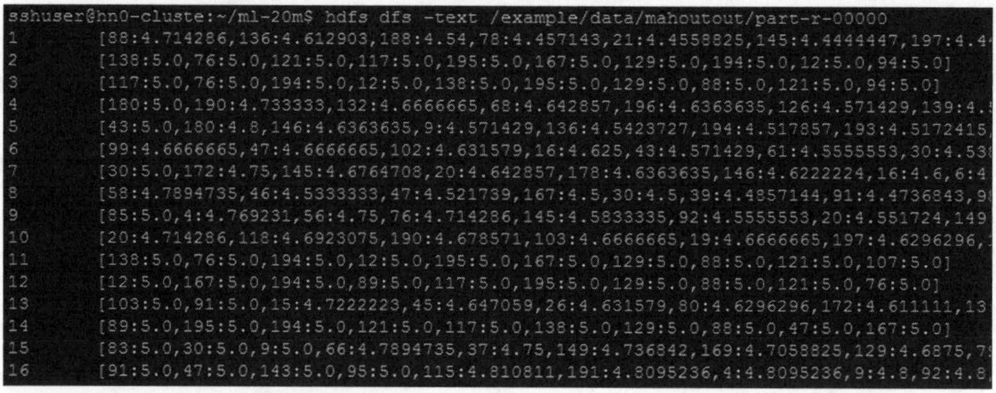

**FIGURE 4-45** First lines of the output file

The fist column is the user id and the second column contains a list of movieID:recommendationScore ordered by recommendation score. In order to interpret these results correctly, further processing is necessary. In this example, you are going to use Spark for reading the output and the moviedb.txt files, and replace the movie IDs with the movie title. Open a new Jupyter Notebook and paste the following code in the first cell:

```
from pyspark.sql.functions import explode

def moviesParser(line):
    movie_id, title = line.split("|")[0:2]
    return movie_id, title

def recommendationsParser(line):
    user_id, recom = line.split("\t")
    # List of IDs of the recommended movies, ignoring predicted score
    recom = [i.split(":")[0] for i in recom.strip("[]\n").split(",")]
    return user_id, recom

# Set loaders and parsers
movies = sc.textFile('wasb:////HdiSamples/HdiSamples/MahoutMovieData/moviedb.
txt').map
(moviesParser).toDF()
recommendations = sc.textFile('wasb:///example/data/mahoutout/part-r
-00000').map(recommendationsParser).toDF()

# Create dataframes
movies_df = movies.toDF("movie_id", "title")
recommendations_df = recommendations.toDF("user_id", "movie_id")
# Recommendations array to rows
recommendations_df = recommendations_df.withColumn("movie_id",
 explode(recommendations_df.movie_id))
```

This code reads both files from the HDFS locations and saves the data in Spark DataFrames. For the recommendations DataFrame another step is performed: the recommendation array is unrolled in rows. Thus, if the arrays contain 10 recommendations per user, there will be 10 rows per user.

If you want, you can visualize the data using the *show* method of the DataFrames (see Figure 4-46).

```
In [2]:  movies_df.show(10)

         +--------+--------------------+
         |movie_id|               title|
         +--------+--------------------+
         |       1|    Toy Story (1995)|
         |       2|    GoldenEye (1995)|
         |       3|   Four Rooms (1995)|
         |       4|   Get Shorty (1995)|
         |       5|      Copycat (1995)|
         |       6|Shanghai Triad (Y...|
         |       7|Twelve Monkeys (1...|
         |       8|         Babe (1995)|
         |       9|Dead Man Walking ...|
         |      10|   Richard III (1995)|
         +--------+--------------------+
         only showing top 10 rows

In [3]:  recommendations_df.show(10)

         +-------+--------+
         |user_id|movie_id|
         +-------+--------+
         |      1|      88|
         |      1|     136|
         |      1|     188|
         |      1|      78|
         |      1|      21|
         |      1|     145|
         |      1|     197|
         |      1|      32|
         |      1|      13|
         |      1|      30|
         +-------+--------+
         only showing top 10 rows
```

**FIGURE 4-46** Fist 10 lines of the loaded DataFrames

The only thing left to do is to filter the recommendations of a specific user, join the two dataframes by movie_id, and show the results. This is what the following code does, and the output is shown in Figure 4-47.

```
def printUserRecommendations(id):
    recommendations_df.where("user_id == {}".format(id))\
        .join(movies_df, recommendations_df.movie_id == movies_df.movie_id)\
        .select("user_id", "title")\
        .show(10, False)

# Show recomendations of user 3
printUserRecommendations(3)
```

```
In [4]:  def printUserRecommendations(id):
             recommendations_df.where("user_id == {}".format(id))\
                 .join(movies_df, recommendations_df.movie_id == movies_df.movie_id)\
                 .select("user_id", "title")\
                 .show(10, False)

         printUserRecommendations(3)
```

```
+-------+----------------------------+
|user_id|title                       |
+-------+----------------------------+
|3      |D3: The Mighty Ducks (1996) |
|3      |Terminator, The (1984)      |
|3      |Sting, The (1973)           |
|3      |Rock, The (1996)            |
|3      |Sleepless in Seattle (1993) |
|3      |Independence Day (ID4) (1996)|
|3      |Usual Suspects, The (1995)  |
|3      |Home Alone (1990)           |
|3      |Bound (1996)                |
|3      |Carlito's Way (1993)        |
+-------+----------------------------+
```

**FIGURE 4-47** Recommendations of the user with id 3

Notice that Mahout does not delete temporary data that is created while processing the jobs, so you need to do it manually. Use the next command for deleting the output folder (indicated by the option `--tempDir` when calling the Mahout command):

```
hdfs dfs -rm -f -r /temp/mahouttemp
```

MapReduce is good for large-scale data processing, but unlike Spark, it does not load the data into memory and keeps it in a cache. MapReduce relies on disk. This is a problem in iterative processes where you have to access disk in each iteration to reload the same data, thus becoming a bottleneck. As you know, machine learning algorithms are iterative processes, so training models with MapReduce is much less efficient than using other approaches like Spark. A Spark implementation of machine learning algorithms can be up to 10 times faster than using MapReduce.

---

**NOTE   MAHOUT: PHASING OUT MAP REDUCE**

For the reasons discussed above, the latest versions of Mahout are gradually phasing out MapReduce. The new algorithms added to the library are being implemented using Spark, H2O, and Flink as underlying frameworks. Check out the currently available implementations at: *http://mahout.apache.org/users/basics/algorithms.html*.

---

# Build and use machine learning models using Microsoft R Server

Historically, the use of R in the machine learning industry has been burdened by three main weaknesses of the language itself:

- Single-threaded processing
- Memory limitation
- Need to move data around in inefficient formats (mainly text files)

In the modern data analytics ecosystem, with ever-growing data amounts and some companies, like Revolution Analytics, started to develop frameworks and tools to overcome these limitations. These tools and frameworks work with Big Data platforms seamlessly, liberating the data scientists of the burden of having to write their own MapReduce jobs or learning other languages, leveraging their expertise and keeping their productivity while taking advantage of massive amounts of data and big clusters.

Microsoft bought Revolution Analytics in May 2015, absorbing and incorporating its technology into new products rapidly. From that acquisition and further developments, Microsoft has formed an R-based stack offering. Its enterprise-grade product, R Server, is 100 percent compatible with base R and offers multiple enhancements, such as:

- Parallel algorithms
- Compressed native data format
- Data chunking to overcome memory limitations
- In-database machine learning analytics

R Server can be used as a standalone product (either in a single machine or as a farm), inside SQL Server with ML Services (see Skill 4.4), or on top of a Spark HDInsight cluster. R Server appears as another R distribution if you are using it in a standalone or inside SQL Server. Therefore, you are able to use it from any IDE you want (e.g. Visual Studio, R Studio, R GUI, etc.).

In this example you go through an example using R code from a local Visual Studio 2017 IDE with R Tools installed (you can find them at *https://www.visualstudio.com/vs/rtvs/*) using the R Server cluster created at the beginning of this skill (Figures 4-1 to 4-4). You will be using the NYC Yellow Taxi Trip Data (available at *http://www.nyc.gov/html/tlc/html/about/trip_record_data.shtml*). The combination of these CSV files stores around 173 million rows and occupies 27GB uncompressed. For the sake of the example, only year 2013 is considered, but you can add other years for your own purposes.

R Server is able to use different compute contexts with minimal code changes. Compute contexts are a representation of where and how computations will be performed. For example, if your compute context is set to your local environment, R Server will understand that all operations over files will be computed using local CPUs, a local file system (whatever the operating system that you are using, R Server works in Windows and Linux) and that there is no cluster structure to take in account. When using a Spark compute context, all these assumptions will be different, and R Server adapts its internal algorithms to the new context.

In order to create the compute context, you need to use the rxSparkConnect clause. With a sample code like the following, you specify the different parameters of your Spark compute context, and a Spark application will be created if the resources you are asking for (worker nodes, memory allocations, and cores per executor) are available. YARN takes care of this. To connect from Visual Studio (or R Studio) you need several items:

- Your cluster to have been created using a public certificate for the sshuser authentication (see Figure 4-48). You can create a public-private certificate using PuTTYgen (see how at *https://www1.psfc.mit.edu/computers/cluster/putty.html*).

The name of the edge node where the R Server engine resides. It will always have the following structure "yourClusterName-ed-ssh.azurehdinsight.net."

**FIGURE 4-48** R Server cluster creation with Public Key for SSH user

```
## Spark context configuration
numberOfWorkerNodes <- 2 # number of worker nodes in cluster
executorCores <- 8 # cores of each executor. In this case, cores of each worker
node
myNameNode <- rxGetOption("hdfsHost")

## Private key has to be created without comment (a space is created in the whole
name and is not supported)
mySshUsername <- "sshuser"
mySshHostname <- "the_edge_node_url_of_your_cluster" #public facing cluster IP
address
mySshSwitches <- "-i your_private_key" #use .ppk file with PuTTY
mySshClientDir <- "C:/Program Files/PuTTY" #your path to PuTTY
myShareDir <- paste("/var/RevoShare", mySshUsername, sep = "/")
myHdfsShareDir <- paste("/user/RevoShare", mySshUsername, sep = "/")

#rxSparkConnect automatically initiates a Spark application and the compute
context
mySparkCluster <- rxSparkConnect(
  hdfsShareDir = myHdfsShareDir,
  sshUsername = mySshUsername,
  sshClientDir = mySshClientDir,
  sshHostname = mySshHostname,
  sshSwitches = mySshSwitches,
  shareDir = myShareDir,
  reset = TRUE, # new Spark application with a fresh resource pool
  numExecutors = numberOfWorkerNodes,
  executorCores = executorCores, #cores by executor
  executorMem = "6g", #Assigned memory to each executor (JVM)
  executorOverheadMem = '2g', ## R process memory
  consoleOutput = TRUE,
  persistentRun = TRUE)
```

If everything is correctly configured, you will see a message like this in the Interactive R window (see Figure 4-49).

```
R Interactive - Microsoft R Server (3.4.1.0)
  reset = TRUE, # new Spark application with a fresh resource pool
+ numExecutors = numberOfWorkerNodes,
+ executorCores = executorCores, #cores by executor
+ executorMem = "6g", #Assigned memory to each executor (JVM)
+ executorOverheadMem = '2g', ## R process memory
+ consoleOutput = TRUE,
+ persistentRun = TRUE)
Parameter 'reset' is set to TRUE. Shutting down existing Spark applications (scaleR-spark-
It may take 1 to 2 minutes to launch a new Spark application.
>
```

FIGURE 4-49 R Server Spark compute context initiated

In the example, your data (only year 2013 of the taxi trip data) is in an Azure Blob Storage. When working with R Server in Spark, although the main storage might be a Blob Storage container you have to explicitly create your folders for R Server to recognize them as part of the HDFS file system. You can do that with the following code sample:

```
# Variable initialization
hdfsFS <- RxHdfsFileSystem()
dataDir <- '/NYCTaxiData'
xdfDir <- '/NYCTaxiDataXDF'
hdfsDir <- '/NYCTaxiDataHDFS'
testDir <- '/NYCTestXDF'
trainDir <- '/NYCTrainXDF'
predsDir <- '/NYCPredictions'
# Ensure that your cluster folders exist
rxHadoopMakeDir(hdfsDir)
rxHadoopMakeDir(xdfDir)

# Copy from the source folder in a blob storage to the cluster source folder.
# Base data needs to be in a cluster folder for R Server to be able to reference
it and convert it into XDF
rxHadoopCopy(dataDir, hdfsDir)
```

Once your data is copied to the HDFS folder, you can start reading the collection of CSVs to convert them into XDF format, the native file format used by R Server, improving compression, allowing data chunking, and increasing overall performance. Every R Server native command (the ones starting with the "rx" prefix) is able to work with XDF files by default. In addition, most of the base R commands (like "head", "summary," or "nrow," to name a few) are overwritten in R Server allowing them to work with XDF files as well.

To read from a collection of CSV files you can specify their structure with a list of fields, as you would do in other technologies or languages like Python or Hive. Then, specify that the desired file system to work with is HDFS. This is important because XDF files are not stored in the same way in HDFS, and in a non-distributed file system. Finally, you can use the rxImport command to go through all of the files and compose a single XDF folder, pointed in the following code sample as "outputData". Note that you can add transformations on the fly while importing the data, like dropping variables, creating new ones or filtering data.

```
#Specify the CSV structure
taxiColInfo <- list(
                    vendor_id = list(type = "factor"),
                    pickup_datetime = list(type = "character"),
                    dropoff_datetime = list(type = "character"),
                    passenger_count = list(type = "integer"),
                    trip_distance = list(type = "numeric"),
                    pickup_longitude = list(type = "numeric"),
                    pickup_latitude = list(type = "numeric"),
                    rate_code = list(type = "factor"),
                    store_and_fwd_flag = list(type = "character"),
                    dropoff_longitude = list(type = "numeric"),
```

```
                        dropoff_latitude = list(type = "numeric"),
                        payment_type = list(type = "factor"),
                        fare_amount = list(type = "numeric"),
                        surcharge = list(type = "numeric"),
                        mta_tax = list(type = "numeric"),
                        tip_amount = list(type = "numeric"),
                        tolls_amount = list(type = "numeric"),
                        total_amount = list(type = "numeric")
                        )

rxSetFileSystem(hdfsFS)

# Once it is copied, the CSV files are located under a new folder called
NYCTaxiData.
 Pointing to the folder will
# go through the files present there
inputData <- RxTextData(file.path(hdfsDir, 'NYCTaxiData'), fileSystem = hdfsFS,
colInfo
= taxiColInfo, firstRowIsColNames = TRUE)

# The output folder will contain one single xdf file, divided in composite mode
(data
 and metadata)
outputData <- RxXdfData(xdfDir, fileSystem = hdfsFS)

# Convert to XDF adding a transformation on the fly to create the binary label and
drop
 the tip amount
rxImport(inData = inputData, outFile = outputData, overwrite = TRUE, rowsPerRead =
1000000
        , transforms = list(
                        # create the label for the binary classification
problem
                        tipped = ifelse(tip_amount > 0, 1, 0),
                        #create the division between train and test
                        set = as.factor(ifelse(rbinom(.rxNumRows, size = 1,
prob
= 0.7), "train", "test"))
                        )
                        #rows from intermediate files that are either empty
or
 headers
        , rowSelection = (vendor_id != "" & vendor_id != "vendor_id")
        #drop unnecesary columns
        , varsToDrop = c("pickup_datetime", "dropoff_datetime", "store_and_fwd_
flag",
                        "pickup_longitude", "pickup_latitude", "dropoff_
longitude",
 "dropoff_latitude")
)
```

This transformation takes several minutes, depending on the size of your cluster. Once the transformation is completed, you have a single XDF folder to point to, to create your analysis. Note that two new variables have been created: "tipped" is the binary label you will be building models for, predicting if a certain taxi trip will receive a tip or not, and "set", that is dividing the dataset in two parts (70-30 percentages, as you did in Chapter 2). This allows you to divide the XDF into two different sets, one for training and the other for testing, as you can find in the following code sample using the rxDataStep command.

```
#point to different folders to store the XDF files
testXDF <- RxXdfData(file = testDir, fileSystem = hdfsFS)
trainXDF <- RxXdfData(file = trainDir, fileSystem = hdfsFS)
predsXDF <- RxXdfData(file = predsDir, fileSystem = hdfsFS)

#separate the original dataset into train and test using the "set" variable
rxDataStep(outputData, outFile = trainXDF, rowSelection = (set == "train"),
           varsToDrop = c("set"), overwrite = TRUE)
rxDataStep(outputData, outFile = testXDF, rowSelection = (set == "test"),
           varsToDrop = c("set"), overwrite = TRUE)
```

Again, you are dropping not useful variables in both datasets and selecting which rows go to each dataset. Now that you have your two datasets you can train a Logistic Regression model using the rxLogit command and a classic R formula, with the "tipped" label as a response variable and some of the features available. You can find an example of the model training in the following code sample:

```
#Create a logistic regression model
model.logit <- rxLogit(formula = tipped ~ vendor_id + passenger_count + trip_distance
 + rate_code + payment_type
    ,data = trainXDF)
```

You are able to check the model training process through the R Interactive window. You see something similar to Figure 4-50.

```
R Interactive - Microsoft R Server (3.4.1.0)
                                    Attach Debugger
+        , data = trainXDF)
======  ed0-cluste (Master HPA Process) has started run at              ======
Picked up JAVA_TOOL_OPTIONS: -Xss4m
                 WARN util.NativeCodeLoader: Unable to load native-hadoop library for your platform...

Starting values (iteration 1) time: 19.439 secs.

Iteration 2 time: 11.336 secs.

Iteration 3 time: 9.673 secs.
131 %
```

**FIGURE 4-50** Logistic Regression training in R Server on Spark

If you are not able to view it by default, you can make it appear going to the main Visual Studio menu, and then R Tools > Windows > R Interactive (see Figure 4-51).

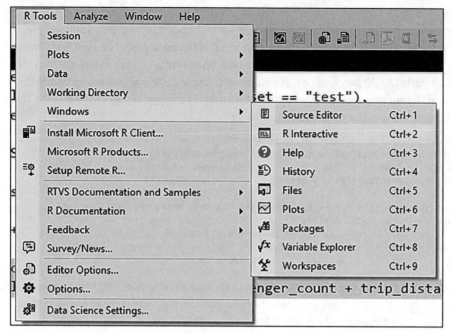

**FIGURE 4-51** R Interactive window in Visual Studio 2017

Once the training process has finished, the object "model.logit" will hold your model. Now is the time to check its performance using the test XDF dataset. In R Server, you use the rxPredict command to create predictions over data using trained models and store them in XDF, or return an R dataframe. You are even allowed to use an alias for the prediction columns and to copy variables either from the model or from the test dataset. This is important because you need to compare the predictions against the observed data. See the following code sample:

```
#Predictions over the test dataset and store them into a XDF file
rxPredict(model.logit, data = testXDF, outData = predsXDF, predVarNames =
"tipped_pred_logit", extraVarsToWrite = "tipped", overwrite = TRUE)
```

Predictions are stored at "predsXDF." Your prediction column will be "tipped_pred_logit" and the actual variable will be "tipped." With all that information you could generate a ROC curve with the AUC score (that you learned how to interpret in Chapter 2 using the rxRoc command.

```
roc <- rxRoc(actualVarName = "tipped", predVarNames = c("tipped_pred_logit"), data
=
predsXDF)
plot(roc)
```

This creates an R plot similar to Figure 4-52.

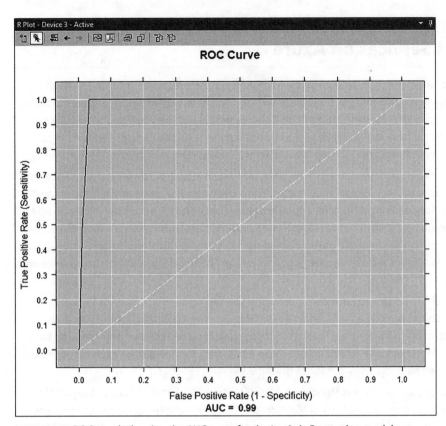

**FIGURE 4-52** ROC graph showing the AUC score for the Logistic Regression model

As shown in Figure 4-52, the model has a very high AUC score and the graph displays a ROC curve very close to the upper left corner of the diagram, denoting a very accurate model. This data science experiment has been designed from a local Visual Studio project, but none of the calculations have been computed in a local environment. The Spark on HDInsight worker nodes has carried all of them out, while the Edge Node has been responsible for the "translation" between the R code into the instructions for the Spark application you have initiated when defining the Spark compute context (see Figure 4-49). This is one of the strengths of R Server: you write your code once, and then deploy it anywhere. Scaling out is fundamental to be able to perform data science on big data: if you need more compute power, just add more nodes to your Spark on HDInsight cluster.

# Skill 4.4: Perform database analytics by using SQL Server R Services on Azure

Developing or even trying out a data science solution can be a resource-intensive task. Many machine learning algorithms, given moderately sized datasets, will take from minutes to hours to train, and if you add this basic delay to an iterative process where you need to visually explore variables, perform statistical tests, and transformations on the dataset and tune algorithm parameters, coming up with a production level model becomes quite time consuming.

In order to minimize development time, minimize architecture/hardware maintenance, and quickly scale up resources in case bulkier algorithms need them, or scale down if the resources are no longer needed, Microsoft offers quickly deployable Virtual Machines on Azure. Some of the major benefits of hosting both an application and the data within Azure is that you automatically can rely on the multiple global datacenters in order to distribute computation, have replicated instances for disaster recovery, or just for load balancing workloads across different resources.

In Skill 4.1 of this book you have configured and worked on the Data Science Virtual Machine,, which comes preloaded with an arsenal of data science tools that enable you to develop anything from a deep learning application to simple graphic interface machine learning solutions in Weka. However, what if you do not require nor are you willing to pay for all those extra resources, while requiring an in-database machine learning service?

Under such scenarios, there is the option of deploying a SQL Server Azure Virtual Machine (SQLVM). The SQL Server Azure Virtual Machine offers a cheaper alternative as compared to the Data Science Virtual Machine, mainly because of the missing associated software plans costs of the DSVM. The advantage of the SQLVM is that, as you see below, the latest versions of SQL Server, SQL Server 2016 and SQL Server 2017, both come with associated R and Machine Learning services, which enables the development of machine learning solutions. These solutions, which are based on R and Python, can be directly executed either from traditional R and Python development environments, or from SQL Server Management Studio as stored procedures close to the relational data. Other advantages of the SQLVM stems directly from the benefits of using an in-database machine learning service: less data movement, real time scoring, TSQL language to process data, columnar storage, and binary model storage and a TSQL PREDICT clause to embed predictions in your queries.

Other reasons to deploy a SQL Virtual Machine come closely associated with why you would move your applications and databases to the cloud. The main two reasons are interoperability and availability: with an Azure SQL Virtual Machine your data will always be backed up, and with high availability in case a server is out of service. As for interoperability, you can easily connect your SQL VM to many other Azure services and amplify the features that are part of your machine learning solution.

Currently there are four machine-learning services available with SQL Server distributions. The name and full features depend on the version of SQL Server deployed:

- **SQL Server 2016 R Services (In-Database)**   This is the initial service version offered with SQL Server 2016 Developer and Enterprise. It incorporates the RevoScaleR functions for faster parallel and distributed R processing, the MicrosoftML algorithms, which perform better than many industry leading algorithms, and an array of R API calls to Cortana Intelligence to complement your R solutions with the Cortana services.

- **SQL Server 2017 Machine Learning Services (In-Database)**   The main addition to the SQL Server 2017 Machine Learning Services is the Python Services, which have been developed similarly to the R Services: The incorporate a RevoScalePy library for parallel and distributed Python computing, as well as the MicrosoftML library with its added functionality.

- **Standalone Machine Learning Server**   This is an optional install when you already have an instance of SQL Server 2016 or SQL Server 2017 installed without R or Machine Learning Services. Essentially, you are able to install the services as standalone software, and then link them to your already existing instance.

- **Azure SQL Databases**   Some Azure regions are starting to support the execution of R scripts and the use of the PREDICT command. Python and MicrosoftML is not yet supported.

---

**This skill covers how to:**

- Deploy a SQL Server 2016 Azure VM
- Configure SQL Server to allow execution of R scripts
- Get started with SQL Server Machine Learning in easy steps
- Execute R scripts inside T-SQL statements

---

# Deploy a SQL Server 2016 Azure VM

In this section you review how to deploy a SQL Server Azure VM from the portal, configure and connect to it for its further use in developing R and Python machine learning solutions closely associated to a SQL Server and its databases.

## Types of Azure VMs

When deciding upon a type of virtual machine for your machine learning solution needs, you first need to consider which version of SQL Server you need. As discussed before, the main difference between the versions is that SQL Server 2017 enables you to develop Python-based solutions in addition to R-based solutions, whereas on SQL Server 2016 you are only able to develop R-based solutions. In addition, SQL Server 2017 comes with a Machine Learning Python library called MicrosoftML. The library has deep pretrained models (like ResNet and AlexNet) that you can easily use for image featurization. Other functionalities such as text featurization and sentiment analysis are also available in the library.

You could deploy SQL Server on a Linux operating system as well, but there are some hurdles to developing SQL R Services related solutions. The current distribution of SQL Server 2017 for Linux does not include in-database R Services, thus if you are a data scientist used to the Linux environment and you wish to use this feature natively on Linux, currently you will not be able to do it. However, you could always deploy SQL Server 2017 on Windows virtual machine hosted on you Linux system, wherein you will be able to use the full features of the Windows SQL Server 2017 that are not yet included in the Linux SQL Server 2017, such as R Services, to Analysis Services and Reporting Services.

Finally, you have to decide the hardware that best suits your needs. As of late 2017 there are six families of virtual machines (*https://docs.microsoft.com/en-us/azure/virtual-machines/windows/sizes*), each aiming to satisfy a particular type of computation task:

- **General Purpose**   Virtual machines with a balanced CPU-to-memory ratio. Ideal for testing and development, for small to medium databases and low to medium web traffic. The following machines fall under this category: B (Preview), Dsv3, Dv3, DSv2, Dv2, DS, D, Av2, A0-7.

- **Compute Optimized**   Virtual machines with a higher CPU-to-memory ratio. Ideal for medium web traffic, network appliances, batch processes, and application servers. The following machines fall under this category: Fsv2, Fs, F.

- **Memory Optimized**   Virtual machines with a high memory-to-CPU ratio. Ideal for relational databases, in-memory cubes, models and analytics. The following machines fall under this category: Esv3, Ev3, M, GS, G, DSv2, DS, Dv2, D.

- **Storage optimized**   Virtual machines ideal for disk IO intensive operations, such as big data, SQL, and NoSQL databases. The following machines fall under this category: Ls.

- **GPU Enabled**   Specialized virtual machines with GPUs ideal for heavy graphic rendering, video editing, and deep learning solutions. The following machines fall under this category: NV, NC.

- **High performance compute**   Virtual machines with the fastest and most powerful CPUs available in the datacenter. Ideal for high-throughput, real time, and big data applications. The following machines fall under this category: H, A8-11.

## Create an Azure VM

You will deploy, configure, and use a SQL Server 2017 Developer on Windows Server 2016 Standard_A4_v2 virtual machine in the rest of this chapter. This machine offers a fully featured free option for developing and testing R and Python solutions associated to a SQL Server and its databases because of the SQL developer edition installed with the machine. The hardware choice stems from it being one of the newest general-purpose machines, with a slight balance toward higher memory for handling moderately sized datasets in R and Python.

FIGURE 4-53 Suggested Virtual Machine Configuration

First, log in to the Azure Portal using your account (*https://portal.azure.com/*). Once the portal launches, click the Create Resource plus sign, click the Compute resources, and then click the See All option, as shown in Figure 4-54.

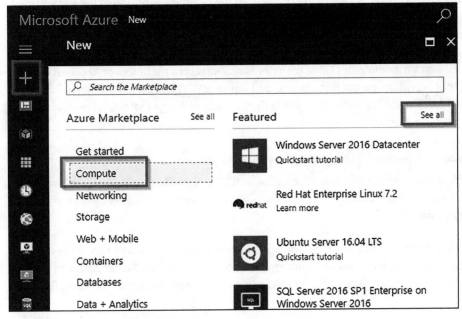

FIGURE 4-54 Azure Portal resource creation

If you cannot see the Free SQL Server License: SQL Server 2017 Developer On Windows Server 2016 virtual machine, search for Free SQL Server 2017 in the search box, and click the indicated virtual machine, as shown in Figure 4-55.

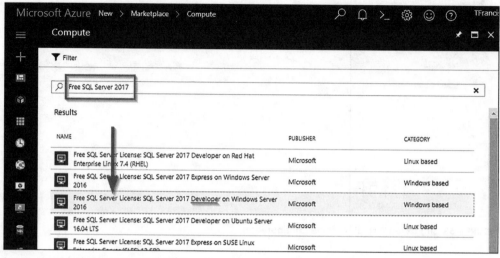

**FIGURE 4-55** Azure SQL Virtual Machines

SQL Server virtual machine images include the licensing costs for SQL Server (and other deployed software, as in the case of the DSVM) into the per-minute pricing of the VM you create. SQL Server Developer and Express editions are exceptions because their SQL licensing costs are zero. SQL Server Developer is a fully featured SQL Server used for development and testing (not to be used in production). SQL Express is meant for lightweight environments and workloads, with a maximum of 1 GB of memory allocation and a maximum of 10 GBs of storage size. Another exception are the Bring Your Own License (BYOL) SQL Server machines. Those VM images will not include licensing costs, you only must acknowledge that you have a valid SQL Server Enterprise license.

> **NEED MORE INFORMATION? SQL SERVER VIRTUAL MACHINES**
>
> Visit the documentation for more information on SQL Server VMs at: *https://docs.microsoft.com/en-us/azure/virtual-machines/windows/sql/virtual-machines-windows-sql-server-pricing-guidance.*

After choosing the virtual machine, you are directed to a general description of the machine, along with links for further information on documentation, SQL Server 2017, and pricing terms. Click Create, leaving the option of selecting a deployment model to its default, Resource Manager.

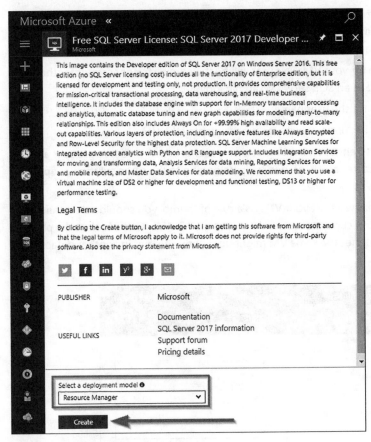

**FIGURE 4-56** VM deployment confirmation

## Configure an Azure VM

After you create the selected VM, you have five final steps to configure the VM:

- **Basics**    Configure basic settings.
- **Size**    Choose virtual machine size.
- **Settings**    Configure optional features.
- **SQL Server Settings**    Configure SQL Server settings.
- **Summary**    Check that everything is correct before deploying.

## Configure basic settings

Under the Basics tab, you are required to input the following values and configurations:

- Enter a name for your VM. Remember that only lowercase names with dashes are accepted.

- Select either SSD of HDD for your virtual machine. If you wish to deploy any of the Av2 family, select HDD as the VM disk type. Those machines are not recommended for SQL production workloads, but are good for this demo because they are cheaper.

- Create a user name for your VM. This user will be the administrator account for the VM, and it will be added as an SQL Server sysadmin login.

- Specify a password for the user name.

- Select the subscription under which you wish to deploy the VM.

- Associate your VM to either an existing or a new user group. A resource group is a collection of related Azure resources, generally belonging to the same solution or application.

- Select a Location that will host your VM. As a rule of thumb, you should select the datacenter nearest to your current client or development PC. Also, take a look at the price estimator, for sometimes the same VM might be slightly cheaper in another datacenter.

- Click OK to save the settings.

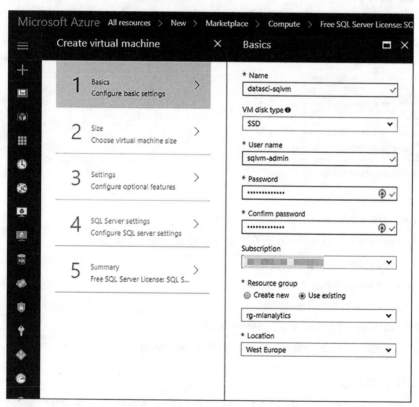

**FIGURE 4-57** Virtual Machine Basics settings

## Configure the VM size

The next step is to configure the VM size. On the Size step, select which virtual machine hardware you wish to deploy. The Choose A Size blade displays recommended sizes based on the selected image to be deployed. Browse all the other available sizes and select one suited to your necessities, or if the purpose is only following this chapter, select the Standard_A4_v2 virtual machine. The estimated monthly cost includes SQL Server and other software licensing costs. However, because you are deploying a free SQL Server Developer Edition with no licensing cost, the cost displayed equals that of the maintenance of the VM alone; this estimated cost will also be the total monthly cost of our deployment.

Choose the machine size and click Select, as shown in Figure 4-58.

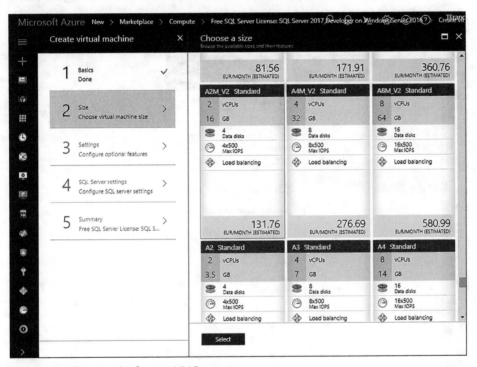

**FIGURE 4-58** Choose a size for your VM Pane

## Configure optional features

The next step in the VM configuration is the configuration of optional features. These include High Availability, Storage Management, Network Settings, Extensions, Auto-shutdown, and Monitoring options. See Figure 4-59 for an example.

- Specify the desired availability set of your VM. Availability sets are managed groups of VMs that are ensured to provide at least one available VM from the group in case of a planned or unplanned maintenance event. Leave this options to None.

- Confirm the Storage mode to use managed disks. Managed disks automatically handle storage accounts, availability, and scaling in case the machine needs to be rescaled.
- Network settings are used to configure the VMs virtual network, subnet, Public IP visibility, firewall security group, and accelerated throughput on the VM network interface. Leave all the options to the defaults specified.
- Extensions allow you to add additional software to your VM, such as antiviruses or backup suites. Leave this option to None.
- Enable the auto-shutdown if you wish to schedule the shutdown of the VM in order to save on resource consumption. Click On, and select a shutdown time and time zone.
- The Monitoring option comes enabled by default. Azure uses the same storage account for monitoring as the one the VM is based on.
- Click OK to save the settings.

**FIGURE 4-59** VM Optional Configuration pane

## Configure SQL Server settings

In this step, you configure SQL Server settings, optimizations, access, and other management settings of SQL Server. Refer to Figure 4-59 as an example.

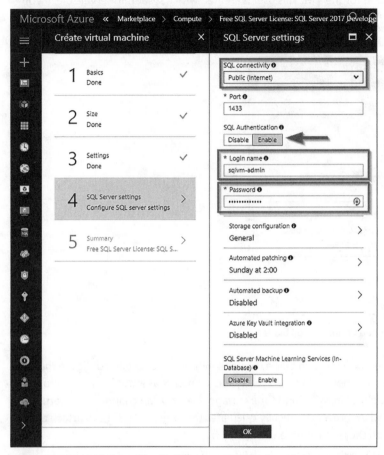

**FIGURE 4-60** VM SQL Server Settings

- Under the SQL Connectivity option, you can specify the type of access you want to the SQL server instance in your VM. You have three options:
- Local (inside VM only) to allow connections to SQL Server only from within the VM.
- Private (within Virtual Network) to allow connections to SQL Server from machines or services in the same virtual network.
- Public (Internet)
- For the purposes of this chapter, select Public (Internet) to allow connections to SQL Server from machines or services on the Internet. Once this option is selected, Azure automatically configures the firewall and the network security group.

In order to connect to your SQL Server instance from outside your VM, you must also enable SQL Authentication. Once enabled, you will be able to specify a different SQL Server admin and password to the default. Otherwise, Azure uses the same user and password as the one for the VM. This user is created with a sysadmin server role. If you do not enable SQL Server Authentication, you can use the VM Administrator account to connect to the SQL Server instance.

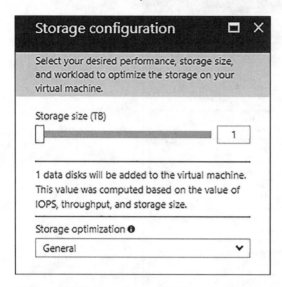

**FIGURE 4-61** SQL Server Storage Configuration blade

- Under the Storage Configuration blade (Figure 4-60), you are able to configure the SQL Server storage requirements. You can specify requirements as input/output operations per second, throughput in MB/s, and total storage size. You can change these settings based on workload. Azure automatically calculates the number of disks to attach and configure based on these requirements.

- Under Storage Optimized For, select one of the following options:

- General is the default setting and supports most workloads.

- Transactional processing optimizes the storage for traditional database OLTP workloads.

- Data warehousing optimizes the storage for analytic and reporting workloads.

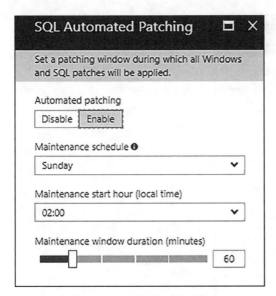

FIGURE 4-62 SQL Automated Patching blade

- Automatic Patching is enabled by default, as shown in Figure 4-61. It allows Azure to automatically patch SQL Server and the operating system. You should specify the scheduled time for maintenance, as well as the window duration.
- Under the automated Backup window, as shown in Figure 4-62, you are able to configure the backup policies of you SQL Server instance. As you click enable, you will be able to configure:
- Retention period (days) for backups
- Storage account to use for backups
- Encryption option and password for backups
- Backup system databases
- Configure backup schedule

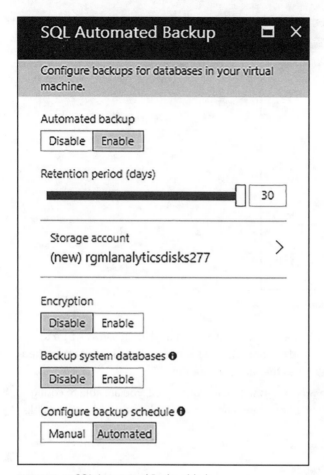

**FIGURE 4-63** SQL Automated Backup blade

- Continuing with the SQL Server configuration, as shown in Figure 4-59, Azure Key Vault integration allows your VM to connect to the Azure Key Vault service for a cloud-based key storage. Leave this option disabled.

- Finally, SQL Server Machine Learning services allows you to install the latest machine learning service with your SQL Server 2017 Developer edition installation. Leave this option enabled.

- Once finished click OK to continue

## Summary pane

On the summary blade, you are able to review the configuration for your SQL 2017 VM and confirm its creation. If this is a reiterated deployment, you can download the template and parameters and deploy similar machines without having to go through the whole setup process. Once you reviewed the settings, click Create.

**FIGURE 4-64** Summary Confirmation blade

## Connect to VMs with RDP

In order to connect to your VM, once it is created, open it within the Azure Portal, as shown in Figure 4-64. On the upper bar of the Virtual Machine window you will find the Connect option. Click it and a RDP file is downloaded. Open the RDP file, on the Remote Desktop Connection click Connect, and then change your credentials to use the admin and password specified during setup, as shown in Figure 4-65. Click OK to connect to the VM.

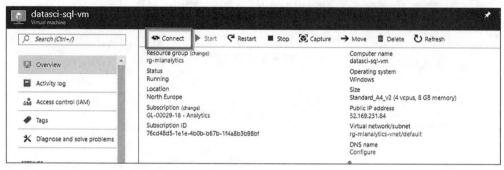

**FIGURE 4-65** Azure Portal Virtual Machine Summary

After you connect to the SQL Server virtual machine, you can launch SQL Server Management Studio and connect with Windows Authentication using your local administrator credentials. If you enabled SQL Server Authentication, you can also connect with SQL Authentication using the SQL login and password you configured during provisioning.

**FIGURE 4-66** Connect to the Virtual Machine using your credentials

Access to the machine enables you to directly change machine and SQL Server settings based on your requirements. For example, you could configure the firewall settings or change SQL Server configuration settings.

## Connect to SQL Server remotely

Previously you configured a Public access for the virtual machine and SQL Server Authentication when deploying the virtual machine. By enabling these two settings, you can connect to the VM's SQL Server instance from outside the virtual machine, by using any client you choose as long as you have the correct SQL login and password. Before being able to do so, you need to enable a couple of features in your VM settings.

1. **Configure a DNS label for the public IP address.**

   Login into your Azure Portal and open your Virtual Machine configurations page. Click DNS Name on the right hand side of your settings summary. A Configuration blade will show up, as shown in Figure 4-67.

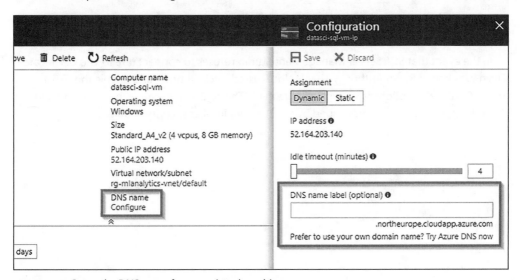

**FIGURE 4-67** Setup the DNS name for your virtual machine

   Enter a DNS Label name. This will be the "readable" Internet address of your virtual machine. Save the full address to a known location, and click **Save.**

2. **Connect to the database engine from another computer.**

   Open SQL Server Management Studio (SSMS), and on the Connect To Server dialog box, specify the DNS Label name you just set up for the VM IP address. Type in the virtual machine login and password (or SQL Server login and password, if different from the main administrator account for the virtual machine), and click Connect.

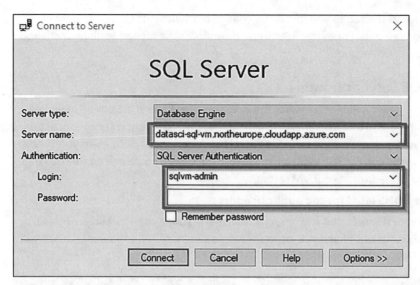

**FIGURE 4-68** Connect to the Server Window

In the event that SQL Server Management Studio refuses to connect due to The Certificate Chain Was Issued By An Authority That Is Not Trusted, click Options, and enable the 'Trust Server Certificate' option, as shown in Figure 4-69. This is just an example, but keep in mind that relying on a certificate not issued by an authority implies security problems.

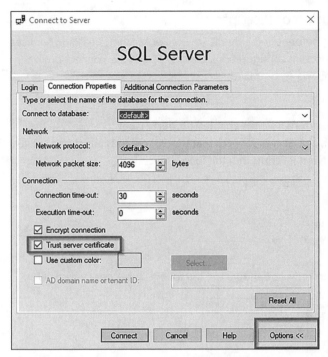

**FIGURE 4-69** Additional Connect To Server options

## Configure SQL Server to allow execution of R scripts

The deployed VM has all the required configurations in order to run R scripts from a query window right from the start. However, depending on your use case for Machine Learning Services you might need to make additional changes and configure the server, firewall, accounts, or database/server permissions.

A few common scenarios that require you to change internal configurations are:

- Verify and configure execution of R scripts
- Unblock the firewall
- Enable ODBC callbacks for remote clients
- Enabling additional network protocols
- Enable TCP/IP for Developer and Express editions
- Add more worker accounts
- Ensuring that users have permission to run code or install packages
- Install Additional R packages

## Verify and configure execution of R scripts

You must always carry out this step before using either R Services or Machine Learning Services because this is one of the most important configurations/checks. Open your connection to the virtual machine and execute the following command:

```
sp_configure
```

Check that the `run_value` for the external scripts enabled property is set to 1. Verify in the SQL Server Configuration Manager, SQL Server Services that the SQL Server Launchpad is running. In order to verify that SQL can run R Scripts, run the following code:

```
EXEC sp_execute_external_script  @language =N'R',
@script=N'
OutputDataSet <- InputDataSet;',
@input_data_1 =N'SELECT 1 AS hello'
WITH RESULT SETS (([hello] int not null));
GO
```

If your machine is configured correctly, you should see the following output (Figure 4-70):

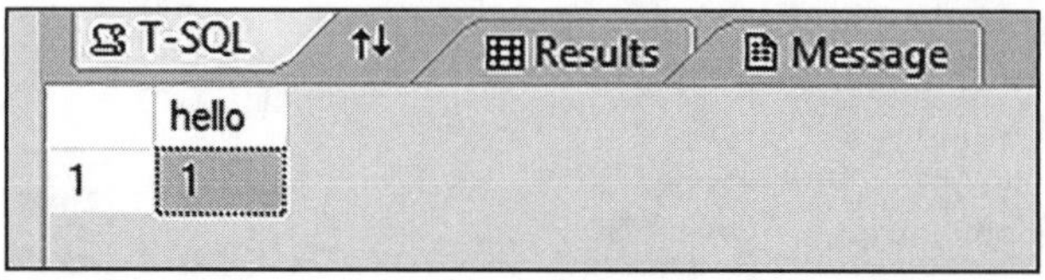

**FIGURE 4-70** Correct output from executing the Hello TSQL R script

However, if your results are different from the above, you need to enable the execution of external scripts. In order to do so, execute the following code with an account that has owner permissions at the instance level (the VM account has these permissions):

```
sp_configure 'external scripts enabled', 1;

RECONFIGURE WITH OVERRIDE;
```

Restart the SQL VM and then re-connect and rerun the 'Hello' code to confirm that external execution has been enabled.

*Mandatory step. Also check Launchpad is enabled on SQL Server configuration. (Easiest way to do it, Server Manager Services)*

## Unblock the firewall

By default, the Azure Virtual Machine firewall blocks network access for local user accounts. Because R is being launched from the umbrella of SQL Launchpad, the operating system sees any R script as being executed by the MSSQLLAUNCHPAD user.

You must disable this rule to ensure:

- That you can access the SQL Server instance from a remote data science client. Otherwise, your machine learning code cannot execute in compute contexts that use the virtual machine's workspace.

- That you will be able to install extra packages from R using the `install.packages()` function.

To enable access from remote data science clients:

- On the virtual machine, open Windows Firewall with Advanced Security.
- Select Outbound Rules.
- Disable the following rule:
- Block Network Access For R Local User Accounts In SQL Server Instance MSSQLSERVER

## Enable ODBC callbacks for remote clients

If you create an R solution on a data science client computer and need to <u>run code by using the SQL Server computer as the compute context,</u> you can use either a SQL login, or integrated Windows authentication.

*For non-admin user.*

- **For SQL logins**   Ensure that the login has appropriate permissions on the database where you will be reading data. You can do so by adding Connect To and SELECT permissions, or by adding the login to the db_datareader role. For logins that need to create objects, add DDL_admin rights. For logins that must save data to tables, add the login to the db_datawriter role.

- **For Windows authentication**   You might need to configure an ODBC data source on the data science client that specifies the instance name and other connection information.

## Add network protocols

In addition to configuring the VM firewall, the following network protocols must be configured in order to install new packages and enabling R scripts to communicate with the rest of the Internet:

- Enable named pipes
- R Services (In-Database) uses the Named Pipes protocol for connections between the client and server computers, and for some internal connections. If Named Pipes is not enabled, you must install and enable it on <u>both the Azure virtual machine, a</u>nd on any data science clients that connect to the server.

- Enable TCP/IP

TCP/IP is required for loopback connections. If you get the error "DBNETLIB; SQL Server does not exist or access denied," enable TCP/IP on the virtual machine that supports the instance, as shown in the next step.

## Enable TCP/IP for Developer and Express editions

When provisioning a new SQL Server VM, Azure does not automatically enable the TCP/IP protocol for SQL Server Developer and Express editions. If you wish to manually enable TCP/IP so that you can connect remotely by IP address, follow these steps:

- While connected to the virtual machine with remote desktop, search for Configuration Manager.
- In SQL Server Configuration Manager, in the console pane, expand SQL Server Network Configuration.
- In the console pane, click Protocols For MSSQLSERVER (the default instance name.) In the details pane, right-click TCP, and click Enable if it is not already enabled.
- In the console pane, click SQL Server Services. In the details pane, right-click SQL Server (the default instance is SQL Server (MSSQLSERVER)), and then click Restart, to stop and restart the instance of SQL Server.
- Close SQL Server Configuration Manager.

## Add more worker accounts

If you think you might use R heavily, or if you expect many users to be running scripts concurrently, you can increase the number of worker accounts that are assigned to the Launchpad service.

## Enable package management for SQL Server 2017

In SQL Server 2017, you can enable package management at the instance level, and manage user permissions to add or use packages at the database level. This requires that the database administrator enable the package management feature by running a script that creates the necessary database objects. To enable or disable package management requires the command-line utility RegisterRExt.exe, which is included with the RevoScaleR package.

- Open an elevated command prompt and navigate to the folder containing the utility, RegisterRExt.exe. The default location is <SQLInstancePath>\R_SERVICES\library\RevoScaleR\rxLibs\x64\RegisterRExe.exe.

- Run the following command, providing appropriate arguments for your environment:

- RegisterRExt.exe /installpkgmgmt [/instance:name] [/user:username] [/password:*|password].

- This command creates instance-level objects on the SQL Server computer that are required for package management. It also restarts the Launchpad for the instance. If you do not specify an instance, the default instance is used. If you do not specify a user, the current security context is used.

- To add package management at the database level, run the following command from an elevated command prompt:

  ```
  RegisterRExt.exe /installpkgmgmt /database:databasename [/instance:name] [/
  user:username] [/password:*|password].
  ```

- This command creates some database artifacts, including the following database roles that are used for controlling user permissions: rpkgs-users, rpkgs-private, and rpkgs-shared. Repeat the command for each database where packages must be installed.

- To verify that the new roles have been successfully created, in SQL Server Management Studio, execute the following query on sys.database_principals. You should see the aforementioned rpkgs groups as shown in Figure 4-71 below.

```
USE AdventureWorksDW2017
SELECT pr.principal_id, pr.name, pr.type_desc,
pr.authentication_type_desc, pe.state_desc,
                  pe.permission_name, s.name + '.' + o.name AS ObjectName
FROM sys.database_principals AS pr
JOIN sys.database_permissions AS pe
    ON pe.grantee_principal_id = pr.principal_id
JOIN sys.objects AS o
    ON pe.major_id = o.object_id
JOIN sys.schemas AS s
    ON o.schema_id = s.schema_id;
```

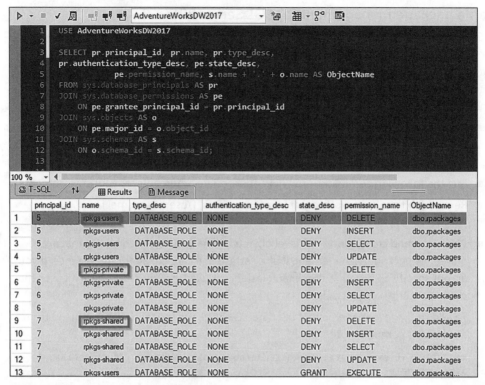

```
USE AdventureWorksDW2017

SELECT pr.principal_id, pr.name, pr.type_desc,
pr.authentication_type_desc, pe.state_desc,
            pe.permission_name, s.name + '.' + o.name AS ObjectName
FROM sys.database_principals AS pr
JOIN sys.database_permissions AS pe
    ON pe.grantee_principal_id = pr.principal_id
JOIN sys.objects AS o
    ON pe.major_id = o.object_id
JOIN sys.schemas AS s
    ON o.schema_id = s.schema_id;
```

| | principal_id | name | type_desc | authentication_type_desc | state_desc | permission_name | ObjectName |
|---|---|---|---|---|---|---|---|
| 1 | 5 | rpkgs-users | DATABASE_ROLE | NONE | DENY | DELETE | dbo.rpackages |
| 2 | 5 | rpkgs-users | DATABASE_ROLE | NONE | DENY | INSERT | dbo.rpackages |
| 3 | 5 | rpkgs-users | DATABASE_ROLE | NONE | DENY | SELECT | dbo.rpackages |
| 4 | 5 | rpkgs-users | DATABASE_ROLE | NONE | DENY | UPDATE | dbo.rpackages |
| 5 | 6 | rpkgs-private | DATABASE_ROLE | NONE | DENY | DELETE | dbo.rpackages |
| 6 | 6 | rpkgs-private | DATABASE_ROLE | NONE | DENY | INSERT | dbo.rpackages |
| 7 | 6 | rpkgs-private | DATABASE_ROLE | NONE | DENY | SELECT | dbo.rpackages |
| 8 | 6 | rpkgs-private | DATABASE_ROLE | NONE | DENY | UPDATE | dbo.rpackages |
| 9 | 7 | rpkgs-shared | DATABASE_ROLE | NONE | DENY | DELETE | dbo.rpackages |
| 10 | 7 | rpkgs-shared | DATABASE_ROLE | NONE | DENY | INSERT | dbo.rpackages |
| 11 | 7 | rpkgs-shared | DATABASE_ROLE | NONE | DENY | SELECT | dbo.rpackages |
| 12 | 7 | rpkgs-shared | DATABASE_ROLE | NONE | DENY | UPDATE | dbo.rpackages |
| 13 | 5 | rpkgs-users | DATABASE_ROLE | NONE | GRANT | EXECUTE | dbo.rpackag... |

**FIGURE 4-71** Query output of added R database roles

- After the feature has been enabled, any user with the appropriate permissions can use the CREATE EXTERNAL LIBRARY statement in T-SQL to add packages.

## Install additional R packages

Although the preferred method to install packages is by calling the install.packages() function directly from an R terminal, here you install packages either locally from TSQL using the xp_cmdshell, or from a remote TSQL terminal with the use of the RevoScaleR rxInstallPackages() function. If you are running a SQL Server 2017 instance, package management must be enabled and the queries must be run either with the db_owner or with a user assigned to one of the roles generated before. Similarly, if you have a SQL Server 2016 instance, be sure to run all these scripts either from an elevated window or with the operating system Administrator account.

- **Install packages from a virtual machine local TSQL query.**

    Connect to your virtual machine and open SQL Server Management Studio as an Administrator. Before installing packages, you have to enable the **xp_cmdshell** stored procedure, which enables you to launch command line commands from a TSQL query. In order to do so, execute the following code:

```
USE MASTER
-- Enable advanced options
EXEC sp_configure 'show advanced options', 1;
GO

RECONFIGURE;
GO

-- Enable xp_cmdshell stored procedure.
EXECUTE SP_CONFIGURE 'xp_cmdshell',1;
GO

RECONFIGURE;
GO
```

*This feels unnecessarily convoluted*

Once the xp_cmdshell stored procedure is enabled, and then execute the following query to call R and pass it to the install.packages() function. As you execute this code, a command line window pops up and the results should be similar to the ones shown in Figure 4-72.

```
EXEC xp_cmdshell '"C:\Program Files\Microsoft SQL Server\MSSQL14.MSSQLSERVER\R_
SERVICES\bin\R.EXE" cmd -e install.packages(''zoo'')';
GO
```

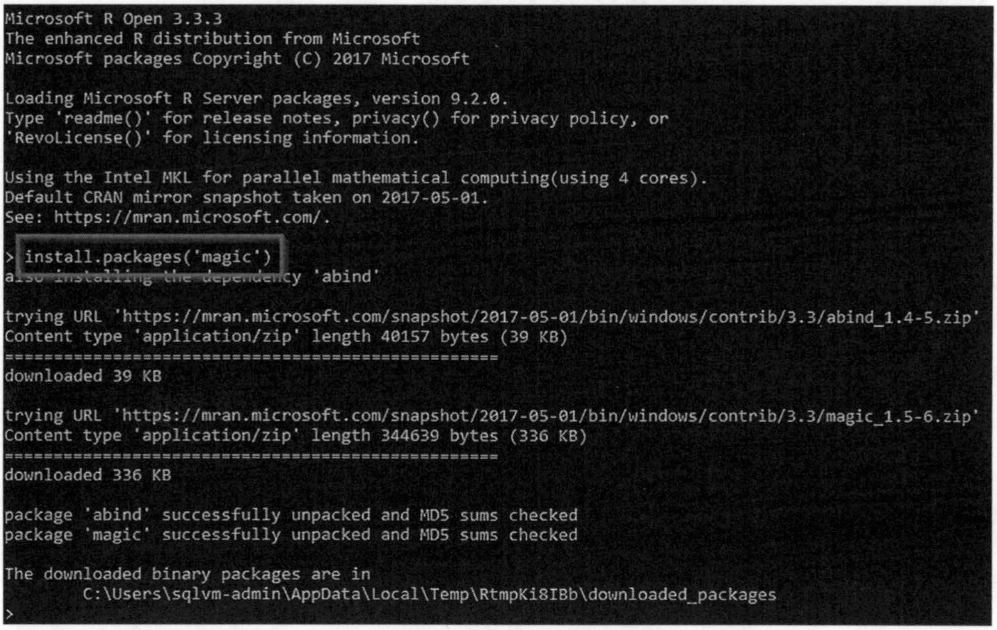

**FIGURE 4-72** Command line window showing the results of installing the package magic

# Install packages from a remote TSQL query.

Connect to your virtual machine SQL Server instance from your chosen IDE. In order to install packages remotely, you will be using the RevoScaleR rxInstallPackages() function. This function, as most of the RevoScaleR functions, needs to have a specific compute context declared; it functions as the execution target for the function. To create a SQL compute context declaration, you call the RxInSqlServer() function with the connection string to your SQL instance and database as shown in the code below. Then you create a variable containing all the packages that will be installed, and finally you will call the rxInstallPackages() function specifying the compute context and the packages to be installed. Additionally, you can specify the package installation scope; "private" (just accessible by the current user) or "shared" (accessible by all users); and the path to the R Services packages library. If the latter is not specified, R will install the new packages to its default library path.

```
EXEC sp_execute_external_script
@language =N'R',
@script=N'
sqlcc <- RxInSqlServer(connectionString = "Driver=SQL Server;
                       Server=MSSQLSERVER;
                       Database=AdventureWorksDW2017;
                       UID=sqlvm-admin;
                       PWD=SQVMadmin2017;")
# list of packages to install
pkgs <- c("dplyr")
# Install a package and its dependencies into shared scope
rxInstallPackages(pkgs = pkgs,
verbose = TRUE,
scope = "shared",
computeContext = sqlcc)'
```

After executing the above code, check that the results are similar to the ones shown in Figure 4-73.

```
83    -- Install Packages Using RevoScaleR Function
84  □EXEC
85    @language =N'R',
86    @script=N'
87  sqlcc <- RxInSqlServer( connectionString = "Driver=SQL Server;
88                                              Server=MSSQLSERVER;
89                                              Database=AdventureWorksDW2017;
90                                              UID=sqlvm-admin;
91                                              PWD=SQVMadmin2017;")
92
93  # list of packages to install
94  pkgs <- c('dplyr')
95
96  # Install a package and its dependencies into shared scope
97  rxInstallPackages(pkgs = pkgs, verbose = TRUE, scope = "shared", computeContext = sqlcc)
```

```
STDOUT message(s) from external script:
Verifying permissions to install packages on SQL server...
Resolving package dependencies for (dplyr)...
Downloading package [1/8] assertthat (0.2.0)...
Downloading package [2/8] Rcpp (0.12.10)...
Downloading package [3/8] tibble (1.3.0)...
Downloading package [4/8] magrittr (1.5)...
Downloading package [5/8] lazyeval (0.2.0)...
Downloading package [6/8] DBI (0.6-1)...
Downloading package [7/8] BH (1.62.0-1)...
Downloading package [8/8] dplyr (0.5.0)...
Installing packages on SQL server (assertthat, Rcpp, tibble, magrittr, lazyeval, DBI, BH, dplyr)...
Downloading assertthat from database...
Downloading Rcpp from database...
Downloading tibble from database...
Downloading magrittr from database...
Downloading lazyeval from database...
Downloading DBI from database...
Downloading BH from database...
Downloading dplyr from database...
Executing operation with description "Soft-delete old packages"

STDOUT message(s) from external script:
Executing operation with description "Install to temporary location"
package 'assertthat' successfully unpacked and MD5 sums checked
For session 222, successfully installed package assertthat
package 'Rcpp' successfully unpacked and MD5 sums checked
For session 222, successfully installed package Rcpp
package 'tibble' successfully unpacked and MD5 sum
package 'dplyr' successfully unpacked and MD5 sums checked
For session 222, successfully installed package dplyr
Executing operation with description "Expose new packages "
Executing operation with description "Hard delete old packages "
Finished chained execution
Cleanup of session 222 succeeded
removing of cleanup tracking for session 222 succeeded
Successfully installed packages on SQL server (assertthat, Rcpp, tibble, magrittr, lazyeval, DBI, BH, dplyr).
```

**FIGURE 4-73** Output of the query containing the rxInstallPackages() function

In order to check that the packages are correctly installed, first query with the following code the location of the packages path. Then follow the path on your virtual machine to check that the directories *dplyr* and *zoo* (the packages you have installed in this section) are correctly created.

```
EXECUTE sp_execute_external_script
    @language = N'R'
    ,@script = N'OutputDataSet <- data.frame(.libPaths());'
```

```
WITH RESULT SETS (([DefaultLibraryName] VARCHAR(MAX) NOT NULL));
GO
```

Finally, whether you installed packages from local or remotely, you can load them into an empty R session to check once again that they are correctly installed and ready to be used in R-TSQL scripts by executing the following code:

```
EXEC sp_execute_external_script
@language =N'R',
@script=N'
# load the binaries in dplyr
library(dplyr)'
```

The output should resemble the one shown in Figure 4-74.

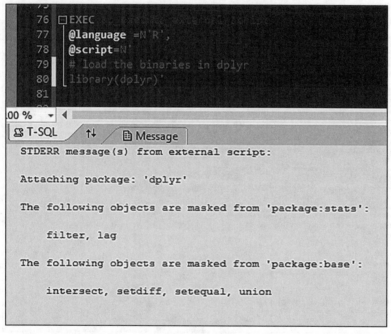

**FIGURE 4-74** Results from loading the dplyr package into an empty R session

**NEED MORE INFORMATION? MACHINE LEARNING SERVICES PACKAGE INSTALLATION**

For more options and details of the procedures followed here, visit the Microsoft documentation on installing additional packages on SQL Server Machine Learning Services at *https://docs.microsoft.com/en-us/sql/advanced-analytics/r/install-additional-r-packages-on-sql-server#bkmk_sqlInstall.*

# First steps in SQL Server Machine Learning

The main purpose of Machine Learning Services in SQL Server is providing data engineers and data scientists with an analytical engine capable of performing data science tasks removing the need to move data unnecessarily, or uploading it to external services that might expose your data to security risks. In order to accomplish this, SQL Server Machine Learning executes as a parallel engine with full connectivity to the relational database system, with the ability to run scripts either from SQL Queries or from the R or Python engine, but with minimum data movement from the relational stores to memory stores that R and Python can handle.

- **Set up SQL Server Machine Learning Services.**

  Follow the previous set up steps if you have not done so. Most importantly, be sure that the *External Scripts Enabled* property has a run_value equal to **1**, otherwise you will not be able to execute Python or R Scripts.

- **Develop your R or Python solutions.**

  Developing R or Python solutions against a development workstation becomes extremely easy with our actual setup. Typically, a data scientist uses R or Python on their own machine to develop a solution with a given set of data. With your actual configuration using an Azure Virtual Machine you are able to connect remotely in order to explore data, build, and tune predictive models and deploy a production quality model to a production scoring scenario directly from your client workstation, without having to move data or ensure that your local scripts will execute on the remote instance. In order to develop your machine learning solutions, you have to:

  - **Choose a development IDE**   Whether you will work remotely or locally there is a multitude of IDEs from which you could choose in order to develop your solution. The main requirement for your IDE is that it should be able to connect to SQL Server Instances in order to execute R and Python scripts embedded in TSQL Stored procedures. A few of the available options are:

    - Visual Studio 2017 with the Data Science and Analytical Applications Workload installed.

    - Visual Studio 2015 with R Tools and Python tools for Visual Studio.

    - Visual Studio Code with the *mssql* Extension installed.

    - SQL Server Management Studio.

    - Others, such as R Studio, IPython / Jupyter Notebooks, or simple notepad editing with command line execution.

  - **Work remotely or locally**   The usual walkthrough for a data science solution requires you to copy a table or dataset to your local machine, load it up in memory, and then start from there the data science cycle. However, Machine Learning Services allows you to develop your scripts remotely pushing their execution to the SQL Server instance without having to copy the data to your local environment. This is done through the RevoScaleR and RevoScalePy libraries, which push many of the loading and computing tasks to the server, avoiding costly local executions. In order to work remotely, configure your IDE to connect to your VM and its SQL Server Instance as you have seen before, and all the scripts developed locally will be executed remotely in the development workstation.

- **Embed R or Python scripts in Transact-SQL stored procedures** Once the developed code is fully optimized, wrap it in a stored procedure in order to avoid unnecessary data movement, optimize data processing tasks, and schedule your machine learning or advanced analytics step into a regular ETL or other scheduled tasks.

> **NEED MORE INFORMATION?** **OTHER MICROSOFT MACHINE LEARNING SERVICES TUTORIALS**
>
> If you wish to further experiment with Machine Learning Services, follow one of the Python or R tutorials specified in the following link. Remember you can also copy a solution from Cortana Solution Gallery and follow its deployment throughout at *https://docs.microsoft.com/en-us/sql/advanced-analytics/tutorials/machine-learning-services-tutorials*.

- **Optimize processes** When the model is ready to scale on enterprise data, the data scientist will often work with the DBA or SQL developer to optimize processes such as:
  - Feature engineering
  - Data ingestion and data transformation
  - Scoring

Traditionally data scientists using R have had problems with both performance and scale, especially when using large dataset. That is because the common runtime implementation is single-threaded and can accommodate only those data sets that fit into the available memory on the local computer. Integration with SQL Server Machine Learning Services provides multiple features for better performance, with more data:

- **RevoScaleR** This R package contains implementations of some of the most popular R functions, redesigned to provide parallelism and scale. The package also includes functions that further boost performance and scale by pushing computations to the SQL Server computer, which typically has far greater memory and computational power.

- **Revoscalepy** This Python library, new and available only in SQL Server 2017 CTP 2.0, implements the most popular functions in RevoScaleR, such as remote compute contexts, and many algorithms that support distributed processing.

Choose the best language for the task. R is best for statistical computations that are difficult to implement using SQL. For set-based operations over data, leverage the power of SQL Server to achieve maximum performance. Use the in-memory database engine for very fast computations over columns.

■ **Deploy and consume**

After the R script or model is ready for production use, a database developer might embed the code or model in a stored procedure, deploy a web service, or create predictions based on a stored model with views and/or stored procedures that make use of the TSQL PREDICT clause, so that the saved R or Python code can be called from an application. Storing and running R code from SQL Server has many benefits: you can use the convenient Transact-SQL interface, and all computations take place in the database, avoiding unnecessary data movement.

After deployment, you can integrate predictions and recommendations of your model with further architecture in other apps that are friendlier to the end user. The most common approach is to consult the deployed machine learning solution through PowerBI, and consume its output directly from the application. This allows you to compare quickly predicted data against other queries, cube queries, and historicals while at the same time developing a graphical interface to convey a complete message about your data science problem and the developed solution.

Although PowerBI is one of the most common consumption applications, you are not restricted to it. Once your model has been operationalized by the data engineer, you can consume it from Reporting Services, Analysis Services, Tableau, command line applications, Azure Services, and any other software that can connect to your SQL Server instance and run queries against it.

> **NEED MORE INFORMATION? SQL SERVER MACHINE LEARNING SERVICES OPERATIONALIZATION**
>
> More information on configuring operationalization, deployment, and consumption can be found at the following Microsoft documentation link *https://docs.microsoft.com/en-us/machine-learning-server/what-is-operationalization*.

# Execute R and scripts inside T-SQL statements

In this section, you work through a full machine learning development cycle, from exploring the data, creating a model, embedding scripts and functions in T-SQL statements, and then using the model to create predictions and plots.

## First steps in embedding R in a T-SQL statement

The following development cycle will be executed from Visual Studio 2017. Visual Studio 2017 should already be configured with the Data Science And Analytical Application and the Data Storage And Processing workloads, as shown in Figure 4-75.

**FIGURE 4-75** Workloads to enable when installing Visual Studio Code

Open Visual Studio 2017 and under the R Tools menu, click Data Science Settings. A dialog box warns you about changing Visual Studio's window layout. Accept and proceed to changing the windows to a more development friendly setup.

Open the new project window (CTRL + Shift + N) and create an R Project. Right-click anywhere on the solution explorer pane and add a new existing as shown in Figure 4-76.

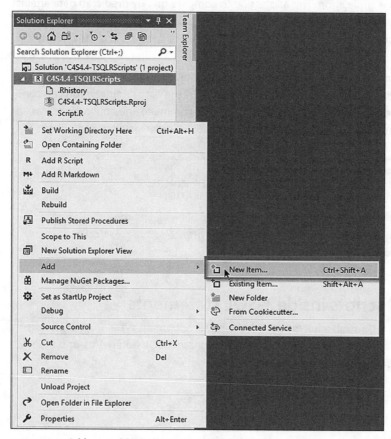

**FIGURE 4-76** Add a new SQL Script to your Visual Studio R Project

Select the SQL Query file, and name your file 01_ExecuteBasic_TSQLR.sql. As soon as the SQL editor shows up, copy and paste the following code:

```
EXEC sp_execute_external_script
@language =N'R',
@script=N'OutputDataSet<-InputDataSet',
@input_data_1 =N'SELECT 1 AS hello'
WITH RESULT SETS (([hello] int not null));
GO
```

In order to execute the code, first you must connect to your virtual machine SQL Server instance. If you try to execute the above script by invoking the keyboard shortcut CTRL + SHIFT + E, a Connect window will be displayed as shown in Figure 4-77.

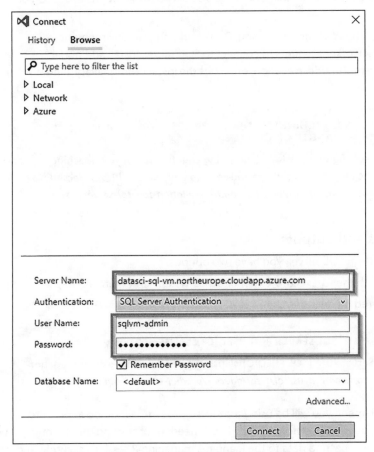

**FIGURE 4-77** Connect to your VM SQL Instance from Visual Studio

Fill the fields with your Azure Virtual Machine DNS address, user name, and password, ensuring to select SQL Server Authentication as your Authentication mode. Click Connect.

If your server is configured correctly, you should see the following output.

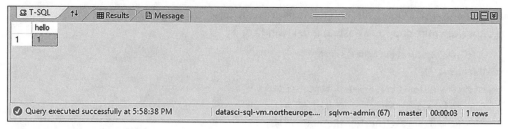

**FIGURE 4-78** Correct output from TSQL R script

If you get any errors from this query, installation might be incomplete. After adding the feature using the SQL Server Setup Wizard, you must take some additional steps to enable use of external code libraries. Refer to the section Configure SQL Server To Allow The Execution of R Script in Skill 4.4.

Make sure that the Launchpad service is running. Depending on your environment, you might need to enable the R worker accounts to connect to SQL Server, install additional network libraries, enable remote code execution, or restart the instance after everything is configured.

> **NEED MORE INFORMATION? MACHINE LEARNING SERVICES INSTALLATION AND UPGRADE FAQS**
>
> If you are having trouble configuring, installing or during your first run of your Machine Learning Services, visit the FAQs for helpful tips and common mistakes at *https://docs.micro-soft.com/en-us/sql/advanced-analytics/r/upgrade-and-installation-faq-sql-server-r-services*.

## Working with inputs and outputs

In order to work with R code in SQL Server, you have two options:

- Wrap the R script with the sp_execute_external_script system stored procedure, or
- Make a call to a stored model using the PREDICT clause of SQL Server 2017.

> **NEED MORE INFORMATION? SQL SERVER 2017 PREDICT CLAUSE**
>
> Details on the new SQL Server 2017 TSQL PREDICT clause can be found in the documentation link at *https://docs.microsoft.com/en-us/sql/t-sql/queries/predict-transact-sql*.

In the following development, you will be using the stored procedure method in order to execute R code from TSQL queries. The stored procedure is needed for starting the R runtime within the SQL Server context, passing data to the R engine, managing R sessions securely, and returning any output to the client connecting to SQL Server.

A first approach to handle R within TSQL is to create a dummy table, query it using TSQL and R within a stored procedure, and make sure the output is the same. First, run the following code in your Visual Studio 2017 SQL script editor to create a test table.

```
CREATE TABLE RTestData ([Pi] int not null) ON [PRIMARY]
INSERT INTO RTestData     VALUES (3);
INSERT INTO RTestData     VALUES (14);
INSERT INTO RTestData     VALUES (159) ;
GO
```

After creating the test table, query the table using first a traditional Select TSQL statement.

```
SELECT * FROM RTestData
```

Instead of querying the table with a regular TSQL query, now you query the table using an R script. The following code first executes the traditional TSQL query and saves the results as the variable InputDataSet in the R session, and then the value is saved to the output variable and returned as a result set to the client executing the stored procedure. The language must be defined as R and the script will always be defined as a string within the **@script** variable.

```
EXECUTE sp_execute_external_script
     @language = N'R'
   , @script = N' OutputDataSet <- InputDataSet;'
   , @input_data_1 = N' SELECT *  FROM RTestData;'
   WITH RESULT SETS (([NewColName] int NOT NULL));
```

Both outputs returned to Visual Studio 2017 should be the same. The WITH RESULT SETS clause defines the schema of the returned data table for SQL Server.

Changing the default input and output variable names can be done by declaring the @input_data_1_name and @output_data_1_name variables, as shown in the next script.

```
EXECUTE sp_execute_external_script
   @language = N'R'
   , @script = N' SQL_Out <- SQL_In;'
   , @input_data_1 = N' SELECT 12 as Col;'
   , @input_data_1_name  = N'SQL_In'
   , @output_data_1_name =  N'SQL_Out'
   WITH RESULT SETS (([NewColName] int NOT NULL));
```

Be careful when writing your R script, because unlike TSQL, R is case sensitive and will differentiate names based on their case. In all cases, variable names must follow the rules for valid SQL statements. Before declaring @input_data_1_name and @output_data_1_name, you must always declare @input_data_1 and @output_data_1 first.

You can also generate data from within an R script and output it to SQL Server and the client used. This is done by using a valid TSQL statement as @input_data_1, but then developing a script that does not use this input, as shown in the code below:

```
EXECUTE sp_execute_external_script
    @language = N'R'
  , @script = N' mytextvariable <- c("hello", " ", "world");
      OutputDataSet <- as.data.frame(mytextvariable);'
  , @input_data_1 = N' SELECT 1 as Temp1'
WITH RESULT SETS (([Col1] char(20) NOT NULL));
```

## R and SQL data types and data objects

Given that you have to match schemas and data types when in- and out-putting data into an R
script, there are a few common issues that usually arise. These are:

- Data types sometimes do not match.

- Implicit conversions might take place.

- Cast and convert operations are sometimes required.

- R and SQL use different data objects.

Becuse R returns its resulting data to SQL Server, it must always return it as a data.frame
object. Any other object used within the R script, whether it be lists, variables, vectors, matrices, or factors, must be encapsulated in a data.frame in order to be passed to SQL Server.
Even a trained binary model must be encapsulated and transformed to a data.frame in order
to store it in SQL Server.  You work through a couple of these transformations in the next code
examples.

Take a look at the following two "Hello World" scripts in R. The first stores a string array in a
temporary variable and later is transformed to a data.frame object. The second script directly
defines a data.frame within the output variable.

```
EXECUTE sp_execute_external_script
    @language = N'R'
  , @script = N' mytextvariable <- c("hello", " ", "world");
    OutputDataSet <- as.data.frame(mytextvariable);'
  , @input_data_1 = N' ';

EXECUTE sp_execute_external_script
    @language = N'R'
  , @script = N' OutputDataSet<- data.frame(c("hello"), " ", c("world"));'
  , @input_data_1 = N'  '
```

The results of these examples can be seen in Figures 4-79 and Figures 4-80 below. As you
execute both examples, you will soon find that the output is completely different. Example 1
outputs a vector with one column and three rows, whereas example 2 outputs a vector with
three columns and only one value in each. Without going into details, the reason for this behavior lies in that R implements 'column-major' order in accessing matrices and data frames. If
you attach the structure function, str(), to any of the scripts you will get additional information
as to the nature of each of the R objects. To view the output of the str() functions, or any other
R functions that return messages and outputs to the command line, switch to the Messages

pane/tab in VS Code, Visual Studio 2017, or SQL Server Management Studio. The following code exemplifies this behavior.

```
EXECUTE sp_execute_external_script
  @language = N'R',
  @script = N' OutputDataSet <- data.frame(c("hello"), " ", c("world"));
    str(OutputDataSet)' ,
  @input_data_1 = N'  ';
```

You can inspect the str() output for both examples in Figure 4-79 and Figure 4-80.

**FIGURE 4-79** str() output from defining a data.frame directly from an array

**FIGURE 4-80** str() output from an R array

R and SQL Server do not use the same data types, therefore when you run a query in SQL Server to get data and then pass that to the R runtime, some type of implicit conversion usually takes place. Another set of conversions takes place when you return data from R to SQL Server. SQL Server pushes the data from the input query to the R process managed by the Launchpad service and converts it to an internal representation for greater efficiency. The R runtime loads the data into a data.frame object and performs the script operations on the data. The R engine then returns the data to SQL Server using a secured internal connection and presents the data in terms of SQL Server data types.

As an example of this engine's mechanics, you can run the following code and examine its output both from SQL and from the R Script implementation. You need to have one of the AdventureWorksDW databases restored.

```
EXECUTE sp_execute_external_script
        @language = N'R',
        @script = N' str(InputDataSet);
        OutputDataSet <- InputDataSet;',
        @input_data_1 = N'
            SELECT ReportingDate
                , CAST(ModelRegion as varchar(50)) as ProductSeries
                , Amount
            FROM [AdventureWorksDW2017].[dbo].[vTimeSeries]
            WHERE [ModelRegion] = ''M200 Europe''
            ORDER BY ReportingDate ASC ;'
WITH RESULT SETS undefined;
```

The results are shown in Figure 4-81.

```
63  ☐ EXECUTE
64       @language = N'R',
65       @script = N' str(InputDataSet);
66          OutputDataSet <- InputDataSet;',
67       @input_data_1 = N'
68          SELECT ReportingDate
69          , CAST(ModelRegion as varchar(50)) as ProductSeries
70          , Amount
71          FROM [AdventureWorksDW2017].[dbo].[vTimeSeries]
72          WHERE [ModelRegion] = ''M200 Europe''
73          ORDER BY ReportingDate ASC ;'
74    WITH RESULT SETS undefined;
75
```

100 %   ▼  ◀

🗃 T-SQL   ↑↓   ▦ Results   🖹 Message

```
     (37 row(s) affected)

STDOUT message(s) from external script:
'data.frame':   37 obs. of  3 variables:
  $ ReportingDate: POSIXct, format: "2010-12-25" "2011-01-25" ...
  $ ProductSeries: Factor w/ 1 level "M200 Europe": 1 1 1 1 1 1 1 1 1 1 ...
  $ Amount       : num  3400 16925 20350 16950 16950 ...
```

FIGURE 4-81 Data types conversion from SQL table to an R data.frame

You can see that the data has been converted from a datetime column into a POSIXct R time data type. The column "ProductSeries," on the other hand, is specified as a factor column; this is a common R transformation on character columns, typical of categorical variables, to a numeric column with a string look up (Factors). Finally, the 'Amount' column has been stored correctly as a numeric column.

In order to avoid any problems when handling data to the R engine or acquiring data from an R script, be sure to follow the following steps to avoid errors:

- Test your data in advance and verify columns or values in your schema that could be a problem when passed to R code.

- Specify columns in your input data source individually, rather than using SELECT *, and know how each column will be handled.

- Perform explicit casts as necessary when preparing your input data, to avoid undesired casts and/or conversions of your data types.

- Avoid passing columns of data (such as GUIDS or rowguids) that cause errors and are not useful for modeling.

## Applying R functions on SQL Server data

Up to this point, you have successfully executed basic R scripts remotely on an Azure SQL Server Virtual Machine within a TSQL stored procedure. Now you can start using the full power of R to leverage many statistical and complex analysis tasks that, if you tried to implement in TSQL, would take many lines of code, as compared to just a few lines in R.

As an example, you first use a function from the internally installed package, stats, to generate an array of normally distributed number given a mean and a standard deviation. The function to generate random normally distributed numbers is called rnorm() and can be called on an R command line like the following:

```
rnorm(<number of samples>, mean = <desired mean>, sd = <desired std deviation>)
```

To call this function from TSQL, encapsulate it in the sp_execute_external_script as you have already done:

```
EXEC sp_execute_external_script
        @language = N'R',
        @script = N'
            OutputDataSet <- as.data.frame(rnorm(100, mean = 50, sd =3));',
        @input_data_1 = N'   ;'
WITH RESULT SETS (([Density] float NOT NULL));
```

In this case, the number of samples, mean and standard deviation are hard coded into the call. If you would like to have different inputs directly from TSQL, you need to define those parameters as variables and pass them to the sp_execute_external_script stored procedure, as shown:

```
CREATE PROCEDURE MyRNorm (@param1 int, @param2 int, @param3 int)
AS
    EXEC sp_execute_external_script
      @language = N'R'
, @script = N'
        OutputDataSet <- as.data.frame(rnorm(mynumbers, mymean, mysd));'
, @input_data_1 = N'   ;'
, @params = N' @mynumbers int, @mymean int, @mysd int'
, @mynumbers = @param1
, @mymean = @param2
, @mysd = @param3
    WITH RESULT SETS (([Density] float NOT NULL));
```

The stored procedure call defines additional parameters that are passed to the R function in the R services. The line beginning with @params defines all variables used by the R code, and the corresponding SQL data types, and the following lines define which TSQL parameters map to which R variables. In order to execute this function call, just copy and execute the following line of code:

```
EXEC MyRNorm @param1 = 100,@param2 = 50, @param3 = 3
```

## Create a predictive model

One of the most powerful uses of R is as a machine learning engine. Many algorithms have been developed to handle different types of machine learning problems, and many problems and algorithms are still better solved from R than from competing languages, such as Python, Julia, or fully implemented machine learning / deep learning services such as TensorFlow. Although algorithms and packages such as XGBoost, e1701, caret, nnet, or randomforest are widely used, you create a simple regression model in this section and store it to the SQL relational engine. Furthermore, you develop the models with Microsoft R Server functions, which are optimized for parallel and distributed computation.

> **NEED MORE INFORMATION? R PACKAGES FOR MACHINE LEARNING AND MICROSOFT R SERVER**
>
> More information on the RevoScaleR package and its functions can be found at: *https://docs.microsoft.com/en-us/machine-learning-server/r-reference/revoscaler/revoscaler*.

The model you will be developing is a linear model to predict the duration of the eruption for the Old Faithful geyser in Yellowstone National Park, Wyoming, USA based on the waiting time between eruptions. The data is part of the sample data that comes with the R installation, and further information can be found by typing ?faithful on an R command line (*see Figure 4-82).

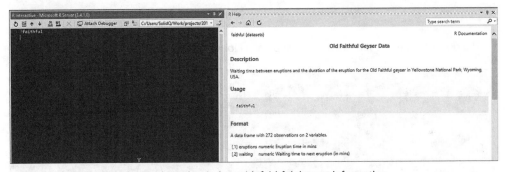

**FIGURE 4-82** R command line and R Help window with faithful dataset information

First, create a table to save the eruptions data.

```
CREATE TABLE Eruptions ([duration] float not null, [waiting] int not null)
INSERT INTO Eruptions
EXEC sp_execute_external_script
        @language = N'R'
        , @script = N'eruptions <- faithful;'
        , @input_data_1 = N''
        , @output_data_1_name = N'eruptions'
```

Inspect the data to make sure it has been copied successfully by querying it with a simple SELECT:

```
SELECT * FROM Eruptions
```

This script essentially copies the faithful data into a relational table. In order to create the model, you need to define a relationship between the columns of your dataset. Because you have a simple regression, the model is duration ~ waiting, which reads 'duration is dependent on waiting'. This formula is defined within the R Server rxLinMod() function in the code below:

```
DROP PROCEDURE IF EXISTS generate_linear_model;
GO
CREATE PROCEDURE generate_linear_model
AS
BEGIN
    EXEC sp_execute_external_script
    @language = N'R'
    , @script = N'lrmodel <- rxLinMod(formula = duration ~ waiting, data =
FaithfulEruptions);
        trained_model <- data.frame(payload = as.raw(serialize(lrmodel,
connection=NULL)));'
    , @input_data_1 = N'SELECT [duration], [waiting] FROM Eruptions'
    , @input_data_1_name = N'FaithfulEruptions'
    , @output_data_1_name = N'trained_model'
    WITH RESULT SETS ((model varbinary(max)));
END;
GO
```

The output should resemble the one shown in Figure 4-83.

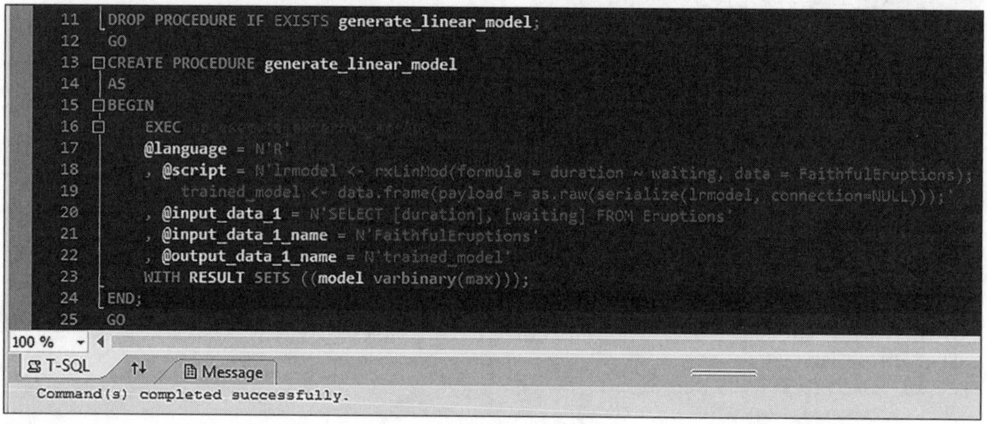

**FIGURE 4-83** Results of creating the train model stored procedure

After you defined the store procedure that trains the linear model, you need to save it to a table for future use. A trained model is essentially binary data that tells a scoring algorithm how to combine the columns of dataset in order to produce an output. As a simple example think of matrix algebra, and let the situation be described as AX=Y, where X is your input, Y your output, and A your model. A is just a matrix that can be hashed and stored as a single value in a table. Generally speaking, models are much more complex than simple matrices, but for this example the abstraction suffices. Create the table running the following code:

```
CREATE TABLE faithful_eruptions_models (
    model_name varchar(30) not null default('default model') primary key,
    model varbinary(max) not null);
```

Finally, you can populate the model table by executing the training stored procedure, and returning the output to the models table, as shown below in Figure 4-84.

```
INSERT INTO faithful_eruptions_models (model)
EXEC generate_linear_model;
```

Unfortunately, this table will not allow you to stored successive trained models because the table has no ID column, and the model is constantly being saved with the same name in its 'model_name' column. In order to sort this problem, you can change the naming scheme to something more descriptive, run the training stored procedure one more time, and query the models table to see the results.

```
UPDATE faithful_eruptions_models
SET model_name = 'rxLinMod ' + format(getdate(), 'yyyy.MM.HH.mm', 'en-gb')
WHERE model_name = 'default model'
GO

INSERT INTO faithful_eruptions_models (model)
EXEC generate_linear_model;
GO

SELECT * FROM faithful_eruptions_models
```

You will be able to see that the models are stored as a hex value under the 'model' column, as shown in Figure 4-84.

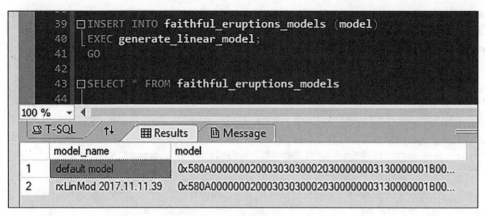

**FIGURE 4-84** Stored serialized linear models in a SQL table

In general, remember these when working with SQL parameters and R variables in TSQL:

All SQL parameters mapped to R script must be listed by name in the @params argument.

To output one of these parameters, add the OUTPUT keyword in the @params list.

After listing the mapped parameters, provide the mapping, line by line, of SQL parameters to R variables, immediately after the @params list.

## Predict and plot from model

Scoring based on the stored models is easily done by recalling the model from the table, applying the model on a new set of data, and storing the output in a table. Scoring is also known as predicting, estimating, or generating an output from a trained model based on the data on which the output or prediction is desired.

The Old Faithful data registers waiting times from 43 minutes up to 96 minutes. However, what would be the expected duration of an eruption if you went to Yellowstone and had to wait 120 minutes? Apart from your disillusion that Old Faithful is making truer its *old* state more that its *faithful*, you could quickly pull out your linear model and give some hope to the people at the area by telling them that longer waits only bring more spectacular eruptions. In order to do so, you must provide the additional waiting times to make a prediction of how long the geyser will erupt. Create a new table with the new waiting times with the following code:

```
CREATE TABLE [dbo].[NewEruptions](
        [duration] float null,
        [waiting] int not null) ON [PRIMARY]
GO

INSERT [dbo].[NewEruptions] ([waiting])
VALUES (20), (25), (30), (35), (40), (100), (105), (110), (115), (120)
```

At this point your models' table must have several different models, all trained on different data, or at different times, or with different parameters. To get predictions based on one specific model, you must write a SQL script that does the following:

- Gets the model you want.
- Gets the new input data.
- Calls an R prediction function that is compatible with that model.

Given that you have generated a model using Microsoft Machine Learning Server functions, you will also generate the scoring / prediction using the `rxPredict()` function, instead of the generic R predict() function. You do this with the following code:

```
DECLARE @eruptionsmodel varbinary(max) = (SELECT model FROM [dbo].[faithful_eruptions_
models] WHERE model_name = 'default model');
EXEC sp_execute_external_script
    @language = N'R'
    , @script = N'
            current_model <- unserialize(as.raw(eruptionsmodel));
            new <- data.frame(ExpectedEruptions);
            predicted.duration <- rxPredict(current_model, new);
            str(predicted.duration);
            OutputDataSet <- cbind(new, predicted.duration);
            '
    , @input_data_1 = N' SELECT waiting FROM [dbo].[NewEruptions] '
    , @input_data_1_name = N'ExpectedEruptions'
    , @params = N'@eruptionsmodel varbinary(max)'
    , @eruptionsmodel = @eruptionsmodel
WITH RESULT SETS (([expected_waiting] INT, [predicted_duration] FLOAT))
```

The initial select statement selects a model from the model table. Once the model is in memory, it is unserialized (converted from a hex binary to a usable R object) and stored as an R variable. Then, applying the predict formula on the new data, and using the stored model, a new set of predicted durations is generated. The str() function is added in order to check that the output dataset matches in schema and data type with the WITH RESULT SET clause. The results of the prediction can be seen in Figure 4-85.

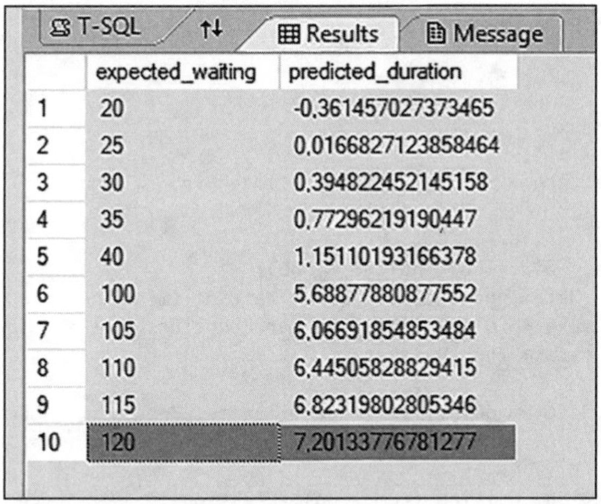

| | expected_waiting | predicted_duration |
|---|---|---|
| 1 | 20 | -0.361457027373465 |
| 2 | 25 | 0.0166827123858464 |
| 3 | 30 | 0.394822452145158 |
| 4 | 35 | 0.77296219190447 |
| 5 | 40 | 1.15110193166378 |
| 6 | 100 | 5.68877880877552 |
| 7 | 105 | 6.06691854853484 |
| 8 | 110 | 6.44505828829415 |
| 9 | 115 | 6.82319802805346 |
| 10 | 120 | 7.20133776781277 |

FIGURE 4-85 Old Faithful predicted eruption durations from estimated waiting times

In the case of a two hour waiting time you will be delighted to have an eruption of little over seven minutes.

An important additional parameter is the @parallel=1 flag. In this example your data is rather small, but suppose you have a large dataset with millions of rows and thousands of columns, you will probably need to optimize speeds by computing in parallel as much as you can. The @parallel flag enables parallel execution for your R script. Parallel execution generally provides benefits only when working with very large data. The SQL database engine might decide that parallel execution is not needed. Moreover, the SQL query that gets your data must be capable of generating a parallel query plan. When using the option for parallel execution, you must specify the output results schema in advance, by using the WITH RESULT SETS clause. Specifying the output schema in advance allows SQL Server to aggregate the results of multiple parallel datasets, which otherwise might have unknown schemas. This parameter often does not have any effect when training a model; it is mostly used when scoring a data set. If you wish to train complex algorithms with large training data, it is recommended that you use Microsoft R Server functions and libraries. The functions and algorithms in these services are specially engineered to train on parallel and distributed data.

Finally, you create a plot of the data and the trained model. Many clients, such as SQL Server Management Studio, cannot display plots created using an R script. Visual Studio and VS Code can display R plots, but these plots are displayed directly from the local memory and a local R session running as a command line window. In your current setup, the process to generate R plots is to create the plot within your R script, write the image to a file, or serialize it and save it in a table and then open the image file or render the serialized table image.

The following example demonstrates how to create a simple graphic using a plotting function included by default with R. The image is saved to the specified file, and it is returned as a serialized SQL value by the stored procedure.

```
EXECUTE sp_execute_external_script
  @language = N'R'
, @script = N'
    imageDir <- ''C:\\Users\\Public'';
    image_filename = tempfile(pattern = "plot_", tmpdir = imageDir, fileext =
".jpg")
    print(image_filename);
    jpeg(filename=image_filename,  width=600, height = 800);
    print(plot(duration~waiting, data=InputDataSet, xlab="Waiting (mins)",
ylab="Eruption Duration(mins)", main = "Old Faithful Geyser Eruptions"));
    abline(lm(duration~waiting, data = InputDataSet));
    dev.off();
    OutputDataSet <- data.frame(data=readBin(file(image_filename, "rb"),
what=raw(), n=1e6));
    '
  , @input_data_1 = N'SELECT duration, waiting from [dbo].[Eruptions]'
  WITH RESULT SETS ((plot varbinary(max)));
```

When executing the code above be sure to go to the C:\User\Public directory to retrieve the image file. The method for creating a plot and saving it to an image essentially is opening a print device, plotting to it, adding the abline, and then closing the device. The resulting plot can be seen in Figure 4-86. From the graph you can quickly identify two trends in the eruptions data:

- There are two clusters of eruptions: short and frequent and long and less frequent.
- There is a linear correlation between waiting time and eruption time, thus the modeling method you have used is valid in this situation.

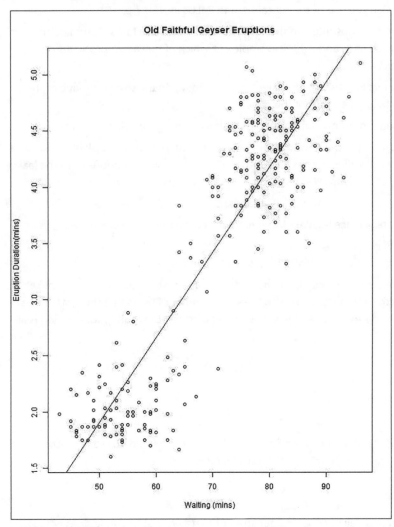

**FIGURE 4-86** Old Faithful plot of waiting minutes vs. eruption minutes, with a linear fit of the points

# Thought experiment

This thought experiment allows you to demonstrate the skills and knowledge gained by reviewing the topics covered in the chapter. The answers are included in the next section.

Answer the following questions for your manager:

1. You need to detect manufacturing errors from photos of factory-produced parts. You have decided to use a deep convolutional neural network because you are going to work with images. What activation would you preferably use in your network: Sigmoid, tanh, or ReLU? Can you use sigmoids, tanhs, and ReLUs in Net#?

2. You are working for a hospital and they ask you to perform two tasks. Assuming that for both problems you have about 100k examples, to which of these two problems deep learning applies best?

   A. Classify tumors into benign or malignant depending on the size and shape of the tumor and the age and sex of the patient.

   B. Classify images of skin lesions as benign lesions or malignant skin cancers.

3. You are collaborating in the development of an application, and your task is to provide a REST service that classifies images. Order the following possible solutions from the least costly to the most costly from a development point of view.

   A. Use Cortana Vision APIs to classify images.

   B. Within a Data Science Virtual Machine, train a convolutional neural network using CNTK.

   C. Define a convolutional network on Azure ML using Net#.

4. You must create a system capable of analyzing in real time the clicks that users make on a website with a lot of traffic. Due to the large number of users that the system must support, you decide to use a cluster. What kind of cluster is best suited for creating real-time systems?

   A. Spark

   B. Storm

   C. HBase

   D. R Server

5. You are using Spark and you have a Spark SQL DataFrame named df. From a Jupyter Notebook you make a SQL SELECT to this DataFrame:

   ```
   %%sql
   SELECT * FROM df
   ```

   After executing that cell of code you get an error that says that the table does not exist. What have you forgotten?

6. You need to periodically analyze the data in one of the tables of an SQL Server. You decide to analyze them by reusing an R script you already have written. To easily schedule the execution of the script you decide to put it in a stored procedure. What is a required step to execute R and Python scripts from a TSQL Stored procedure?

   **A.** Define the input and output variable names.

   **B.** Encapsulate the procedure call in another custom procedure.

   **C.** Enable external scripts execution in the SQL Server engine.

   **D.** Execute the full R and Python script from the command line prior to executing it form TSQL.

# Thought experiment answers

This section contains the answers to the thought experiment.

1. ReLU, because it does not suffer from the vanishing gradient problem. Sigmoids are the default activation function in neural networks created by Net#, but you can change it for tanh activations. However, ReLUs cannot be used in Net#; that is one of the reasons that makes Net# not suitable for building deep neural networks.

2. Although we consider images to be unstructured data because they are not in the form of a table, such as the database tables we are used to handle, in a certain way they are structured. An image has pixels correctly organized in two dimensions: width and height. The proximity of the pixels helps us to identify what appears in the image. Data in table form is very well structured, but they are not structured in the way that the pixels of an image do (nearby columns in the table do not provide extra information) so that no advantages can be seen when applying deep neural networks with convolutions (CNN).
   When we talk about tabular data, fully connected neural networks work well but do not usually provide better performance than a SVM, random forest or xgboost, and if you add that they are computationally expensive to train and difficult to fine tune, they end up being less used in this type of problems.
   So, task B is best suitable for deep learning.

3. The correct order is A, C, B.

4. See Skill 4.3 Perform data sciences at scale by using HDInsight.

5. You must create a temporal table using that DataFrame:

   ```
   df.registerTempTable("MyTable")
   ```

   And make the SELECT to that table:

   ```
   %%sql
   SELECT * FROM MyTable
   ```

6. See Skill 4.4 Perform database analytics by using SQL Server R Services on Azure.

# Chapter summary

In this chapter we have set aside Azure Machine Learning to discuss other alternatives when generating models and processing large amounts of data. Among all that has been reviewed, some key points stand out:

- You have reviewed CNTK, a Microsoft deep learning library that allows you to efficiently create and train deep models. The acceleration provided is mainly due to the parallelization of operations using GPUs. In addition, self-differentiation allows you to optimize models without the need of differential calculus.

- Throughout the chapter you have reviewed how to create virtual machines in Azure. The Deep Learning Virtual Machines, in addition to GPUs, has a number of pre-installed tools for data science and deep learning. The Data Science Virtual Machine does not focus so much on deep learning and has tools commonly used in the data science community.

- You have seen how to clone solutions from others to speed up your machine learning developments or share your own using the Cortana Intelligence Gallery.

- The main features of the clusters have been listed and you have seen which Azure HDInsight cluster type to create to tackle different analytics workloads that may arise in your business.

- You have reviewed how to use a cluster with Spark SQL for exploratory data analysis, with MLLib to create machine learning models using Spark, with Mahout to train a recommender using MapReduces, and with R Server to build machine learning models.

- In addition to R server over a cluster, you have used R server (Machine Learning Services) in a Data Science Virtual Machine. You configured additional options within your Virtual Machine and its SQL server instance that allowed you to execute R (and Python) scripts remotely from a TSQL query in a remote database client of your choosing.

- With the correct execution of R-TSQL scripts, you experimented with R data types, understood the mechanics behind the R-TSQL procedure call, and then trained and stored a linear model and predicted future data based on the eruptions of the Old Faithful Geyser in Yellowstone National Park.

# Index

# About the authors

**GINGER GRANT** is a managing consultant at SolidQ, where she provides advanced analytic solutions and training. Ginger started working in data science to provide machine learning solutions across a wide range of industries including insurance, education, healthcare, finance and transportation. She was able to leverage expertise gained by developing business intelligence projects, where she applied the knowledge gained through her MCSA certification in SQL Server. These efforts encouraged her to pursue the greater analytic capabilities in data science and Azure Machine Learning. She is a prolific blogger at *http://www.desertisesql.com* and frequent speaker at data conferences and events worldwide on topics such as R, Power BI, Python and Azure Machine Learning to introduce more people to current developments and future trends in data science and machine learning. Microsoft has recognized her technical contributions by awarding her a MVP in Data Platform. in You can follow her on Twitter at *http://twitter.com/desertisesql*.

**JULIO GRANADOS** from Barranquilla, Colombia is DPE, a data platform engineer at SolidQ. He has been a collaborating professor at EAE Business School in Barcelona and speaker at SolidQ Summit. He completed his degree in Computer science specialized in information systems at the University of Alicante, Spain and a Master in Business Intelligence in Microsoft Technologies taught by SolidQ You can follow him on linkedIn: *https://www.linkedin.com/in/julio-granados-barros-398ba4a4/*.

**GUILLERMO FERNÁNDEZ** Vizcaíno is Data Platform Specialist at SolidQ, where he works every day on BI and data science projects. Guillermo is a graduate of University of Alicante with a degree in computer engineering. Since his university days, he has been focused on the study of AI algorithms, especially machine learning and deep learning. He recently completed a master's degree in Business Intelligence with Microsoft tools at SolidQ.

**PAU SEMPERE SÁNCHEZ** is Mentor at SolidQ, participating in SQL Server, BI, Big Data and Data Science projects. Pau is a computer engineer graduated at University of Alicante, being awarded as Microsoft Active Professional in 2012. He started working with SQL Server relational databases and switched to OLAP analytical models, data mining models, cloud technologies, big data and AI systems. He participates regularly as speaker at Microsoft events, SolidQ Summits and Data Platform community events. He is member of the PASS Spanish group, being founder and organizer of SQL Saturday Spain.

**JAVIER TORRENTERAS** is Mentor at SolidQ, leading the business analytics department. Javier is a computer engineer graduated at University Politécnica de Madrid, as long as having a Masters degree in education and e-learning by the University of Alcala. He has been working in the IT business since 1996, mainly involved in data analytics projects. As a specialized BI professional he has also been involved as a speaker in public events and also as a teacher on some business schools and universities.

**PACO GONZALEZ**, based in Atlanta, is a Microsoft Data Platform MVP and Managing Director for SolidQ North America. He is a speaker at relevant conferences such as: Ignite, PASS BA, PASS Summit, DevWeek London, PAW Chicago and London. Paco holds a BS in Computer engineering and a Master's degree in Artificial Intelligence from University of Murcia, Spain.

**TAMANACO FRANCISQUEZ** is a DPS with SolidQ. A physicist by formal training, he has a Master's Degree in Molecular Nanotechnology and during his academic research worked extensively with Matlab. Having switched his interest and focus into R, R Server, machine learning and citizen data science, he has extensive experience with analytical models, statistical methods and machine learning. He is currently finishing a Master's Degree in Business Intelligence and is pursuing his first MCSA Certification.

# Visit us today at

# microsoftpressstore.com

- **Hundreds of titles available** – Books, eBooks, and online resources from industry experts

- **Free U.S. shipping**

- **eBooks in multiple formats** – Read on your computer, tablet, mobile device, or e-reader

- **Print & eBook Best Value Packs**

- **eBook Deal of the Week** – Save up to 60% on featured titles

- **Newsletter and special offers** – Be the first to hear about new releases, specials, and more

- **Register your book** – Get additional benefits